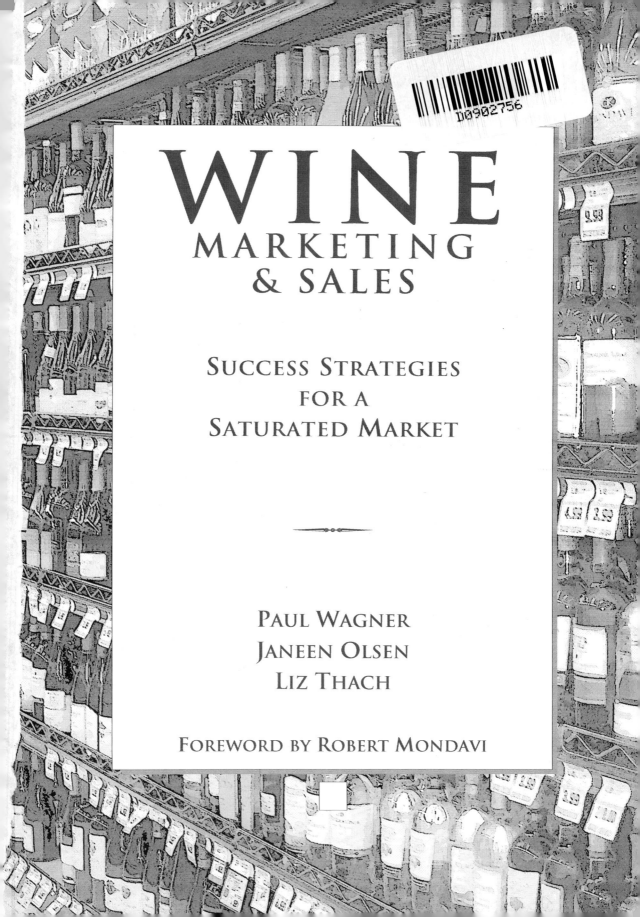

WINE
MARKETING
& SALES

SUCCESS STRATEGIES
FOR A
SATURATED MARKET

PAUL WAGNER
JANEEN OLSEN
LIZ THACH

FOREWORD BY ROBERT MONDAVI

Other Books by The Wine Appreciation Guild

"The Best Wine Publisher in the US."
—Edward Cointreau, Gourmand World Cookbook Award

A Century of Wine, Edited by Stephen Brook (ISBN 1-891267-33-7)
A Wine Growers' Guide, Philip M. Wagner (ISBN 0-932664-92-X)
Africa Uncorked, John and Erica Platter (ISBN 1-891267-52-3)
Armagnac, Charles Neal (ISBN 1-891267-20-5)
Champagne and Sparkling Wine Guide, Tom Stevenson (ISBN 1-891267-41-8)
Cheese, Gabriella Ganugi (ISBN 1-891267-69-8)
Chip Cassidy's Wine Travels, Chip Cassidy (ISBN 1-891267-34-5)
Chow! Venice, Shannon Essa and Ruth Edenbaum (ISBN 1-934259-00-4)
Concepts in Wine Chemistry, Yair Margalit (ISBN 1-891267-74-4)
Concepts in Wine Technology, Yair Margalit (ISBN 1-891267-51-5)
Favorite Recipes of California Winemakers, (ISBN 0-932664-03-2)
Fine Wine in Food, Patricia Ballard (ISBN 0-932664-56-3)
Ghost Wineries of the Napa Valley, Irene Whitford Haynes (ISBN 0-932664-90-3)
Grands Crus of Bordeaux, Hans Walraven (ISBN 0-932664-94-6)
Icon: Art of the Wine Label, Jeffrey Caldewey and Chuck House (ISBN 1-891267-30-2)
Imagery: Art for Wine, Bob Nugent (ISBN 1-891267-30-2)
Napa Wine: A History, Charles L. Sullivan (ISBN 1-891267-07-8)
New Adventures in Wine Cookery, (ISBN 1-891267-71-X)
Northern Wine Works, Thomas A. Plocher (ISBN 1-891267-66-3)
Olive Oil, Leonardo Romanelli (ISBN 1-891267-55-8)
Pasta, Fabrizio Ungaro (ISBN 1-891267-56-6)
Portugal's Wines and Wine Makers, New Revised Edition, Richard Mason (ISBN 1-891267-01-9)
Prosciutto, Carla Bardi (ISBN 1-891267-54-X)
Red & White, Max Allen (ISBN 1-891267-37-X)
Rum, Dave Blume (ISBN 1-891267-62-0)
Sauternes, Jeffrey Benson and Alastair McKenzie (0-856673-60-9)
Secrets of Patagonian Barbecue, Robert Maiño (9568077324)
Secrets of Peruvian Cuisine, Emilio Peschiera (9568077251)
Tasting & Grading Wine, Clive Michelsen (9197532606)
Terroir, James E. Wilson (ISBN 1-891267-22-1)
The Bartender's Black Book, Stephen Kittredge Cunningham (ISBN 1-891267-31-0)
The Champagne Cookbook, Malcolm R. Herbert (ISBN 1-891267-70-1)
The Commonsense Book of Wine, Leon D. Adams (ISBN 0-932664-76-8)
The French Paradox, Gene Ford (ISBN 0-932664-81-4)
The Global Encyclopedia of Wine, Edited by Peter Forrestal (ISBN 1-891267-38-8)
The New Italy, Daniele Cernelli and Marco Sabellico (ISBN 1-891267-32-9)
The Science of Healthy Drinking, Gene Ford (ISBN 1-891267-47-7)
The Taste of Wine, Emile Peynaud (ISBN 0-932664-64-4)
The University Wine Course, Marian Baldy (ISBN 0-932664-69-5)
The Wine Atlas of New Zealand, Michael Cooper (1-86958-921-1)
The Wine Buyer's Record Book, Ralph Steadman (ISBN 0-932664-98-9)
The Wines of Baja California, Ralph Amey (ISBN 1-891267-65-5)
The Wines of France, Clive Coates (ISBN 1-891267-14-0)
Tokaj, Alkonyi Laszlo (ISBN 1-891267-50-7)
Understanding Wine Technology, David Bird (ISBN 1-891267-91-4)
Wine Heritage, Dick Rosano (ISBN 1-891267-13-2)
Wine in Everyday Cooking, Patricia Ballard ((ISBN 0-932664-45-8)
Wine Investment for Portfolio Diversification, Mahesh Kumar (ISBN 1-891267-84-1)
Wine Lovers Cookbook, Malcolm R. Herbert (ISBN 0-932664-82-2)
Wine, Food & the Good Life, Arlene Mueller and Dorothy Indelicato (0-932664-85-0)
Winery Technology & Operations, Yair Margalit (ISBN 0-932664-66-0)
World Encyclopedia of Champagne and Sparkling Wine, Tom Stevenson (1-891267-61-2)
You're a Real Wine Lover When..., Bert Witt (1-891267-25-6)
Zinfandel, Cathleen Francisco (1-891267-15-9)

WINE
MARKETING
& SALES

SUCCESS STRATEGIES
FOR A
SATURATED MARKET

PAUL WAGNER

JANEEN OLSEN

LIZ THACH

FOREWORD BY ROBERT MONDAVI

THE WINE APPRECIATION GUILD
SAN FRANCISCO

Wine Marketing and Sales
Success Strategies for a Saturated Market

The Wine Appreciation Guild
360 Swift Avenue
South San Francisco, CA 94080
(650) 866-3020
www.wineappreciation.com

Managing Editor   Bryan Imelli
Copy Editor   Margaret Clark
Assistant Editor   Jason Simon
Book Design   Diane Hume

Library of Congress Cataloging-in-Publication Data

Thach, Liz, 1961-
Wine marketing and sales : success strategies for a saturated
market / Liz Thach, Janeen Olsen, and Paul Wagner.
p. cm.
Includes bibliographical references and index.
ISBN 978-1-934259-45-0
1. Wine industry--United States. 2. Wine--Marketing. 3. Selling
--Wine.   I. Olsen, Janeen. II. Wagner, Paul, 1952-   . III. Title.
HD9375.T43 2006
663'.200688--dc22
2006017552

CONTENTS

ILLUSTRATIONS

Thank you to Dita and Gary Blackwell of Blackwell's Wines & Spirits on Geary Blvd. in San Francisco for allowing us to photograph their store to create the illustrations fronting Chapters 4 (p. 66), 7 (p.144), and 12 (p. 262).

Thank you to Maher Abudamous for allowing us to photograph his restaurant, Layaly, on Clement St. in San Francisco to create the illustration for Chapter 9 (p. 198).

Thank you to Jeff Beach for his help with photographing various retail establishments and providing the Golden Gate Bridge image fronting Chapter 13 (p. 282) as well as other images.

Thank you to Robin Lewis of Balzac Communications & Marketing for the label and packaging illustrations in Chapters 5 and 6.

Thank you to all the other organizations; wineries, wholesalers, research groups, etc. for the use of their illustrations and contributions to this book.

FOREWORD

I'm honored to be asked to write a foreword to a book on wine marketing, because for my first fifty years in the wine business we talked mostly about growing grapes and making wine, and went around the country trying to educate people and sell what we were making. We didn't think about marketing, and we suffered for that lack of knowledge.

Wine is a wonderful beverage that combines agriculture, science and business, and it also has many cultural aspects in cuisines and the traditional arts. But now anybody in the wine industry, or any other highly competitive business, must address all of wine's aspects in a way that earns credibility and makes a profit, too.

There are an estimated 60,000 labels available in the American market, so it's crucial to understand how to make a winery stand out from the crowd, and yet fit into people's lifestyles in a enjoyable, meaningful way. This book does all of that...and more. It can help any marketer look for tips and tactics, and understand how to succeed.

The authors have hands-on marketing experience complemented by the work of California's leading wine marketing professors. The book is both credible and authoritative, and very, very helpful.

—Robert Mondavi
Napa Valley

PUBLISHER'S PREFACE

My first job out of college was as a "marketing analyst" in the regional office of a multinational conglomerate. We had no computers, electronic calculators, nor fax machines. It was slide rules, adding machines and the telex.

My office was in the "financial district" of San Francisco. It was a different world then. It was the era of "men only" lunch bars and women were not permitted to stand up on cable cars. The Drinking Man's Diet and beatnik poets were all the rage and topless bars were making their debut.

San Francisco had five daily newspapers but no wine columns. Gossip columnist Herb Caen was king and a brief mention in his daily column could launch any new product in San Francisco and perhaps nationally.

Wine marketing was approaching sophistication and San Francisco wine impresario, Ed Everett, knew how to build a new wine brand. Ed's Trumpeter Cabernet Sauvignon from Argentina had all the right stuff: a memorable name, endangered species picture on the label, exotic origin and an easy, quaffable texture. Besides, it was on all the right wine lists at that time; Ernies, The Old Poodle Dog, The Leopard Café, and it was mentioned several times in Herb Caen's column.

Wine marketing fundamentals are still the same; catchy label, good publicity, and distribution to the right places. But it's now an alternative universe from the quaint world of marketing I entered 40 years ago. The authors of this groundbreaking work have provided a concise, scholarly and fascinating gift to this fundamentally different era of wine marketing. In fact, the breadth and utility of this book is reflective of this new age. It can, quite possibly, improve the fortunes of not only wineries, wine marketers and students of the craft, but wine brokers, negotiants, brand managers, sale reps …and Walmart employees.

—Elliott Mackey
Publisher
Former Marketing Analyst

ACKNOWLEDGEMENTS

We would like to thank all of the very supportive people who have encouraged us in the creation of this book. First among those have to be our students and colleagues at Napa Valley College and Sonoma State University.

A heartfelt thanks to Robert Mondavi for his inspiring forward, and to all of the other wine executives and managers who provided information, images, and anecdotes for this book.

We extend a very grateful thank you to our families as they supported us through long days and some nights typing away at the computer.

To Paul's family: his wonderful wife Margaret, and two daughters, Liz and Estelle.

To Janeen's family: Russ, Yoshiko, Karen, Ken, Jeff and to Rodney.

To Liz's family: her husband Michael, daughter Zia, and supporting relatives and friends.

INTRODUCTION

The US is soon to become the largest wine market in the world. It would seem that this is the very best time to be in wine marketing. The quality of wine in the bottle has never been higher, or more consistent. The selection of wines, from every part of the world, has never been greater, or more interesting to the consumer. Per capita consumption, long a disappointment to American wine producers, has grown appreciably in the last few years. It is the best of times.

And yet...

There are enormous challenges to marketing wine—challenges not faced by marketers in other industries. These challenges often frustrate those marketing executives who are new to the wine industry, because they seem to work against some of the basic tenets of marketing. What works in other industries doesn't always work with wine.

As a result, many wineries look for marketing help from those who have worked their way up through the complicated value system of the wine industry: to retailers, distributor salesmen, sommeliers, or connoisseurs. All too often, however, these wine experts do not have the academic background in marketing to really solve the problem.

The challenges remain...

Some of these challenges are general, and must be faced whether you market wine in Austria or Australia; or are selling Amarone or Zinfandel. Compared to other packaged goods, there is virtually no consumer brand loyalty in wine. Consumers love the choices they are offered, and try a different producer, different grape varietal, or different appellation with every bottle. Faced with a similar situation, most packaged goods marketers would throw up their hands in frustration.

The lack of brand loyalty is compounded by the complete saturation of the market. With more than 2,000 wineries in California alone, and wineries now producing wine in all fifty of the United States, the competition for shelf space and consumer attention is brutal. As wine marketers from Australia, Italy and elsewhere have shown, competition is not limited to American producers. There are more than 60,000 different wines for sale in the US today, and no retailer can possibly stock them all. Furthermore, the continued globalization of the wine industry will only make the competition for shelf space more intense.

Adding to the confusion is the tradition of the wine industry that often limits production to smaller lots of wine from specific appellations or even specific vineyards. While this information becomes the lifeblood of the true connoisseur, most consumers find it difficult to master. The result is that they find wine so intimidating that they would prefer not to talk about it in a social setting. Furthermore, since most quality wines are also vintage dated, each year presents a new challenge, and a new group of SKUs for the market. These layers of complexity reach into the truly bizarre for most consumers.

These smaller lots of wine carry with them an additional burden, that of limited budgets. Some of the most famous wineries in the world produce fewer than 10,000 cases, and many of the top wines are made in lots of 500 cases or fewer. Marketing budgets for such wines must, by definition, be tiny, and yet the marketing goals frequently aim at national or even international recognition, awareness, and purchase.

For those marketing wine in the US, a Byzantine distribution system, which emerged from the repeal of Prohibition, makes it very difficult for all but the very biggest brands to gain leverage. Distribution is regulated into three-tiers, and each state has very different requirements for each tier. These laws have consolidated much of the marketing power of the wine industry into the hands of a few large distributors, who are frequently more interested in volume than in developing new markets for smaller producers. Though admirable efforts have been made in opening up direct-to-consumer shipping in some states, there are still many legal hurdles to leap in this part of the wine marketing equation.

The combination of these factors has made wine marketing one of the most challenging subjects in business today. However, the solutions to these challenges are among the most creative strategies in marketing. What is learned in wine marketing today can, indeed, be successfully applied to a wide range of entrepreneurial businesses.

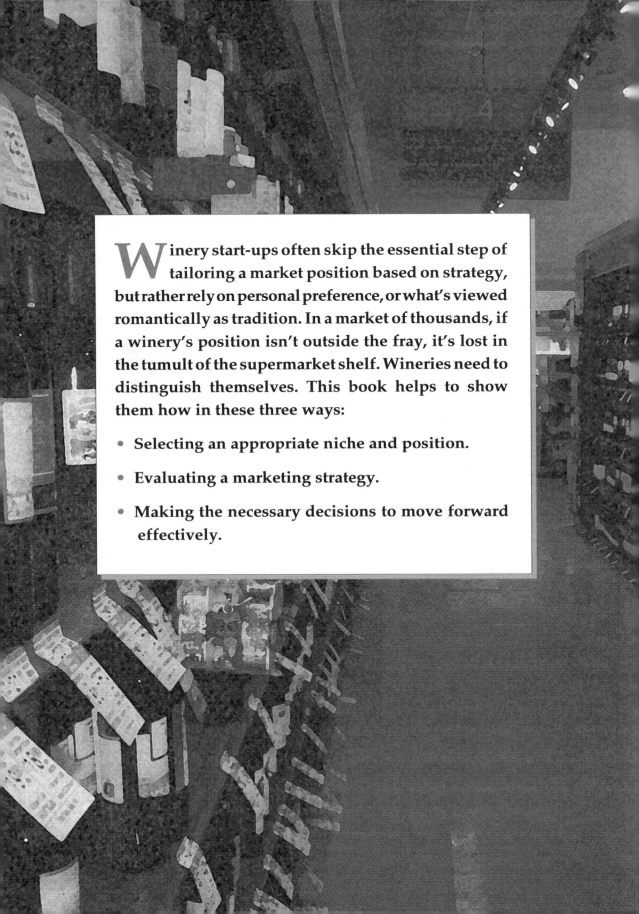

Winery start-ups often skip the essential step of tailoring a market position based on strategy, but rather rely on personal preference, or what's viewed romantically as tradition. In a market of thousands, if a winery's position isn't outside the fray, it's lost in the tumult of the supermarket shelf. Wineries need to distinguish themselves. This book helps to show them how in these three ways:

- Selecting an appropriate niche and position.

- Evaluating a marketing strategy.

- Making the necessary decisions to move forward effectively.

1

BASIC WINE MARKETING PRINCIPLES

Historically the wine industry has been a business dominated by the mentality of production rather than marketing. For every international brand that has achieved name recognition and consumer mindshare, there are literally thousands of producers who grow grapes and make wine without really thinking through the marketing implications and ramifications of the decisions they make every day.

With the explosion of wineries and wine brands around the world, the market has become overly saturated. The result is that many of the small producers who make a few thousand cases of wine to sell are suddenly swamped by very competitively priced wine from around the world—and they are suffering.

For years, wineries have produced wine under a simple philosophy—to produce a high quality wine that will drive sales. Unfortunately, it is no longer enough to simply make good wine. Today, most wineries produce good quality wine. But that is just the baseline. In today's wine market you also have to know how to sell your wine. This calls for a basic understanding of marketing principles and practices. Perhaps most importantly, just as you always want to make your wine better than your competitors, you also have to market your wine better than your competitors do.

It's a new world of wine, with enormous challenges. Small wineries often operate under severe competitive disadvantages when vying with big brands and wine companies:

- They do not have the large budgets.
- They do not have the same in-house marketing expertise.
- They do not have the same leverage, in terms of volume or affiliated products and brands.

But their most important disadvantage is one that can be solved. They do not bring a disciplined marketing approach to the wine business. Without that approach, wineries simply cannot be successful in this market. The good news is that the basic rules of marketing are by far the most important, and they can be understood fairly quickly and easily. The real challenge for most companies is not to understand the rules—it is to live by those rules when it seems so easy to do something else. Yet the companies that show consistent success and growth over the years are those that approach marketing with iron discipline and a single-minded focus on the basic rules.

WINE MARKETING PRINCIPLES

To begin exploring wine marketing, it is useful to start with a definition of marketing. According to the American Marketing Association (2005) **marketing** is defined as follows: "The performance of business activities that direct the flow of goods and services from producer to consumer ." This can be translated into a simple definition of wine marketing as "how you define your wine product, promote it, distribute it, and maintain a relationship with your customers." In the end, wine marketing can be defined as everything a company does in terms of its customers.

From this basic definition of wine marketing, the next step is to review the five aspects of marketing activities, which are often referred to as the "five P's." Each of these will be covered in more depth in future chapters, but it is useful to have a high-level overview to begin the process. The five aspects are: **Product, Placement, Price, Promotion,** and **Positioning.**

Figure 1.1: The Five "P"s of Marketing

Product	What You Sell
Placement	Where You Sell it
Price	What it Costs
Promotion	How You Support it
The sum of the above four elements creates the consumer's perception and creates the fifth P—Position:	
Position	How Do You Compare?

1. *Your Wine* **Product:** This is the specific type of wine and services that you offer to your customers. You should be able to describe your product clearly, and explain how it is different from your competitors' products.

2. *Distribution Channel*—**Placement:** How you make your wine available to customers. In the wine industry, there are multiple distribution channels, and the process can be very complicated due to many regulations, both in the U.S. and abroad.

3. *Wine* **Pricing:** How much you charge for your wine and related services. It is critical to understand your position before setting prices. If it is too low, the customers will not take you seriously. Conversely, if it is too high, customers may not be willing to take the risk.

4. *Wine* **Promotion** *and Advertising:* How you choose to promote and sell your wine. There are many avenues, including direct-to-consumer sales, public relations, sales promotions through distributors, and many others.

When you add up the total of these elements, you can then talk about how your wine or brand is perceived in the marketplace. The sum of these perceptions is your position.

5. *Your* **Position:** The combination of these factors determines how your target customers define you in relation to other winery competitors. It is what makes you truly unique, and makes your wine stand out from others.

It is important that wineries understand and internalize these basic wine marketing principles. Anything less will not generate true marketing and sales success. In addition, there are a few key steps in the ongoing process that should be identified, so that they can be used to guide the reader through the rest of this book.

- The winery must perform a complete SWOT analysis (see Chapter Three) on its assets to determine exactly what kinds of opportunities may exist for future strategic marketing efforts. The analysis of these assets and the creative work on future plans will then drive the winery to focus on the next few steps of the strategic process.

- Using this analysis, the winery must develop a unique position—one that defines the winery and its brands in a way that is attractive to consumers, clearly distinguishes the winery from all competition, and is capable of being summarized in fewer than ten words. This is a key concept that is integral to its products and marketing, which will drive future decision-making at the winery, and resonate with trade and consumers. It will become the unique selling proposition for the brand and its wines.

- The winery must apply these concepts to everything that it does, and must do so ruthlessly. Any variation from these concepts will dilute the message just as surely as adding water will dilute the quality of your wine.

- The winery must identify a clear marketing goal that not only defines the strategy for the future, but also provides clear guidelines for evaluating progress.

THE GOAL OF WINE MARKETING

The **goal of all marketing is to enhance the value of the brand**, to make it worth more than your investment of time, money, and energy has cost. It takes a clear vision, a good understanding of the rules of marketing, and the dedication and discipline to avoid making the easy and obvious mistakes that can cost your brand its image and its value.

In the end, there are a few very specific goals that a brand should adopt for its marketing efforts. These few goals are the only ones that really matter, and any marketing effort that does not have one of these goals as its final objective is flawed. All of them are based on a single concept: that your brand should stand out from the crowd—that it should own a distinct position in the mind of the consumer and the market.

In short, every winery should be able to answer this question as succinctly and poignantly as possible: What makes you so different? The best answers will have fewer than ten words. This is the famous "elevator conversation" philosophy that every marketer is forced to learn in his or her first marketing class. But most wineries haven't learned it. They cannot give a short, simple answer to the question: what makes you different?

Many wineries simply don't know where to begin. In many cases, the winery began as a dream to participate in a lifestyle that was both attractive and potentially profitable. Critical decisions were made about vineyard plantings, product mix, and price points based not on marketing or strategy, but on personal preference and a desire to fit in with the larger sense of what traditional wineries should do.

This philosophy is obviously completely at odds with marketing theory. You cannot follow in the footsteps of hundreds, if not thousands, of other wineries and then expect to be able to create something that is unique or even slightly different. Instead, wineries find that they have created something that mimics the rest of the wine world. Thousands of wines have been launched into the market in this condition. The market can hardly be blamed for not caring or for not paying attention.

In this book, we will spend considerable time working through the process of selecting an appropriate niche and positioning for wineries. We will provide guidelines and procedures for helping wineries evaluate their marketing strategy, and make the necessary decisions to move forward more effectively.

Pure and simple, the best of all marketing goals is to become the industry leader. This establishes your company and brand in a position of enormous value and power. Of course, within such a saturated industry as wine, that goal is beyond the reach of all but a very few companies. The solution, however, is not to settle for a position far short of that ambitious goal. This is the mistake that many companies make. There is no marketing reward at all for being the 76th (or 924th!) most important winery in the market. Marketing theory tells us that there is no point in being anything other than first, second, or third in the market. This is a critical fact: you must be either first, second, or third. There is no other alternative. In a market with more than 10,000 wines, what is a small winery to do? Classical marketing theory has a clear directive in this situation: where you cannot become the leader, you must create a category (a smaller market segment) where you can become the leader. This is a reasonable and viable strategy for any winery, but is where most wineries fail.

IDENTIFYING YOUR MARKET CATEGORY

The question is simple: if the best of all marketing goals is to become the industry leader, how do we achieve that goal? First, you must identify your category. Most wineries cannot explain this critical element of their marketing plan. They do not have a clear definition of their category, and as a result they have no concept of how to gain leadership of that category.

Without a clear goal, and without a clear path to that goal, there is no focus, discipline, or hope of positive results from their programs. The fault lies not in the execution of their promotions, the appearance of their label, or the work ethic of their sales team. The fault lies in their complete lack of a strong and focused marketing strategy that will build the brand into the leadership of a category.

So what is a category? **A category is a segment of the market that is statistically significant to the consumer.** When you ask consumers about beverages, they will usually note that soda pop is a category— everyone knows about it, and most people buy it. And that category has a clear competition for leadership, between Coke and Pepsi.

In the wine industry it is more complicated. Some obvious examples of wine categories are such segments as Napa Valley, sparkling wine, or Chardonnay. But even within those categories, there are significant smaller segments. Most consumers buy wine based on a price point—those who normally buy wines for $5 a bottle do not generally also buy wines at $25 a bottle. The category leader for Chardonnay should then also be defined by price point.

At the supermarket level this becomes quite evident. There are clear leaders in the area of $5 varietal wines, for example, and they have worked hard to get that recognition in the market. There are also comparatively few wines in those categories, because they are very competitive, and the risks for failure are high. The rewards can also be quite high.

The situation is far different when we speak about wines at some of the higher price points. There are more than 500 Chardonnays in the

US market, and more than 200 of those sell between $12 and $22. There are certainly leaders in that category; but what about the rest of the wines? How are they seen by the market? By consumers? They are lost and are struggling against all odds to gain some kind of recognition, but they have no real hook to hang their hat on. That is a problem. In fact, for most wineries, that is *the* problem.

Here is where marketing sophistry can sometimes come into play. While It is true that the goal of brand marketing is to become a category leader, some marketers try to take the easy way out by simply coming up with a definition of their category that allows them to claim leadership. It does no good to define your category as "Dry Creek Valley Viogniers with Korean winemakers." That's not a category. No consumer ever entered a store asking for wines in that category. It does the winery no good to become the leader of a category, if neither the consumer nor the trade recognizes the category.

Most wineries cannot become category leaders because they cannot even define the categories they hope to lead. Without such direction, they cannot target their marketing to accomplish their goal. In other industries, these wineries would be driven out of business in a very short time. In the wine industry, thanks to industrious salespeople, hardworking winemakers, and emotionally involved owners, these wineries can linger for years. But they will not achieve real marketing success until they more effectively define what they are trying to accomplish, what category they wish to lead.

So what are some good examples of innovative brands that have redefined their categories and become leaders with enviable results? Randall Grahm and his Rhone Rangers stand as the epitome of good strategic marketing in a saturated market. Rosenblum has established category leadership in vineyard designate Zinfandels from Sonoma County. Stone Hill has taken category leadership in producing high quality wines made from the Norton grape. The products, marketing efforts, and even packaging have all worked to create a new and very viable category, and an enviable position as a category leader. Other newer categories include organic wines, new varietals, innovative packaging, and new regions or appellations. All of these bring new categories to the mind of the consumer, and offer leadership opportunities to smart wine marketers.

As of this writing, there are over 9,300 wineries in the USA (Wine Business Monthly, 2006), but fewer than ten percent of this number have clear marketing strategies to achieve category leadership. Without leadership strategies, they will fall far short of their potential.

It is ultimately the responsibility of the winery management to address this issue. If the management of the winery is unwilling to do this, that decision will have long-lasting effects on every marketing effort the winery undertakes.

EMBRACING STRATEGIC WINE MARKETING

Why don't wineries think strategically? There are many reasons, and most of them originate in the initial business plan for the winery. The original business plan usually calls for the winery to achieve success similar to other wineries in the same region, using similar strategies. Some would argue that in some parts of the Wine Country, these business plans have become so formulaic that they can be written without any experience in the business at all.

The irony is that such business plans work well with financial institutions and lenders, who like the idea that a new business is a predictable investment that will pay dividends precisely because it does not vary from existing models. But marketing teaches us exactly the opposite. If you want to achieve marketing success, you must create a new and different model. You must take the risks associated with that innovation for you to successfully establish a unique positioning for your brand and products. If you do not, then you will never truly distinguish yourself from the rest of the market, and you will be at the mercy of general market fluctuations that ripple through the industry every few years, claiming the lives of a few wineries and the careers of a few individuals who never saw it coming.

In the world of marketing, it is not enough to take our place on the field, and glory in the sunshine. In the world of marketing, it is our job to react to the ball, move into the right position, and score goals. We are not on the field to be part of the game; we are on the field to win.

The good news, of course, is that winning is fun, and playing the game with people who want to win is really rewarding. It is more fun than just being on the field. The importance of this philosophy becomes clear when we think about the large strategic decisions that every winery must make from time to time. These are the decisions about vineyard plantings, wine styles, product mixes, label design, and messaging that really define the winery and its role in the industry.

But there are other decisions, some of them made on a daily basis, that must also be guided by this same philosophy. Without a clear strategic direction, smaller decisions are also likely to be flawed. While the negative impact of these flawed decisions may be delayed over time, they will accumulate to the point that the winery is no longer able to function effectively in the marketplace. The history of our industry is littered with the stories of wineries that didn't really make any big mistake—just lots of little ones, over time.

This becomes quite clear when we examine the winery pipeline. This is the vast system of distributors, salespeople, retailers, restaurateurs, chain stores, direct mail programs, and all of the other ways that your wine will eventually find its way into the hands of a consumer. In the best of all worlds, this pipeline performs flawlessly, with old customers buying the wines on a regular basis, new customers coming into the fold, and all the stages of the delivery system in between working like a well-oiled machine.

But every winery knows that this is not accurate. A bad cork, bad bottle storage at a retailer, scuffed labels, an off-vintage, a poor review in the media, an email crash, unexpected snowstorm, or a winemaker's messy divorce can all throw a wrench into the works.

As we look at wine marketing programs, we must first assure ourselves that the strategic decisions are appropriate. Once that is done, the next step is to understand that marketing strategy applies to each of the situations we must solve in the pipeline. Not only must our strategy be well conceived, but our execution must also be consistent with that strategy.

Each pipeline problem will have solutions. Only one of those solutions will be consistent with the long-term marketing strategy of the brand. If that strategy is not in place, and well understood by the winery staff, the wrong solution will often be taken.

As the sales team requests that the winery make efforts to establish better brand recognition, the strategic marketing of the brand will determine how these are developed and what tactics are appropriate. Every element of the winery's marketing efforts, from media samples to participation in special events or donations to key charities, will all need to be evaluated through the matrix of the strategy. It becomes the driving principle behind everything that the winery does.

HOW ARE MARKETING AND SALES RELATED?

Marketing prepares the ground; sales harvests the crop. Any good salesperson can go out and find a few customers. But the difference between that and a good strategic marketing campaign is the difference between a hunter/gatherer society and modern agriculture. If you ask your salespeople to work without good marketing support, you are putting them at an enormous disadvantage.

You want your salespeople to harvest their sales leads, not have to track each one down. You want their sales calls to be with people who are fully ready to buy, not hiding under a bush. Finally, you want each sales call to be as efficient and effective as possible, not a battle over a total of three cases.

But marketing takes time and money. Often there is a conflict between salespeople, who want immediate results (and are often paid for immediate results) and the marketing team that wants to make sure that the ground is perfectly prepared. It is not enough to simply sell the wine. The best solution is one that sells every bottle to the right customer, at the right price, and at the right time.

Unfortunately, there is a paradox built into wine marketing: wine marketing is slow. It takes time for the gentle (and you must be gentle!) massaging of the market to pay off in increased sales, higher price points, and enhanced image. When the winery is struggling, this investment of time and money is not only disheartening, it is potentially ruinous financially.

A sale, on the other hand, is fast. There is no question that a good salesperson can sell a lot of wine very quickly. Reduced prices, bargain bin placements, and special volume discounts can quickly turn a winery's aging inventory into hard cash. Those increased sales come as a result of a simple equation: The salesperson is taking a very good product, one that is worth $X, and selling it very quickly for $X-5. Customers leap at the bargain. They rejoice in buying a wine for far less than its usual high price.

Figure 1.2: Marketing and Sales Compared

Marketing	Sales
Prepares the Ground	Harvests the Crop
Takes Time and Money	Happens Now, Happens Fast
Increases the Value of the Brand	Reaps the Value of the Inventory
Is Hard to Measure	Is Tracked by Cases, Dollars, and Cents
Is Strategic	Is Tactical

The paradox, however, arises from the long-term impact of that effort. Once consumers and the trade get accustomed to seeing your wine at that reduced price, the bargain no longer seems attractive. You no longer have a wine that is perceived as one that is worth $X. Your brand is worth far less than it was before the fire sale.

You have may achieved your short-term sales goals, but you have put your long-term brand marketing efforts far behind.

HOW IS THE AMERICAN WINE BUSINESS DIFFERENT?

If you explained how wine is sold throughout the US to someone who does marketing at a major packaged goods company, they would throw up their hands in disbelief. The regulations and requirements surrounding alcohol sales in America provide an enormous layer of complexity over what is already a complicated business. Why does each state, and in some cases even each county, have different laws and regulations concerning alcohol sales? It all goes back to that grand failed experiment called Prohibition.

Prohibition was repealed in 1934 because it didn't work. In fact, it was so ineffective that consumption of many kinds of alcoholic beverages actually *increased* during Prohibition. While Americans could not legally buy wine, beer or spirits during Prohibition, they had no trouble purchasing those same beverages through a vast network of illegal producers, distributors, and retailers. That network was developed and managed by organized crime, and in most markets, it was a perfect vertical monopoly—the same family controlled the production, distribution and sales of the product from beginning to end.

When it came time to repeal Prohibition, politicians in Washington were quite worried that they would give that same organized crime network the opportunity to continue to dominate the industry. They designed a plan that would make it almost impossible to create any kind of vertical monopoly, and required registration and licensing at every level that made it illegal for anyone with a criminal record to play a role in the industry.

Producers were required to be bonded by the federal government. Wholesale distributors were required to be bonded by each individual state government. Every retailer or restaurant was required to be licensed by the government of that state, and also to be reviewed by local authorities. To avoid any possible vertical monopoly, it is illegal for any individual to hold more than one kind of license. You cannot be a distributor and run a retail shop. You cannot be a producer and also own a distributorship. The involvement of organized crime in the business was effectively limited by these laws.

But the authors of Repeal knew that they would need the support of every state to be successful. They included a condition that every state would have the authority to control the sale of alcohol as it saw fit. This is why some states only allow wine to be sold through state-owned stores, and others allow it in grocery stores. Some states took that idea and passed it along down the line, so that each county in the state has the right to regulate alcohol in that county. The list of long and unusual state laws would be amusing, if it didn't create so many challenges to the simple business of selling wine in America.

These laws create a complicated system of distribution for any wine company. The complexity of the situation also means that many times there are real limitations to the kinds of marketing programs and campaigns that can be executed on a national basis. Too many wineries have discovered that because of these local regulations, their wonderful national plans will not be legal in Texas or New York, let alone smaller markets like Utah and Oklahoma.

National campaigns on behalf of wine companies face other challenges as well. With a few notable exceptions, few other industries face the issue of producing and marketing a completely different product every year. In the wine industry, each vintage brings its own character to the wines. The media, the pipeline, and the consumers all have become accustomed to vintage reports that change the perception of particular brands, products, or even entire regions based on these vintage differences.

Wineries have learned that they must manage not just a product line of three or four or six wines, but that each of those product lines will be affected by the weather, their own winemaking expertise, and the response of the market to those factors. A great review can sell out a single wine in weeks, while a poor response can suddenly change the annual plan by many months. The careful management of inventory as these vintages transition from one to the other in the fifty different states requires a spreadsheet of Herculean proportions.

In terms of classic marketing techniques, this means that a simple brand extension for a winery is often far more than just that. In addition to the usual concerns about cannibalization from the existing product line, wineries must consider that line extensions really can create logistical and administrative problems that may far outweigh any real increase in case sales or perceived increase in brand image.

At the same time, most wineries in the US produce far fewer than 50,000 cases of wine. Such production levels mean that they must be quite selective in how and where they sell that wine. It is a continual challenge to balance the desire to sell as much wine as any individual market will bear with the need to keep your markets diversified and stable.

Such small production lots mean that wineries have very limited marketing funds available. However, most wineries believe that they must compete on a regional if not national basis, because the top wine consumers are not located in only one or two markets. While the wine market is quite focused in many ways by demographics, the geography of the major wine markets in the US is daunting. Any attempt at a national brand would require a winery to have a presence in California, New York, Florida, Illinois, Texas, and other markets. The amount of wine sold in those markets is usually not significant enough to justify any major advertising campaign, and so wine marketers cannot rely on the traditional brand marketing approaches of the packaged goods industry.

Complicated laws, vintage transitions, limited budgets, and national goals—these are not reasons to despair or concede defeat. They are simply another fact of life in the world of wine marketing—and one that only underscores the important of solid strategic work. When your options are so limited, it is critical that everything you do be as effectively targeted as possible.

There are some who will argue that such a strategic approach is diametrically opposed to the spirit and tradition of the world of wine. We would suggest, first of all, that if a winemaker wants to sell his or her product anything that distinguishes a wine from the rest of the market should be seriously considered. That is, after all, the primary point of this chapter: You must make your wine or winery stand out as different. That is the premise of wine marketing theory and practice.

But we also recognize a number of very strong consumer perceptions about wine. Wine is seen by most consumers as a hand-crafted product, the result of loving care in the vineyard and in the winery. It is seen as the personal expression of an individual: a visionary owner, a remarkably gifted winemaker. It is seen as the unique expression of a single piece of earth: a terroir that cannot be replicated.

All of these things are true. It is equally true that if the marketing efforts of the product are not held up to that same standard, then those very producers will find their wines lost in a sea of wine. Their painstaking work, their years of investment, their dedication to quality will be wasted. Their wine will become nothing more than a commodity that is bought and sold based on the design of the label or the discount coupon on the necker.

The role of marketing in the wine industry is not to corrupt the process of making great wine. It is to make that process clear and understandable to the market. If the market cannot see or know what makes your wine the unique expression it is, then it cannot fully appreciate your wine. If you do not give the market the marketing strategies, tactics and programs it needs to understand your product, then much of your effort in making that wine will have been wasted.

IS YOUR WINE MARKETING SUCCESSFUL?

So how can you tell if your wine marketing is successful? It is a simple equation. If you were to sell your company, how much would the brand name be worth? Once you have sold all of the tangible assets of the company, how much would someone pay just for your brand name? That amount is exactly equal to the quality of the marketing you have done.

SOME BASIC WINE MARKETING TERMS

Like any other discipline, marketing has a special language that can be confusing. Following are some basic terms that are helpful to understand as you enhance your wine marketing efforts.

- **Brand:** A name you can trust, it stands for a family of products. The entire focus of your marketing efforts should be to make your brand more valuable.

- **Brand Awareness:** Getting on the short list in the customers' minds. The top brands are remembered by customers, while lesser-known brands fall by the wayside.

- **Brand Equity:** The value of the intangible assets of a brand.

- **Brand Extension:** Adding new products, sizes, or packages to the initial brand offering.

- **Brand Visibility:** The first step in awareness. Either your products or your marketing campaigns must create visibility for your brand.

- **Category:** A segment of the market that both customers and the trade recognize as being important. Leadership in a category is a key goal for any marketing campaign.

- **Distribution Channel:** The institutions and partners such as wholesalers and retailers that are used to make your product available to customers.

- **Label:** In the wine business, another name for brand. Also a graphic design concept that gives the brand a visual image.

- **Leverage:** Using the strength of your brand or company sales volume to get more attention from the pipeline, and to generate more sales to consumers.

- **Market:** A way of describing a collection of customers.

- **Marketing:** The performance of business activities that direct the flow of goods and services from producer to consumer.

- **Pipeline:** Everything between you and the person who actually opens the bottle; this includes the distributor network, retailers, and restaurateurs.

- **Position:** How customers perceive your brand compared to other products that compete in the same category.

- **Pricing:** How much you charge customers in exchange for your products.

- **Product:** A specific type of wine for sale, e.g. 2002 Cabernet Sauvignon, Alexander Valley, XYZ Winery. Usually labeled as one SKU for inventory purposes.

- **Promotion:** How you convey the distinct message of your brand to target customers.

- **Segment:** A way of breaking the market into more manageable parts.

- **SKU:** Stock keeping unit. Generally includes a barcode number to identify a specific wine product in inventory.

- **Target:** A way of refining the description of the market.

- **Trial:** Getting customers to try the product. Many marketing programs aim to have customers try the product, fall in love with the product, and as a result become loyal to the product. This philosophy is frequently misapplied in the wine industry.

REFERENCES

"Marketing Definitions." Available at: http://www.marketingpower.com/content4620.php. American Marketing Association, 2005.

"Number of U.S. Wineries Tops 5300." *Wine Business Monthly*, Vol. 13, No. 2, Feb. 15, 2006.

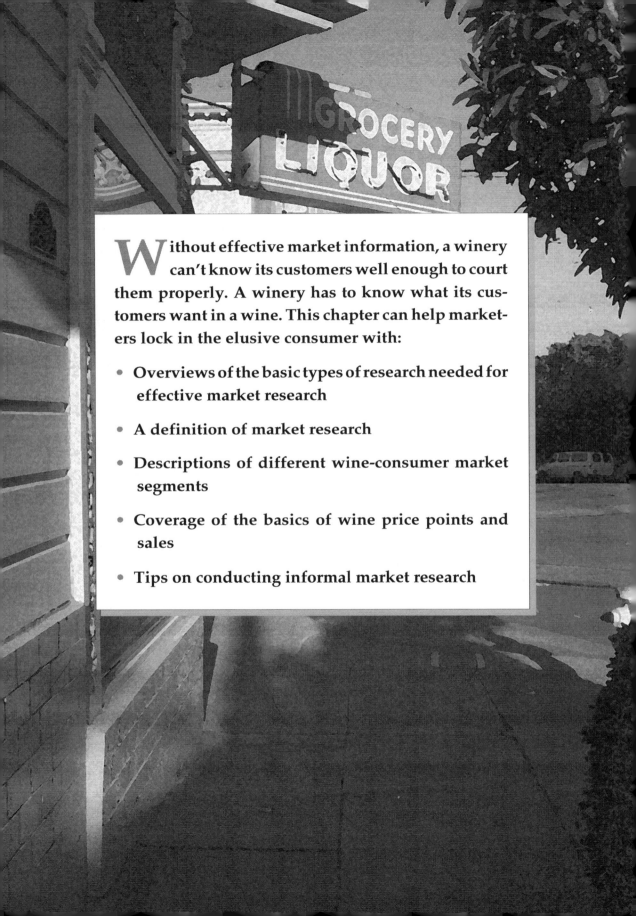

Without effective market information, a winery can't know its customers well enough to court them properly. A winery has to know what its customers want in a wine. This chapter can help marketers lock in the elusive consumer with:

- Overviews of the basic types of research needed for effective market research

- A definition of market research

- Descriptions of different wine-consumer market segments

- Coverage of the basics of wine price points and sales

- Tips on conducting informal market research

C H A P T E R

RESEARCH & DEMOGRAPHICS: WINE CONSUMERS TODAY

How much do you know about your wine customers? Can you answer the following questions: Where do your customers live and what are their characteristics? What are the motivations they have for purchasing wine? What drives their interest in wine? How can wine make their lives better? What are the benefits they seek in a bottle of wine—especially your wine? What are the important attributes customers want in the wine they drink? How do they want wine to look and taste? If you can answer the above questions, you are well on your way to building a good market research database for your winery.

What Is Market Research?

Marketing research has become a critical component of marketing for wineries. **Marketing research** is defined as the use of information to connect marketing firms with their customers. Information is gathered that can identify new opportunities for marketers, solve problems, improve marketing actions, and delineate how marketing delivers the benefits that consumers expect. More specifically, marketing researchers first must identify the exact information that will be helpful, decide how best to collect the data and then conduct the appropriate analyses once that data has been gathered. Once these steps are finished, the findings must be reported with the implications for managers clearly stated (American Marketing Association, 2005).

Marketing activities are performed in an attempt to satisfy the wants and needs of people in a way that provides an adequate profit to the company. However, this implies that marketers know and understand the needs and wants of its customers. The more we know about the wants and needs of potential customers, the better we can meet or exceed our customers' expectations.

To gather information that can help us understand our wine customers, wineries rely on market research information. Companies can either conduct their own marketing research studies , a process called **primary research**, or they can rely on research already conducted by someone else, a process called **secondary research.** Most wine companies use a combination of both primary and secondary research to help them formulate their marketing plans.

Figure 2.1: Consumer Wine Consumption in the U.S.

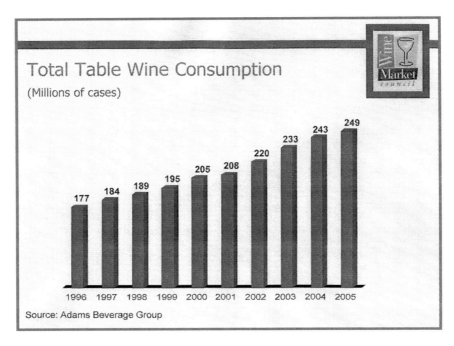

It is important to have clear goals and objectives when developing a marketing research program, as conducting marketing research requires a commitment of both human and financial resources. Designing and implementing a relatively simple primary research study can easily run over $10,000, depending on the scope of the study. In the case of secondary research where the data has already been collected by others—for example, sales data collected from retail scanners—costs are also involved, as you will most likely have to purchase the data from an outside vendor. Even if you rely on information that is available for free—for example statistics located on the internet—there still must be someone assigned to finding the information and interpreting the data before it can be of any use to your winery. Because you don't want to see the money budgeted to marketing research wasted, it is very important that much thought go into deciding what information is necessary and how it will benefit your wine business. The following sections highlight some of the types of marketing research data that wineries usually rely on to formulate their marketing plans.

WINE CONSUMER SEGMENTATION

One important objective of marketing research is to better understand the consumers the winery wants to target with their marketing programs. Wineries use research to develop a profile of their customers and create detailed descriptions of the market segments they are interested in reaching. Typical data that are used to describe customers and markets include the following four categories, which are described in the next section:

1. **Geographic market data:** Showing where purchases of wine occur.

2. **Behavioral:** Based on usage rates, occasions, benefits, readiness stage.

3. **Demographic:** Including gender, age and ethnicity.

4. **Psychographic:** Including lifestyles and involvement, attitudes, or interest in wine.

Table 2.1: Four Major Types of Market Segmentation and Questions Addressed

Types of Segmentation	Questions Addressed
Geographic Segmentation	**Where do our consumers live?**
Behavioral segmentation	**How are our products consumed? How often do consumers drink wine, on which occasions?**
Demographic segmentation	**Who drinks wine? What is their gender, age, income, education, ethnicity, and other descriptive factors?**
Psychographic segmentation	**Why do people drink wine? What are their motivations, their attitudes, involvement or interest in wine?**

Geographic Market Data: Where Is Wine Purchased?

Very few wine companies are large enough to sell to customers in every country throughout the world, or even to all locations within the United States. Most companies prefer to identify a smaller number of markets and concentrate their marketing activities in geographic areas where they feel they can be most successful. When making the decision on where to sell wine, companies often look at marketing research figures to see where wine is already being sold. Consumption and export data are used to identify countries where the potential for wine sales exists and is discussed in Chapter 13 on exporting wine.

The US is the third most populous country, and has wine consumers from coast to coast. In a survey taken March 2003, 39% of US adults had purchased wine in the previous 3 months (*Scarborough Research*).

The wine market in the US is predicted to be the largest market in the world by 2008 (www.winebusiness.com 2005). But where in the US would a wine marketer find the largest number of consumers? Sales data have identified that in 2004, the states with the largest markets are California, New York, New Jersey, Texas and Florida (Gomberg, Fredrikson & Associates, 2004).

These findings are probably not surprising as these states all have relatively large populations and are also popular tourist destinations. On a per capita basis, Nevada tops the list in terms of wine consumption, and again the figures probably reflect the tourism found in Nevada. Other cities in the US that sales data indicate have high wine sales per capita include Los Angeles, New York City, Chicago, San Francisco, Boston and Washington, D.C. Of course, not all wineries choose to target the cities with the largest number of consumers, but instead may look for markets that have fewer competitors. For example, many small wineries with production of less than 10,000 cases focus on selling wine only within their state or region. This is often because people from a particular state are proud to drink the wine produced from that state, and will visit the winery, as well as purchase the wine in local restaurants and wine shops.

Behavioral Market Data: Usage Segments and Their Characteristics

While it is important to know in which regions wine is sold, it is also important to know who is purchasing the wine and how much they buy. Market research has been collected to provide a better profile of the US wine drinker (Wine Market Council, 2000, 2003).

Core Drinkers drink wine the most, usually several times a week, or at least 3 times a month. Currently, there are about 25.4 million US consumers, or about 12.5% of the population who fit into this category. Obviously this group is very important to wine marketers—they drink 88% of the wine sold in the US. Market research has shown us

Figure 2.2: US Wine Consumer Segments

Consumer Segments

(Percentages, ages 21+ HHI $35K+)

	% Sample	% Volume
Core Wine Drinkers	13.7	87
Marginal Wine Drinkers	18.9	13
Beer/Spirits Drinkers	24.7	0
Non-Drinkers	42.7	0
TOTAL	100	100

Source: Merrill Research

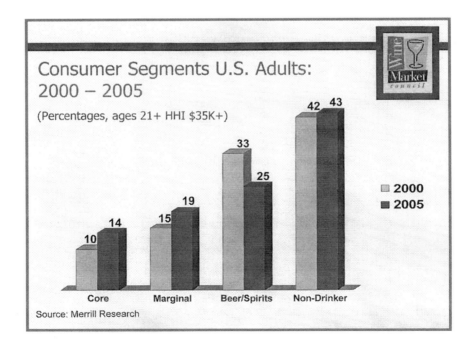

Consumer Segments U.S. Adults: 2000 – 2005

(Percentages, ages 21+ HHI $35K+)

Source: Merrill Research

that of core consumers 60% are women, 85% of the group's ethnic background is white, and 71% are over age 40. This market segment tends to be better educated and more affluent than the average American.

Marginal Drinkers are wine drinkers who enjoy wine, but they drink it less often, usually once or twice a month, or at least once a quarter. Wine is usually a beverage that they associate with a special occasion instead of a beverage they would enjoy with a regular meal. Currently, about 14% of the American population, or 28-million consumers, fall into this category. In terms of their demographic characteristics, marginal drinkers are very similar to Core Drinkers, but slightly younger. On average, 59% are women, 84% are white, and 58% are over 40. There has been a lot of interest recently in developing marketing campaigns to increase the amount of wine that Marginal Drinkers consume. For example, advertisements that show wine being consumed with everyday foods are, in many cases, targeted toward Marginal Drinkers.

Non-Wine Drinkers drink alcoholic beverages but do not drink wine. Consumers in this group often say that they do not like the taste of wine because they prefer beer or sweeter drinks. People in this category tend to be much younger on average; most are between ages 21 and 39. This group is predominately male, at 55%. There have been a few attempts to develop products that this group might like, such as wine coolers and flavored wines.

Abstainers do not drink alcohol at all. This is a large group of consumers in America, with 43% of the population, or close to 90 million consumers. There are many reasons why people avoid alcohol, including their religious beliefs that advocate abstinence and health issues they face, such as interactions with medicines, allergies, pregnancy and recovery from addictive behavior. Wine marketers for the most part would probably see these as valid reasons for not consuming wine, and therefore marketing efforts are usually directed at the other three segments of the population.

Figure 2.3: Change in US Wine Consumer Segments

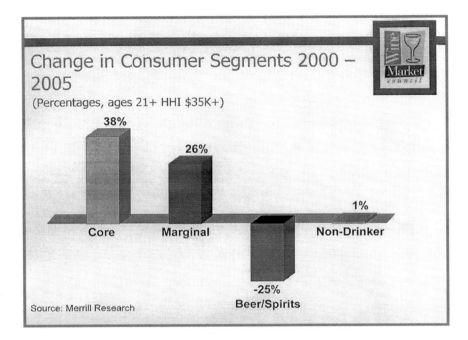

Demographic Market Data:
What Do Wine Consumers Look Like?

Demographic variables include consumer characteristics such as gender, income, education level, ethnicity, household size, etc. As wine consumers are found in many different demographic groups, marketers must identify the segment(s) of the market that they hope to target. Demographics are then often used to describe the segments that are of interest. For example, a marketer may decide that they would like to target African-American women who are age 40–55. In addition to providing wine firms with descriptions of the segments of potential customers, demographic factors are useful from a promotion standpoint, as they often relate to the media preferences of the chosen target market.

Figure 2.4: US Wine Consumption by Gender

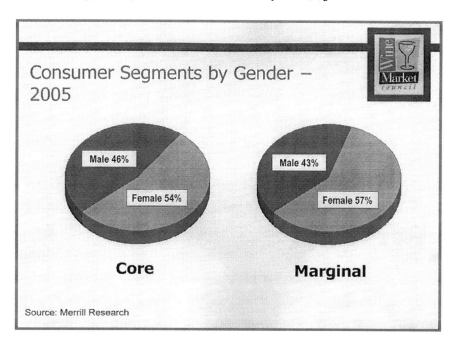

One demographic variable that has been used to describe wine consumers is their **gender**. In the US, women are more likely than men to purchase wine, accounting for more than 60% of all of the wine purchased (Reynolds 2005). Some of the wine they purchase they drink themselves, and, as women often do the shopping for the household, some of the wine is likely purchased for men. However, women typically drink wine more often than men; as about 60% of consumers who drink wine several times a week or more are women. Women give different reasons for drinking than men. Women are more likely to claim that they drink wine in a social setting and dining context, and women appear to have less interest than men in collecting wine and following wine scores.

These market research findings have inspired several wineries to introduce wines targeted specifically at women. For example, Beringer Blass Wine Estates (BBWE) has introduced the first premium California wine ever to be designed by women expressly for the U.S. female

Figure 2.5: US Wine Consumption by Age

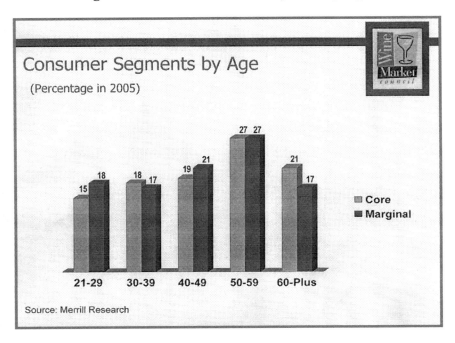

consumer. White Lie Early Season™ Chardonnay, trademarked because of the groundbreaking way in which the wine is made, is a great-tasting wine that is low in calories, sugar and alcohol, meeting the needs of today's dynamic women who want to "have it all." (Beringer Blass Press Release, happyhours.com)

Age is another demographic characteristic that marketers use to segment the wine market. People of all ages do drink wine; the questions are how much does each age group drink, and how much are they typically willing to spend on wine. Although the ages included in one group or another differ slightly from one source to another, wine consumers can currently be placed into four different age groups: Older Americans (60 and above), Baby Boomers (40-60) Generation X (28-39), and Echo Boomers or Millennium Generation (21-28). Interestingly, older Americans often drink wine, especially red wine, to realize associated health benefits, yet at the same time, many older consumers limit or abstain from wine for health reasons, often due to possible interactions with medicines they take. This age group has been relatively small in terms of overall population, but as the Baby Boomers begin turning 60, its importance to marketers will increase.

The Baby Boomers account for the largest percentage of the US population, and historically, they have been the primary consumers of wine. Due to the group's large size of 80 million consumers, and its favorable consumption habits, this is the age group that most wineries have felt has the most potential, and therefore many wineries have targeted Baby Boomers in their marketing plans. With so many companies focusing on Baby Boomers, this has been an extremely competitive segment of the market. It is likely that this age group will remain an important customer for wine in the future.

Generation X has been a difficult market to sell wine to for many reasons. The size of the market is smaller than the Baby Boomers, and Generation X consumers' consumption rates have not rivaled the Baby Boomer's. Many wineries optimistically hoped that as this group aged, their wine consumption would increase to the levels of the Baby Boomers, but so far that has not happened. Of course, there are members of Generation X who drink wine, and even though their numbers may be fewer than other groups, the Generation X group should not be written off completely.

Echo Boomers, or Millennial consumers, as they are sometimes referred to, are an age group that has shown much promise for wine marketers. This group has shown an interest in wine at an early age, and they drink a lot of it. Unlike many older groups where consumers first developed a preference for white or rosé wines before moving on to red wines, many people in this age group prefer red wines over white wines. Millennial consumers often complain that they find many wine brands to be too snooty and arrogant, and they appreciate most those wines that are fun and approachable. Many wine companies are developing products that appeal to this group. For example, Jake's Fault, a new Shiraz wine, was targeted for the Millennial generation. It is red, fruit-forward in taste, and has appealing, quirky graphics for the label. It is well-priced at approximately $9.99 a bottle, and is selling well to this demographic.

Marketers are also realizing that there are many ethnically diverse consumers who also appreciate wine, and marketing research is providing tantalizing evidence of the potential of these market segments based on ethnicity. For example, the Hispanic market has become the largest ethnic market in the US, and research shows that they are one of the fastest growing segments in terms of wine consumption (Gallup News Organization, 2005). One study found that Hispanics in several markets are willing to spend slightly more for a bottle of wine than are other consumers (Scarborough Research, 2003). Researchers suggest that this may be due to the fact that Hispanics often hold celebrations where wine is provided.

African-American consumers are also consuming more wine. There are now groups such as Wine Divas that organize events to educate African-American consumers about wine. Consumers of Asian backgrounds in the US have not been heavy consumers of wine for the most part, yet recently, more and more attention is being paid to this group. Asian-Americans have the highest level of income of all ethnic groups in the US (U.S Census Bureau, 2003), and many Asian-Americans live in areas where wine consumption is already high. In order to increase wine sales to Asian-Americans, wine experts are identifying wines that complement Asian foods and are putting together wine lists for Asian restaurants. These attempts to broaden the wine market in the US clearly show that wineries recognize the diversity of wine consumers in this country.

Although the market for wine is becoming more ethnically diverse, it should be noted that not all wine marketers feel that creating special marketing programs is necessary to reach consumers of different ethnic backgrounds. Marketers point out that the profile of ethnic wine consumers with regards to other demographic characteristics, such as income, education, and occupation, tends to mirror those of traditional consumers. Since developing a specialized marketing campaign entails additional costs, there is little advantage to spending extra money creating a special marketing program if it is not necessary. However, other marketers argue that the lifestyles, foods, or media habits of ethnic consumers are quite different, and wine marketing programs that recognize and capitalize on the differences will have a competitive advantage in the marketplace.

PSYCHOGRAPHIC MARKET DATA: WHAT ARE THE MOTIVATIONS FOR DRINKING WINE?

Psychographics refer to people's lifestyles, including how they live, what interests them, and what activities they like to do (American Marketing Association, 2005). The analysis of psychographic data helps marketers understand consumers' motivations for drinking wine. There have been numerous marketing research studies investigating the various segments of wine drinkers and the reasons why they purchase wine. One approach has been to segment consumers by their **level of involvement in wine** (Lockshin and Spawton, 1997). For example, wine marketers have identified three involvement groups.

The first group consists of **Connoisseurs**—people who are highly involved with wine and enjoy learning about wine. They often attend wine events such as wine tastings and winemaker dinners, they take wine tours to different wine producing regions, and they often are involved in collecting wine.

The second group, with medium involvement levels, is comprised of **Aspirational Drinkers** who feel that wine fits nicely with their image of themselves and the image they want to portray to others. They often drink wine to gain social acceptance, and because they like the image it conveys to important peers, they see wine as a way to fit in with people whose lifestyle they admire. As with

Connoisseurs, they attempt to learn about wine, but the motivation is primarily because they don't want to make a mistake and embarrass themselves in important social situations.

The third group, **Beverage Drinkers,** with low involvement levels, see wine as a beverage, and they don't want to work at learning about wine. They often rely on mental shortcuts to make wine purchasing and consumption easy. An example of a shortcut they might use would be to always buy the same brand whenever they purchase wine, or the same varietal in an acceptable price range. Note that involvement levels are not necessarily related to wine consumption rates, as beverage drinkers may drink as much or more than people in the other categories. For example, a person may have been raised in an Italian household where wine is consumed with meals, and as an adult, he or she may continue to drink the same wine each night without giving it a lot of thought.

Somewhat similar to involvement segmentation, but focusing on the *motivations based on the nature of the occasions* in which people often drink wine, five segments have been identified (Questar and Smart, 1998; Hall and Lockshin, 2000). These are as follows:

1. **Social Wine Drinkers** who drink wine because they feel it enhances a social situation. These people primarily consume wine at parties, weddings and other celebrations, or when out at bars and pubs.

2. **Image-Oriented Wine Drinkers** often order wine when out at restaurants with peers or business colleagues, and because the correct image is important to them, they often engage in risk-reduction strategies by purchasing known and trusted brands.

3. **Ritual-Oriented Wine Drinkers** are those consumers who enjoy trying new wines at tastings and festivals. They enjoy wine-education classes and special events as these give

them opportunities to increase their knowledge about wine. They also read wine-related magazines and pay attention to wine ratings.

4. **Premium Wine Drinkers** are high-end wine consumers who are very knowledgeable about wine. They are often into wine collecting and having an impressive wine cellar. For these consumers there is immense satisfaction in scoring the exclusive wine that others do not have—the more rare or valuable the wine the more interested these consumers are likely to be.

5. **Basic Weekend Wine Drinkers** are at the other extreme. They see wine as a beverage to have at weekend parties, BBQs and while socializing with friends. As with the Beverage Drinkers, they have low levels of involvement and do not want to spend time or effort learning about wine, but prefer to buy wines that are convenient and within their budget.

By understanding the basic motivations and demographics of people who drink your wine, you will be able to focus your marketing efforts more effectively. For example, if you discover through market research that the majority of people who drink your wine live on the West Coast, are women, part of the Millennial generation, and fall into the category of social wine drinkers, you can then focus your advertising and promotion campaigns to appeal more broadly to this audience.

MARKET RESEARCH DATA:
SALES OF WINE AND DIFFERENT PRICE POINTS

Marketers rely on sales data to track the amount of wine that has sold. Of course, the marketing approach needed to sell wine varies by the price of the wine, so marketers are not only interested in how much wine is sold and to whom, but how much is sold in the various price categories. Marketing research data that tracks the sales of wine by price point is available, but care should be taken in analyzing the data because many of the popular sources of this information rely on scanner data of sales at supermarkets and similar retail stores, and do not include wine sold in specialty wine stores or in restaurants. For this reason, the figures may distort the true picture of the amount of wine sold, especially by not capturing the sales for a lot of higher-priced wines that tend not to be sold in supermarkets.

Price categories are defined in different ways by different marketing research organizations, but most are similar in approach even if the cutoff points vary slightly. At the most inexpensive level, the **Super Value Wines** are now tracked. These are wines that sell for less than $3 per 750ml, and probably the most famous example of a Super Value wine is Charles Shaw, sold at Trader Joe's for $1.99 in California. In other states the price might be slightly more due to taxes and regulations. The success of Charles Shaw has encouraged other retail outlets to offer store brand sold at similar prices.

The next level up in terms of price is the **Basic or Sub Premium Wines** which usually sell for $3-6.99. Popular brands include Beringer, Woodbridge, and Sutter Home. At the next level are the **Premium Wines** which typically sell for $7-9.99 and include brands such as Turning Leaf and brands from Fetzer. **Super Premium Wines** usually sell for $10-$13.99 with well-known brands from Kendall-Jackson, Clos du Bois, Mondavi, and Gallo of Sonoma. **Ultra Premium or Deluxe Wines** sell for $14 and above and include a variety of wine brands such as Moët & Chandon, Franciscan's Magnificat, and Chateau St. Jean. Finally, some market research reports have a separate top category for those wines selling for more than $50, called the **Icon Wines.** Examples of well-known Icon Wines include Dom Perignon, Penfold's Grange and Silver Oak Cabernet Sauvignon. Consumers are very conscious of price/quality relationship although recently many consumers are showing a willingness to spend more and purchase wines at higher price points than they did in the past (*Wine Business Monthly*, 2005).

Table 2.2: Common Wine Price Segments

Super Value Wines	**Less than $3.00**
Basic or Sub Premium Wines	**$3.00–6.99**
Premium Wines	**$7.00–9.99**
Super Premium Wines	**$10.00–13.99**
Ultra Premium or Deluxe Wines	**$14.00–49.99**
Icon Wines	**$50.00 and greater**

ONGOING NEED FOR MARKETING RESEARCH

The findings mentioned above have been some of those used by wine marketers in developing their marketing programs. However, it is important to note that the wine market in the US is constantly changing. The profile of a wine consumer that has served the wine industry well in past years may not accurately reflect the new consumers now adopting wine. Marketers themselves alter the landscape as well, because they are constantly developing new advertising campaigns and product innovations. All of these changes underscore the importance of developing an on-going marketing research program to provide data that is timely and meets the needs of the wine industry. As the wine market becomes more competitive, it is safe to say that marketing research will only become more important.

SIMPLE SUGGESTIONS TO
CONDUCT INFORMAL MARKET RESEARCH

Common wisdom suggests that if you want good market research data, you will have to pay for it. For the most part this holds true, and it is recommended that you find a good market research firm to assist you in designing and implementing market research to fit your specific needs. However, there are also some basic and informal market research techniques you can use that are low cost and will result in some useful data. These are often useful in conjunction with a more formalized market research agenda:

- **Tasting Room Customer Feedback:** If you have a tasting room, you already have a built-in research facility. Why not take advantage of it? Consider using customer comment cards requesting feedback on what consumers enjoyed in your tasting room, their favorite wine, why they visited you, and suggestions for improvement. Some wineries employ this concept by setting up a computer kiosk station in the tasting room. To encourage customers to participate, consider giving them a discount on purchases or tasting fees, or sponsor a monthly drawing for a merchandise gift (don't use wine, because you cannot ship to all states). Also, by tracking your wine purchases in the tasting room, you will have a clear idea of what brands and price points are selling well. Compare this data with information from your other sales channels. What does this tell you?

- **Wine Club Consumer Feedback:** Similar to your tasting room, your wine club customers are an excellent source of data. Therefore, consider including a short survey in your wine club newsletter or online announcements. Gather data on why the customers have selected your wine club, their favorite wines, and suggestions for improvements.

- **Retail Observation Surveys:** The story of Ernest and Julio Gallo visiting the retail stores in which their wine was sold to talk with customers and shop owners is an inspiring one. They kept close tabs on the buying preferences of their customers, and gained valuable information from talking with wine shop owners. This type of casual observation—though not standard quantitative research—can yield fascinating qualitative information about your wine brand. Therefore, consider visiting grocery stores, wine shops, and restaurants where your wine is sold. Observe customers as they attempt to select a wine, and consider asking them about their selections. Some small winery owners do this at least once a month, whereas others do it weekly.

- **Focus Groups:** Another qualitative research technique is to pull together a small focus group of 6-10 wine consumers. Though this is usually run by a professional market research firm, you can also do this informally with customers who visit your tasting room or events. Generally you will need to schedule this in advance, and offer the customers something for their time, e.g., merchandise or discounts. You will also need to have developed focus group questions in advance, and may want to ask an impartial friend to facilitate the session, as you may be too emotionally involved in the responses.

- **Internet Surveys:** Finally, it is now possible to launch an inexpensive internet survey with the assistance of some of the online survey companies such as www.surveymonkey. com, www.insightexpress.com, and www.zoomerang.com. You will also need access to a list of consumer emails. These may be from your own database, or you can also purchase email lists from other groups. For example, you can buy an email list from frequent-flyer programs, because people who fly a lot often drink wine. Most important, however, is to come up with relevant survey questions that can be quickly and easily answered online. Since 99% of wine consumers have internet access (Stallcup, 2005), you often receive a decent response rate as long as the survey is not too long. Again, offering some type of incentive for completing the survey, such as entering them in a drawing, can increase response rates.

A final caveat when conducting informal market research is to have clear research objectives that tie directly to your marketing and business objectives. Therefore it is important to know what questions you want answered. Finally, don't conduct research if you aren't going to use the findings in some meaningful and constructive way.

CHAPTER REFERENCES

"Dictionary of Marketing Terms." Available at: www.ama.org, American Marketing Association, 2005.

Hall, J., and L. Lockshin. "Using Means-End Chains for Analyzing Occasions-Not Buyers," *Australasian Marketing Journal, 8(1)*, 45-54, 2000.

Gallup News Organization, "Wine Gains Momentum as Americans' Favorite Adult Beverage" Available at www.gallup.com, 2005.

Gomberg, Fredrikson & Associates. "Annual Wine Industry Report." Woodside, CA, 2004. Available at www.wineryexchange.com.

Lockshin, L., G. Macintosh, and A. Spawton. "Using Product, Brand, and Purchasing Involvement for Retail Segmentation," *Journal of Retailing and Consumer Services, 4(3)*, 171-183, 1997.

"Product Innovation Focus Leads to First California Wine Designed by and for Women." HappyHours.com Inc. 49 Commodore Road, Chappaqua, NY 10514.

Quester, P. G., and J. Smart. "The Influence of Consumption Situation and Product Involvement Over Consumers' Use of Product Attribute," *Journal of Consumer Marketing*, 15(3), 220-238, 1998.

Reynolds, Gavin. "Wine and Women" Available at http://www.13wham.com/news/. 2005.

Scarborough Research, "New Wine Market Segments," Presentation at the 2003 Unified Wine & Grape Symposium, Sacramento, CA.

Stallcup, J. "Staying Close to Your Customers: Simple & Inexpensive Ways to Get Consumer Feedback." Presentation at the 2005 Unified Wine & Grape Symposium, Sacramento, CA.

U.S. Census Bureau, "Facts and Figures," Available at http://www.census.gov/Press-Release/www/2003/cb03-ff05.html . 2003.

"Retail Sales Analysis." *Wine Business Monthly*, Available at www.winebusiness.com. July 15, 2005.

"U.S. to Become World's Largest Wine Market by 2008 Study Shows." www.winebusiness.com. 2005.

Wine Market 2000: Trends and Analysis. Published by the Wine Market Council, Greenbrae, CA, Oct. 1, 2000.

"Wine Consumer Tracking Study Summary—2003." Wine Market Council (2003). Available at: http://www.winemarketcouncil.com/research_summary.asp.

A proper brand is a trusted name, which customers remember and seek out. Brands don't storm consumer consciousness overnight; it takes time and strategic skill. A lean, mean brand is built through effective market positioning. Chapter Three shows you how to build one:

- Defines position and competitive set

- Describes the seven steps of the positioning process

- SWOT analysis

- Strategies for competing within a category

- How brand strategy springs from the position-defining process.

CHAPTER 3

WINE
BRANDING

If a random group of consumers were brought together in a focus group and asked to name the top five wine brands in your category—category being the varietal, price point, appellation or other defining characteristic of your wine—would they mention your brand? If the answer is yes, then you should celebrate and dance around the vineyard, because you have achieved something that is quite difficult to do in the wine industry. You have developed a strong and compelling brand name. If the answer is no, don't feel bad, because you are among the ranks of hundreds of other small wineries that are still striving to develop a brand that is known to consumers.

DEFINING POSITION & COMPETITIVE SET
Positioning refers to how a product is viewed relative to competing products in the same category. It is how your target customers define you in relation to other winery competitors. It is also what makes you truly unique, and makes your wine stand out from others. Examples of different positions in the wine industry are outlined in Figure 3.1 below.

Figure 3.1: Matrix of Potential Wine Marketing Positions

Common Positioning Strategies	Execution of Positioning Strategy
Product Attributes: How is our product unique compared to others in the category?	A winery can use special grapes coming from distinctive vineyards, unusual varietals or different winemaking techniques to create a wine that unique and sought after.
User Characteristics: Does our wine appeal to smaller segment of the market more than other products?	A winery can create a product for a special segment of the market. For example, the wine and its image may be created to appeal to younger women who like to socialize often with friends.
Situation: Is our wine seen as the best choice for special occasions or events?	A winery can create a product for a specific situation. For example, the wine can be marketed as a perfect choice for a picnic on the beach.

A **competitive set** is a group of products that compete with each other with similar products, sold at similar prices. Competitive set is related to position, because customers compare wines in order to make the best choice. When deciding upon a wine to purchase, customers will first look at which of the products are available from the competitive set, and select the one that best fits their needs. It would not be possible for a consumer to consider every wine product available each time he or she went to make a purchase, nor would it even be desirable. Each consumer has their specific set of needs that they are seeking to fulfill, and many of the products available would not be able to fulfill all those needs. The consumer will narrow their search and look toward the product category that is most likely to contain products that meet their individual needs.

For example, a consumer may be looking for a lighter body red wine within the $7.00 to $9.00 price range. Within this category there are usually only a few products that are seriously considered—this is the so-called competitive set for any product. Consumers just do not have the time or energy to seriously consider most products, so they engage in a quick process of elimination until they finally select the one product that fits.

It is not enough to be a good choice; a wine has to be the best according to the criteria used by that particular consumer if it is to be the one selected. Being second or third isn't good enough, much less number 30 or 50 on a consumer's list. That is why it is so important for wine marketers to understand how they are viewed by consumers relative to other wines that are likely to be considered at the same time. Rather surprisingly, most wineries are not sure what category they are actually in. As the goal of any marketing campaign is to become the leader of a category, you are at a real loss if you can't even identify the proper category consumers see you in.

The goal is to be considered the best in a category. But just what does "being the best" really mean? To answer this question, it is important to look closer at the product positioning process.

THE POSITIONING PROCESS

The positioning process consists of seven major steps that are described in the following paragraphs. (Table 3.1 provides a graphical depiction of this process.) One important caveat, however, is to recognize that the position of any existing winery has already been established. This is because the winery has already created a brand image, a label, a package, a price point, etc., and they have communicated this to their consumers. So when established wineries analyze positioning, they should bear in mind that it is actually *re*-positioning that they are considering. Unless they have never released wine on the market before, they already have an image in the customer's mind, and they already have baggage to carry into the marketplace.

Table 3.1: Overview of the Positioning Process

Step	Developing a New Brand	Re-Positioning a Brand
1. Conduct Marketing Research	Research the segments you would like to target.	Research the segment you are targeting.
2. Identify Key Attributes	Understand what key attributes consumers are looking for in wine.	Understand what consumers are looking for in a wine and determine if your wine is fulfilling this need.
3. Identify Similar Products	Which products are competing in the category you intend to serve?	Which products are competing in the category you currently serve?
4. Collect Consumer Data on Category	How do consumers perceive the products in the category?	How do consumers perceive the products in the category?
5. Create a Perceptual Map	How do brands in the category currently compete?	How does your brand compete with brands currently in the category?
6. Identify Competitor Positions	Are there attractive openings where no other brands are competing?	Is your brand in a good position relative to competitors?
7. Identify Your Position Strategy	Determine if there are openings in which you have the strengths to compete effectively.	Decide if you should remain where you are, or move the brand to a new position with more potential.

1. Conduct Market Research

The process of creating a unique position for your brand begins with solid research on wine consumers, their needs and on the competition. Chapter Two describes in more detail the research that is used to describe wine consumers and their needs. It is important to recognize that the positioning process cannot begin unless a marketer has a clear understanding of his or her consumers, their needs, their buying habits, and how they view the various products competing for their pocketbook. It is critical to remember that the positioning process should always be done from the customer's perspective, and it is unlikely one can do this in a meaningful way without research focused on the consumer.

2. Identify Key Attributes Your Consumers Seek

One of the outcomes of the research should be the ability to identify the attributes that consumers are evaluating when they make a choice. Following is a list of the common attributes consumers seek when selecting a wine.

- *Price:* Usually one of the most important attributes that consumers first consider:"Is this wine selling for a price I can afford?"

- *Price/quality relationship:* Here consumers are asking, "Is it a good deal?"

- *Product features:* With this attribute consumers are interested in the style of wine and its taste. "Is it sweet, dry, tannic, etc?" Is it the varietal they are looking for?

- *Origin:* Here, consumers are asking where a wine comes from. Some consumers may be looking for a wine from a particular country or region.

- *Benefits* the product can fulfill, such as how well a wine might complement a particular meal.

- *Endorsements* or recommendations from others may be important. In this case, consumers may be searching for wines with high ratings or medals.

- *Parentage* of the winery could be an important consideration for some people who are fascinated with buying wines associated with well-known celebrities. An example could be Niebaum-Coppola wines, because the winery is owned by Francis Ford Coppola.

The list could go on and on, but until the marketers fully understand what key attributes their consumers are looking for, it is almost impossible to derive a positioning strategy that will appeal to the chosen market segment.

3. Identify Similar Products in Your Category
The next step of the positioning process is to identify similar products that compete in the same category as you. A temptation is for the winery to make a long list of the wineries they feel are the competition. However, consumers should be researched to find out which wines come to mind when thinking of a particular type of wine at a particular price point. This group of wines is referred to as the **evoked set,** and in many cases, you will be lucky if a consumer can name more than two or three wines for each category.

4. Collect Consumer Data on Your Category
Once you have determined who the competition really is, the next step is to collect customer data about their perceptions of the products they see competing in the category. What are the key criteria used by consumers to select a wine, and how do the products compare to each other on these key criteria? Too often wine marketers only ask how consumers view their own brand and do not consider how other similar brands are viewed. You will not be able to locate your position unless you know where you stand compared to others.

5. Create a Perceptual Map

When the data have been gathered, marketers then create a graphical depiction of how the brands are related to each other. This depiction is referred to as a perceptual map. The axes measure the criteria that consumers find important, and the location of each brand shows how it is positioned relative to others on these criteria. Oftentimes a circle is drawn to represent each brand's market share. The benefit of drawing a perceptual map is that the marketer can clearly see how brands are positioned.

Figure 3.2: Example of a Perceptual Map for Chardonnay

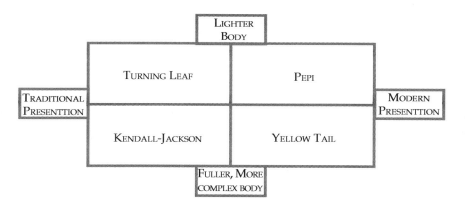

6. Analyze Competitor Positions

The next step is to use the map to analyze the current position of the companies that compete in the category. You should be able to see where competitors have positioned themselves relative to others. This informs you of their position and yours. It may be a position of low cost in a specific varietal category, or a luxury-priced wine in four traditional varietals. The key is to determine where you fit on the map in relationship to your competitors. The next step is then to determine your position strategy.

7. Identify Your Position Strategy

After analyzing the map, you might be quite content with your current position and decide to stay there. It is possible that you already have a competitive advantage, and that there are not many other wineries in your space. However you may also find that there are empty spots on the map where consumers do not see the current brands residing. These openings deserve further attention, although not all will prove opportunities to act upon.

Sometimes there are openings because the attributes described by the axes in the map are just not of interest to consumers. Other times, however, there may be openings where consumers would be interested in making a selection, but the current competitors are not seen as especially strong. This situation would provide an opportunity where a new brand could enter and take advantage of the weak position of competitors.

To build a strategy to capitalize on an opportunity requires the wine company to develop strengths and overcome weaknesses so that it can provide consumers with the products they are seeking. Therefore the next form of analysis to be considered is a SWOT analysis, which gives marketers the tools to do just that.

SWOT Analysis

As you can see from the previous description of the positioning process, developing a clear position in the marketplace requires a wine marketer to synthesize and to integrate a large amount of information about their company, competitors and customers. Perhaps one of the most popular methods for analyzing all of this data is called a SWOT analysis. SWOT stands for Strengths, Weaknesses, Opportunities and Threats, and the overriding purpose of a SWOT analysis is to develop a strategic plan to position a brand successfully.

Figure 3.3: SWOT Diagram

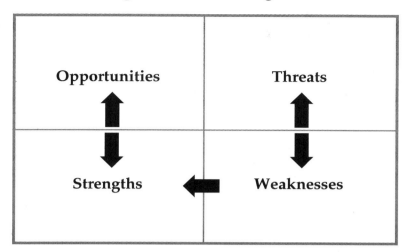

Pros/Cons of SWOT Analysis

One of the nice factors about SWOT analysis is its flexibility as an analytical tool. SWOT is widely used both in and out of the wine industry because it can be adapted to fit most situations. It can be used by wineries, wine distributors and retailers, and other companies that service the wine industry to create a competitive advantage in the marketplace. SWOT is also a relatively simple tool to understand and employ, and this has led to its wide acceptance by marketers. You do not need special statistical training nor expensive computers and software to use a SWOT analysis.

However, the ease in which SWOT can be used has led to its misuse at times. For the misinformed, SWOT analysis becomes nothing more that a list of firm and environmental characteristics, with little effort given to how these factors fit together and what the strategic implications are. To really be able to contribute to the positioning and branding process, the analysis aspect of the procedure needs to be performed carefully.

THREE STEPS OF THE **SWOT** ANALYSIS PROCESS

The first part of a SWOT analysis is the identification of the company's strengths and weaknesses. These are internal characteristics of the firm. The second part of the analysis is the study of opportunities and threats. These are characteristics of the environment that are external to the firm. The third part of the SWOT analysis is to see how these four categories can be matched together to identify the direction the firm should be taking in its marketing program.

Step 1: Analyzing Strengths and Weaknesses

Strengths and Weaknesses are internal characteristics of the firm. **Strengths** are areas where the company has a comparative advantage over the competition. **Weaknesses** are areas which are important to customers but where competitors hold a relative advantage. It is important to note that being good at something isn't enough to be considered a strength. Making good wine in the Napa Valley isn't a strength, because just about everybody makes good wine. To be a strength, it has to be something that sets you apart from the competition, such as being the only winery in Napa to make award-winning Cabernet Franc. More importantly, a strength is something that sets you apart in the eyes of the consumer—not something you say about yourself because you believe it.

Strengths can exist due to many factors. The amount of **financial resources** is one source of advantage because it can be used to develop advantages in many key areas. For example, resources can be used to purchase high quality fruit from sought-after appellations. Money can also be spent on advertising to improve the reputation of the company and make the wine's image seem more attractive.

Although financial resources are often the first advantage to come to mind when conducting a SWOT analysis, others resources possessed by the firm may be equally important. For example, **human resources** can provide a firm with a tremendous advantage if the skill set possessed by employees is difficult for others to duplicate. Certain winemakers have earned a reputation for their ability to make exquisite wines, garnering celebrity status.

Other employees in the company can also have special talents that customers appreciate. Event planners can create such fun and unique wine events that customers may want to join the wine club just to receive invitations. Marketing talent can also set one winery apart from others by creating catchy labels and collateral. Some salespeople have a talent for developing close personal relationships with distributors and retail buyers. When looking at the strengths of the company, it is important to keep a broad perspective on the different sources of advantage so that important sources of strengths are not missed.

Weaknesses, areas where competitors outperform the firm, must also be considered. It may be difficult at times to honestly admit that there are areas where customers view competitors more favorably, but denial only increases the chances that changes to the strategy will not occur. Questions that need to be asked include: Are your competitors' brand names better known? Do they have an image that customers appreciate more? Do they deliver a better price/quality ratio? Are they able to spend more on developing innovative packaging? Do they have access to distribution that you cannot duplicate? These questions illustrate the type of honest assessment the firm must make.

Step 2: Analyzing Opportunities and Threats

Opportunities and Threats refer to trends or changes in the external environment that a firm may seize upon or be hurt by. Specifically, **Opportunities** are breaks that open up, allowing the company to pursue its strategy more aggressively. Examples include openings to win market share, rising buyer demand for products, and expanding products. **Threats** are factors that pose threats to the organization's profitability and competitive well-being, such as the introduction of better products by rivals, entry of lower-cost foreign competitors, onerous regulations, and other issues.

In order to differentiate between internal and external effects, you can ask yourself whether the condition would continue to exist if your winery were no longer in business. If the answer is yes, the factor should be considered an external trend. The study of the external environments is referred to as a **situation analysis** in marketing.

Marketers need to conduct a thorough situation analysis to insure that they do not miss important changes, both positive and negative, in the external environment. Typically, a situation analysis includes factors such as 1) economic conditions, 2) cultural trends, 3) technological advancements, and 4) legal or regulatory changes. Each of these areas of the external environment can have an impact on wine consumption, and therefore should be considered in a situation analysis.

Economic conditions can have an immediate effect on the sale of wine. Wines at different price points may feel the impact of economic growth or slowdown differently. Often when people are feeling less confident about the economy they may still continue to purchase wine, but trade down to lower-priced wines than they would have purchased otherwise. When economic growth slows, businesses often cut back on employees' expense accounts. This may hurt wines that are sold at restaurants since businesses may spend less entertaining clients. A good example for the economic conditions that could create a threat is the currency rate exchange, which has, over the years, changed the market for European wines in the USA. Currently, Italian wines are discovering that the new higher exchange rate for the Euro is putting their wines into new price categories—and since consumers don't cross price categories very often, it means that they have to launch these wines and brands all over again to a new audience.

On the other hand, when economic times are good, people may be willing to splurge on more expensive wines for special occasions, and even buy wine more often for everyday consumption. Travel and tourism is another sector of the economy that may suffer in a down-turn. This could have an impact on the number of visitors to tasting rooms and the money that is spent on wine-related travel.

Cultural trends are also important to watch closely. Dining and food trends are especially relevant to wine marketers. One trend that has had a positive effect on wine consumption is the Slow Food Movement, which encourages people to spend more time enjoying the meals they eat and to eat locally grown foods. Another trend that is having a positive impact on wine consumption is the focus on a healthy diet. People in the US are eating more fish and chicken as part of a healthier lifestyle, and this has changed the wine market from one that drank primarily red wines to one that drinks more Chardonnay. However, red wine is also recognized as playing a positive role in many health issues, especially heart disease. As people become more aware of the health benefits of wine it is expected this will encourage more people to drink wine.

Another cultural trend affecting wine reflects the more active lifestyle of wine drinkers. More people are consuming wine at the beach, backpacking, or sailing. This has created an opportunity for wineries to create newer closures and packages that can fit into the active lifestyles.

Technology can also introduce change into the wine industry. Technology is changing the ways wines are made, the way they're packaged, and the way business is conducted. Technology is bringing consumers new forms of closures that make wine more approachable. Business technology is also important to wineries. It was not feasible for most wineries to sell wines over the internet until consumers were comfortable purchasing wine over the computer, and until the wineries had the ability to handle the databases with addresses and credit card information.

Finally, the **legal and regulatory environment** bears constant monitoring. The laws affecting direct shipping of wine to consumers in the United States are a prime example of how changes in this environment can create opportunities and threats to wineries. In some states, consumers can now receive shipments from out-of-state wineries, whereas in others, the consumers cannot receive the shipments they could from in-state wineries.

Step 3: Prioritization and Action Planning

Once strengths, weaknesses, opportunities and threats have been identified, the next step is to prioritize each item in terms of importance and to potential impact on the firm. Which of the strengths that the firm currently possesses are critical to the long-term success of the wine firm? Once the most important strengths are identified, the resources to sustain these strengths must be continued or even increased. Which weaknesses appear to put the company at the greatest disadvantage relative to its competition? Firms should look for ways to address the most critical weaknesses first.

Once there has been an attempt to prioritize the strengths and weaknesses, the next step is to look for ways to grow the business. This can be accomplished by matching the strengths to the opportunities that were identified. Which of the opportunities that were identified best fit the strengths the company now has, or at least, has the resources to obtain quickly? Is it possible in areas where there are weaknesses, to correct the weaknesses so that the firm can take advantage of the opportunities? This may be more difficult to do, but in some cases it may be the only choice. One very important caveat to SWOT analysis is that opportunities should not be pursued if the company does not have sufficient financial and organizational resource capabilities. This could just make matters worse, as they would not have the backing to compete well against others with stronger resources.

The most damaging threats that face the firm also need to be addressed. If there is a weakness where the company is vulnerable to the threat, changes must be considered. If changes are not possible due to lack of resources, the firm may have to exit the category alltogether.

The end result of the SWOT analysis is to develop an action plan to capitalize on strengths matched to opportunities, and to find ways to improve weaknesses and offset threats. The action plan is based primarily on items that have been prioritized. It then needs to be assigned to specific people within the winery, those who have accountability, to complete the actions by a set deadline. Progress checks should be installed to verify that action plans are being implemented and moving along smoothly.

STRATEGIES FOR COMPETING IN A CATEGORY

Once an opportunity that matches the firm's strengths has been identified, the firm must decide how it wants to compete in that category. (A category is a group of similar products that compete against each other.) For consumers, the single major factor determining a category is price. It overwhelms all other factors. So the first criterion for determining the competitive set for any consumer is the price point. Once a marketer has decided on the price category they wish to compete in, they can start to figure out how to differentiate themselves in this pricing arena. Classical positions in which companies compete have been identified as **differentiation, low-cost,** and **stuck in the middle.** Each of these, however, can be further subdivided into specific markets and products.

Differentiation

The best strategy is to compete with a clearly differentiated product. Consumers see your product as possessing some unique difference that competitors are unable to duplicate and that they find desirable. Because the product is unique in their minds, substitutes are seen as inferior, and consumers are willing to pay a premium to obtain the products with the attributes they desire.

Low-Cost

If a firm does not have any unique features that differentiate it from the competition, the battleground usually becomes the pricing field, the one area that consumers usually can grasp easily. Competing by having the lowest price is not necessarily an undesirable place to be, as long as the firm has the lowest cost structure that allows it to capture adequate margins and remain profitable. However, when price wars break out, the firm that does not have a low-cost structure will usually find itself in a precarious position.

A low-cost structure can result from economies of scale, which give larger wine firms advantage in competing with low prices. Smaller wineries do not usually have the ability to offer the lowest prices and stay profitable over the long term. Therefore, smaller to medium size wineries would prefer to compete by selling a differentiated product.

Stuck in the Middle

Companies that do not possess a differentiated product nor do they have the ability to offer the lowest prices, are said to be stuck in the middle. Firms stuck in the middle usually have the lowest level of profitability in any industry. In order to be successful, you must always be better than the competition in some way.

Of course, it is easier to stand out when there are few other competitors in the marketplace. Finding a way to differentiate your brand is not as difficult when there are not so many choices. But what about conditions in the wine industry? This is a mature industry that is saturated with brands. It is much more difficult to find a way to differentiate your brand when there are so many other firms trying to do the same.

There are a few truths to remember when you are dealing with a saturated market. First, there will be more and more product categories defined by marketers. No longer will it be red wine or white wine; there will be rosé. Then there will be rosé that is sweeter, and rosé that is dryer. Then there will be rosé that is sparkling. Of course, you can have sparkling rosé in bottles or you can have rosé in small cans or single serving packaging. In each of these new categories, leaders will emerge.

Market Segments

Those that appreciate each of these new categories will be the focus of marketers' attention. The groups may be smaller, but if developed to their full potential, could provide attractive returns. Market segmentation has been one approach to dealing with the problem of more brands than there are categories of products. Each company selects a different market segment to focus their efforts toward.

So the question remains, how do you compete in a category when there are so many brands and everyone is trying to capture the attention of consumers? The key to long-term success has to do with your ability to build the brand's value to customers. This includes not only the final consumers; it also includes the wholesalers and retailers who will help you sell your wine.

COMPETING AS A SMALLER WINERY

How can smaller wineries add value to their brands when their marketing budgets are not nearly as large as a national brand's? The answer is that they must go outside traditional methods of marketing and make use of word-of-mouth advertising and the internet; emphasize wine clubs; and build relationships to support their brand. It is their creativity, not the extent of their spending that will determine success. In short, your marketing must stand out. You must have better ideas for relationship marketing. You must execute those ideas better than anyone else. Your personal style will become the marketing message...rather than the product itself. Ultimately, your **marketing** must not only **create** the point of difference it must **be** the point of difference.

CREATING YOUR BRAND

Now that you've determined the best position for your wines, you are at the point where branding becomes your major focus. Remember your **brand** is the name consumers trust and can remember, but **branding** refers to all of the aspects of your wine and winery that identify your products and differentiate them from the competitors. While the positioning process and the SWOT analysis should show you where you want to be located in the minds of consumers, branding is the process used to create this position. So now it is time to create or **re-**create your brand.

Table 3.2: Key Brand Definitions

Brand: A name you can trust, it stands for a family of products. the entire focus of your marketing efforts should be to make your brand more valuable.
Brand Awareness: Getting on the short list in the customer's minds. The top brands are remembered by customers, while lesser-known brands fall by the wayside.
Brand Equity: The value of the intngible assets of a brand.
Brand Extension: Adding new products, sizes or packages to the initial brand offering.
Brand Visibility: The first step in awareness. Either your products or your marketing campaigns must create visibility for your brand.

Branding includes the name, story, label, collateral, images, relation-ships and all other ways in which the winery communicates with its customers. You need to have a succinct brand position, and you need to communicate it effectively to your customers. Therefore, the fol-lowing chapters describe in detail how to make the brand come alive with appropriate advertising, promotion, labels, packaging, graphic design, and public relations. Later chapters then describe the process of taking your "brand" to market and creating budgets, as well as working with distributors and selling your wine direct to consumers.

Your advertising must convey a unique marketing message—one that consumers will want to care about—and you must do it in a way that is more effective than your competitors' messages.

- The medium of advertising

- Pros and cons of advertising

- Tips for the small winery

- The myriad alternative pathways of ad messages

WINE ADVERTISING AND PROMOTION

The codfish lays ten thousand eggs
The homely hen lays one
The codfish never cackles
To tell you what she's done.
And so we scorn the codfish
While the humble hen we prize
Which only goes to show you
It pays to advertise.

—Anonymous, 19th Century

The concept of advertising is simple. You pay a publication to deliver your message to their audience. In fact, it would help to remember that the way publications make money is to deliver that audience to their advertisers.

In any industry, there are some basic strategies for advertising that make a lot of sense. It is important to focus your advertising message on the benefits your product brings to the consumer, not the features that it offers. All too often, wineries tell their story in words that matter not to the consumer or the trade, but to themselves. As you create your ads, there is one single question you should always ask: *Why will any consumer care about this message?*

Most wine advertising fits into the category of <u>image enhance</u>ment, rather than <u>immediate response</u>. However, please bear in mind that every winery does this type of advertising. Every winery wants to enhance its image. In most cases, consumers and the trade are bored with these ads, and tired of the same old "still-life-with-wine" school of graphic design. That is not good marketing. Following the traditions of the past doesn't create new categories, open new markets, or build new consumer loyalties.

Your advertising must convey a <u>unique marketing message</u>—one that consumers really care about—and it must do it in a way that is more effective than any of your competitors. Therefore the purpose of this chapter is to outline how to do effective advertising and promotion. It begins with some definitions, and then describes the medium of advertising, as well as the pros and cons of advertising. Next it provides tips on advertising for small wineries, then offers specific details on how to do advertising and promotion with alliances, donations, sponsorships, charities, trade associations, trade shows, and wine festivals.

DEFINING PROMOTION, ADVERTISING AND PUBLIC RELATIONS

Before we dive into the practicalities of how to deliver high impact advertising and promotion for your winery, it is useful to begin with some basic definitions and distinctions:

Promotion is the particular blend of advertising, public relations, and sales promotions a winery uses to achieve its marketing strategy. Done effectively, promotion maintains the specific wine brand in the mind of the customer and helps stimulate demand for it. Thus advertising and public relations are both subsets of promotion.

Advertising is bringing the wine brand to the attention of customers, usually through a variety of media including print ads, brochures, radio and TV commercials, internet and/or email ads, direct mailing, signs, and even personal contact. In general, wineries usually have to pay for advertising.

Public Relations (covered in Chapter 7) is more specific in that it relies on news about the winery and its wine brands, and attempts to get that news placed in journals, print, TV, and other media via press releases, special events, personal contact, and other mechanisms. According to Posert and Franson (2004), professionals in wine public relations are experts in the art of "spinning" a message within the media to promote a particular wine business. Public relations advertising can often be free, except for the salary or consulting fee to obtain a public relations professional.

ADVERTISING AS A MEDIUM

One of the greatest quotes from the world of marketing comes from Lord Leverhulme. Concerned about his advertising budget, and knowing that the ads were never as perfectly targeted as he would like, he said, "I know that half the money I spend on advertising is wasted, and the trouble is I don't know which half (Kilburn, 2004, p.1)."

Advertising does allow you to get your message to the audience. Public relations programs are far more sensitive to the turn of events in the news. Your ad—once you have paid your money—will appear in the publication just when you expect it to. It will appear just the way you drew it up—your message the way you wrote it, delivered to the publication's readers exactly when you specified. You can't say that about a public relations campaign.

On the other hand, there are some drawbacks to advertising in general, and some very specific challenges to advertising in the wine industry. In fact, wine advertising faces some unique challenges. They are the same challenges that the wine industry faces in other marketing and communications disciplines, but in advertising they are even more critical.

1. Wineries usually have a limited budget. The revenue from selling 22,000 cases of wine is simply not enough to fund national advertising campaigns. When advertising executives learn of the budgets that most wineries use for their campaigns, they quickly lose interest in the business. The overall scale of the wine industry does not justify the volume, revenue or budgets to really tackle national advertising campaigns.

2. Wineries usually have a national sales target. While most California wineries still sell fifty percent of their wine in California, the rest is sold in a collection of smaller markets across the country. This requires a national marketing approach to develop a national presence for the brand.

3. Frequency is the only way to make sure people get your message. As advertising genius Hal Riney once said, "In advertising, less isn't more, it's less." Advertising requires frequency: lots of ads over an extended period of time, to accomplish the goal. These ads are expensive.

So what is a good ad campaign? It's one that achieves your marketing goals and positions you effectively with the trade, the media and with consumers. It is one that positions you above your competition. If you are going to compete against them, you have to compete at every level, including advertising. And if you are a small winery, remember that your ads have to compete against the big firms in size, creative content, and frequency. That's not usually a challenge small wineries can meet.

WHAT'S RIGHT ABOUT ADVERTISING?

Advertising can be an incredibly powerful weapon. A really well done creative campaign can really capture the attention of every level of the market, from distributors and retailers right through to the consumer. It can create a positive image for your company that will sell product and resist a huge amount of damage.

Some examples of highly successful advertising campaigns in the wine industry include Corbett Canyon radio ads, and Blackstone's ads which feature a cartoon character relaxing on the couch with a glass of wine after a long day at work. Another advertising campaign that was quite successful was Sutter Home's ads featuring a strong public relations message that a portion of the money spent on the purchase of every bottle of wine would be donated to breast cancer research. All of these ads linger in the minds of consumers and encouraged increased sales.

Figure 4.1: Sutter Home Ad

Really good ad campaigns can even become news in their own right—how many times have we heard someone say, "Oh, I love those ads!" Of course, loving the ads and buying the products are two different things. All too often the ads that most people remember are ones that don't really deliver the complete brand message—they have sacrificed brand message for entertainment. And they will ultimately fall short of the goal because of this. Our world is full of memorable ad campaigns for companies that went bankrupt because their sales did not improve. Never confuse clever ads with good marketing.

The perfect ad campaign can have a huge positive effect. In the end it can achieve one of the great marketing goals—it can help you own a word in the buyer's mind. Of course, such advertising campaigns usually cost a lot of money, both for the creative work (there is no such thing as a great, cheap, creative agency) and for the media placement itself. The ad needs to get placed everywhere it needs to be seen, and seen with great frequency by the target market. If that is not possible, then it will not generate the kind of success you would like. And every year we see ad campaigns that fail simply because the company doesn't plan to spend the money necessary for the market to see the ads. Repetition is the key. Repetition costs money.

WHY ADVERTISE?

Every serious publication on the face of the planet will deny this, but in the right circumstances, and with the right publisher, a significant advertising campaign can help buy editorial coverage. That can be very important to your sales team and to your customers. But such a relationship must be handled with great delicacy. No editor likes to get a phone call from an advertising client (or the publisher, forwarding the message) asking for a special feature article in return for a major new ad placement contract. And most resist the idea, with varying degrees of success.

At the same time, if the editor is doing an article on wines from a certain region, and one of the wineries in that region is a major advertiser, the editorial staff will (and should!) make every effort to taste the wines from that advertiser. They may even taste them with a slightly less critical palate—or taste more wines than from other producers. In other cases, they may even take advantage of the relationship they have with the advertising winery to get an extra quote, another photo, or a sidebar story. On the defensive side, many times major advertisers will get advance notice about a negative story, and may even be given more opportunity to respond to their critics than a non-advertising winery.

Table 4.1: Reasons to Advertise

Why Advertise?
• To support your distributor sales force in a market, or nationally.
• Because it can sometimes buy editorial coverage in some publications.
• It can create a long-term image for the brand.
• It guarantees that your message will be seen when you want and as you want it. It keeps your name in front of the target market.

Some publications that will remain nameless (Would you give out the names and locations of your best secret trout streams?) will take direct input from an advertiser, and print long and large feature stories about those wineries. Some will not print feature stories about any winery that does NOT advertise. It's the way the game is played.

There is also a deeper reason to advertise on behalf of a winery—a reason that goes well beyond simple brand name promotion. Every winery in America will tell you that they have a favorite wine publication, and often a least favorite one. Yet few will actually develop a strategic plan to support those publications they wish to succeed. This should be part of any strategic plan for the winery. If those publications organize large consumer or trade events, attending or participating in those events can also send a strong message of support to the publication. But never confuse that message with a signed contract for ad placement. That takes money. But money sends a message.

Many publications in the wine industry that are considered to be consumer wine magazines are really more influential with the trade than with consumers. It is important to understand how this impacts the audience and message of your advertising. A solid and well-funded advertising campaign in these publications can play a key role in distributor support. It is tangible evidence that you are supporting your brand in their markets, and that is pretty powerful stuff—provided you are doing better than your competition. It is unlikely that such a campaign will drive large numbers of consumers to buy your product. They are far more likely to rely on the editorial content in the publication for that decision.

Finally, for those wineries that really have no budget to undertake a major national advertising campaign, there are small victories to be won. Even small listings in the classified ads page can help you get your message out. Such ads will also keep your name in an admittedly small spotlight, and show your flag to customers who are ready to buy. Cleverly worded and placed, they can accomplish some modest advertising goals for very small amounts of money. Those are all advantages of advertising. Don't overlook them.

WHAT IS WRONG WITH ADVERTISING?

For the wine industry, most advertising is simply not cost effective. Wine companies don't have the dollars to go after national campaigns, or anything close. While cosmetics and car companies can advertise on national TV, wineries don't have the budget for that. And the ugly fact about wine in general is that not enough people in the US drink it. Forget about half of Lord Leverhulme's budget being wasted—if you are advertising wine on national TV, you are lucky if only 75% of your budget is being spent reaching people who don't drink wine. That is tough to justify in a budget meeting.

Table 4.2: Advertising Cautions

Why Shouldn't You Advertise?
• It is hard to target your message to the right audience.
• It is very expensive for most wineries.
• It can can tie you to an outdated or ineffective position.
• Many consumers distrust it or don't believe it.
• There are often more cost-effective ways to achieve similar goals.

Even with the most sophisticated media analysis, it is tough to come up with a radio or television show that will deliver an audience that is composed of people who drink wine on a regular basis. The same is true for newspapers, general interest magazines, and the kind of lifestyle publications that feature ads for all sorts of other inspirational purchases. Which means that in the wine industry, our list of potentially targeted publications is pretty small. And we all know most of them by name. It is pretty safe to assume that the readers of such publications as *The Wine Spectator, Wine Enthusiast,* and *Wine & Spirits* are interested in wine. Now the question we have to ask is, "Does advertising in those magazines convince their readers to buy our products?" The jury is definitely out on that question.

Such advertising can encourage more activity from retailers and distributors, and that will certainly increase sales. But there is also a very common theme through almost all wine market research that indicates many wine consumers in this country resist advertising at almost every level. In one way or the other, these consumers seem to say, "If a winery is big enough to advertise, then it is too big to make good wine." They actually resist buying wines because of the ads. And while those consumers tend to buy at the higher end of the market, it must be considered that most of the influential wine magazines are aiming much of their issue directly at those very consumers.

A second concern about advertising is that any customer who can be won over to your products by your ads can just as easily be lost to a competitor by their, better ads. And since many smaller wineries simply can't afford the kind of professional advertising of their larger competitors, they are at a huge disadvantage. They don't have the money to create memorable, effective advertising, and they don't have the budget to slather those ads all over the top magazines. In a battle of perceptions, these smaller wineries are trying to fight a war with a pitchfork and a peashooter.

Even larger wineries run certain risks by spending too many of their dollars on national ad campaigns. In a wine world that is constantly in flux, a national ad campaign can force a company into a static position, defending a hopeless cause while the rest of the industry has moved on. And even worse are those wineries who invest heavily in personality ads, only to see the key personnel leave or pass away, leaving the marketing message completely at sea. Sadly, when it comes to advertising, one of the biggest challenges of all is that the ads do not provide any third party credibility. What you say about yourself is often open to debate in the eyes and ears of the buying public. Even worse, they can even react with disagreement or even ridicule in the right (wrong?) situation.

This resistance to advertising messages is captured in some sense by Michael Phillips & Salli Rasberry (2005), in their book, *Marketing Without Advertising.* They are obviously not big supporters of advertising, and they warn consumers against taking any advertising claims too seriously: "We've all heard these (popular ad) slogans for so many years, and they're so familiar, that you have to concentrate to even hear them and pay attention to understand why they are either hype or simply not true." That's not exactly the response you are hoping to get to your carefully crafted and extensively placed advertising campaign!

Of course, it would be easy to make your ads more believable by quoting independent third parties. But in the end, those kinds of ads start to look an awful lot like a supermarket shelf, where every wine has a rave review. There is no product differentiation, and there is no unique selling proposition to the consumer. Given that you are spending a lot of money to get this message in front of the consumers, you really ought to be able to explain how and why you are different in a way that stands out from the crowd. These ads rarely do this.

All too often, wineries put an inordinately large portion of their budget into the advertising bucket. They know it is expensive, and they really want to make sure they have enough money to do it well. The only problem is, they don't really know what the goal of that advertising is. If you carefully define what your expectations for your advertising are, then you will quickly realize exactly what kind of advertising is cost effective, and what kind is simply a massive drain on your finances, with no real hope of return on investment.

ADVERTISING SUGGESTIONS FOR SMALL WINERIES

So based on the above, there are pros and cons for advertising in the wine industry. What then is the solution if you are a small winery with a limited advertising budget? Following are a few tips, based on the above information, which will provide the biggest bang for your buck.

Tip 1: Be clear about your objectives, target audience, and budget. Don't try to solve all the problems of the winery with one ad. Focus on a single communications goal with a single audience, and then develop a plan to achieve that goal.

Tip 2: Dare to be different. If your ad looks just like all the other winery ads, with a different label on the bottle, then you have not accomplished your goal. Most wine ads feature a bottle image prominently placed in the ad. What most consumers see in those ads is a nice bottle of wine. They don't really see the label. How will your ad be different?

Tip 3: Make sure your ads really convey the overall marketing strategy of your winery. This assumes, of course, that you have a strategy. Each ad should stand on its own, but each should also clearly be part of a larger campaign that positions the winery and its wines effectively against the competition. If your ad doesn't do this clearly, it is not a good ad.

Tip 4: Spend the money to make sure people see your ad. If you are going to advertise, then you must be committed to making sure that the target audience has a chance to see your ad many times. Only after repeated exposure to the ad will they be able to internalize the message.

Tip 5: Always include some kind of tracking device to see what works. An 800 number, a special offer, or a website promotion will give you an idea of how your ad is really reaching people. If it elicits no responses, then you will have to redesign your ad, or re-think your strategy.

These are solid techniques, and represent legitimate goals for the marketing programs for any winery. If you combine these advertising strategies with an effective campaign that integrates public relations, promotions, and direct marketing, this can play a key role in making your winery successful. Even more importantly, advertising can play a critical tactical role in supporting the other, more creative elements of your marketing campaigns. How that works will determine, by and large, how these other elements communicate your marketing messages to their audiences

In the rest of this chapter, we address three major promotion activities which can complement your advertising campaign. These are: 1) Strategic alliances, donations, and sponsorships; 2) Trade associations; and 3) Wine festivals.

STRATEGIC ALLIANCES, DONATIONS AND SPONSORSHIPS

Targeting your marketing and donation dollar and getting the biggest bang for your bottles is a full-time job, requiring strategic planning, creativity, and an iron discipline. Whether these programs are part of a charity donation, or building a strategic alliance with a corporate partner, your goal should always be the same: to get the biggest and best possible result for your efforts.

Every winery has the same problem. Some wineries receive as many as 100 requests for wine donations every week. And most, if not all of them, are from very worthwhile organizations who are working hard to make our country and our community better. For smaller wineries, it would be quite easy to give away the entire annual production just to support these charities.

Most wineries take a rather reactive approach. Each letter requesting a donation is reviewed and judged on the merits of the organization and the potential benefits the donation might generate for the winery. Then the decision is made, and either the wine is donated and delivered, or the request is denied. The challenge to all of this, of course, comes at the end of the year. How do you judge the effectiveness of your donation budget? How do you measure the results you achieved? And how do you justify the expenditures for these donations, when you can't really measure the results they achieve?

So what are the answers to these questions? First of all, some are quite obvious. While all of these organizations are doing good works, not all are appropriate to the wine business. A donation of wine to an organization that is dedicated to the reinstatement of Prohibition is just not in the cards—not unless you are really looking for the wrong kind of publicity. Other organizations are simply too far away. While you might well consider making a small donation to help raise funds for a library in your community, you would probably not support the same efforts to buy books for a library in Bulgaria.

But those are the easy ones. And what every winery really struggles with are the hard ones. The real solution to the issue of donations begins at the very beginning, when you take a reactive approach. Because a good donations program should begin not with letters from charity organizations, but with your marketing and communications plans. You need to have that plan in hand, and use it ruthlessly. Begin by defining your category and positioning in that category. That should go a long way towards helping you determine what kinds of events and organizations you want to cultivate.

The first level of selection should be the demographics of the organization. This assumes that you know the demographics of your target market well enough to judge. The classic matches with the demographics of wine are fine art, classical music, food and wine societies, public radio and television, and the like. The only problem here is that every other winery also wants to appeal to these same audiences. Remember that one of the basic rules of marketing is that you should try to be the leader in everything that you do. It's a big pond out there, and most wineries are pretty small fish.

Of course, this gives rise to the classic marketing question—should you be where everyone else is, or should you strike out on your own to find new audiences? The question is a complicated one, but for most wine donations, it is simply not very effective to be one of one hundred in a crowd of people who don't know what they are drinking or why. It is far better to find your own group, build a long-term relationship, and have a few close friends that are exclusively yours.

You can ask for exclusivity with an organization, and hope that this will give you the leadership position you want. As you do this, please bear in mind that such positions are valuable enough that other wineries might well outbid you for the next year. If you do a great job of taking advantage of the opportunities presented by an exclusive sponsorship, your efforts are often rewarded by increased competition for this spot in the future. Plan for that, and make sure that you won't have to reinvest every year in a new relationship.

Negotiating a Strategic Relationship with Donation Request Organizations

The relationship is the key. You should be looking for organizations that want a long-term relationship—one that is equally beneficial to both parties. If you provide all of the money and wine, and you don't receive good value in return, then you are wasting more than your wine and money, you are also wasting your time. And your competition is gaining on you. The ideal partner for a winery donation program would be an organization with demographics that correlate very closely to the wine industry, and that can offer a wide range of opportunities and media to help you build rewarding relationships with their members. Following is a list of opportunities you should seek or request when agreeing to give wine donations and build a strategic partnership.

- **Joint newsletter exposure:** A newsletter that goes out to all their members is a great place to tell the story of your winery, position your products, create some brand awareness, and encourage experimentation. See if you can explore the various opportunities in a newsletter with the organization. Can you suggest wine and food pairings? Can you have a regular column in the newsletter to talk about your interest in the organization? Can you get a feature story on your donation in the newsletter? Those are real, measurable goals—goals that will help you get ahead of the competition. Likewise, if you have a newsletter, it is the ideal medium to promote this relationship to your customers, and achieve those goals as well.

- **Your winery name at their event:** If the organization does exclusive membership events, can you provide the wine for these events in return for some higher visibility? Charity organizations are always happy to receive free wine—but you want to negotiate their price. In the best case scenario, your winery would be the title sponsor of the event, would have signage that clearly showed your support, and would have something for each member to take home that reiterates your winery name and the reason that you have so much in common with the members.

- **Opportunity to speak about your winery at their event:** Furthermore, you should request an opportunity to provide a speaker at their event. Ideally this speaker can tell the story of the winery and its relationship to the members and the organization's cause.

- **Your name on event publicity:** As publicity for the event unfolds, you should ask that your name be positioned prominently in all releases and information. While it is true that this "shared attention" can take away from the primary goal of the organization, you should be able to negotiate some kind of a solution that will make you both happy.

- **Linked website information:** Websites for both your winery and the charity organization should have links and share content to explain your relationship and why it is important.

- **Share with wine media:** The media are another example of shared attention, and while you would love to be featured in stories about the charity organization and its work, you should also share with wine journalists the interests and concerns of your selection organization. You may well find that your support has built a much stronger bond with a key wine writer—one that you can explore further with other elements of your PR campaigns.

- **Create POS material:** In return, you might offer to give the organization more visibility by creating bottle neckers or other POS (point-of-sale material) about the organizations for your retail displays. This gives them great visibility with a new audience, gives new customers a reason to try your product, and gives your existing customers another reason to buy your product. That's the kind of attention that most charities would deeply appreciate—and it doesn't cost much, either.

A Caveat on Usual Alliances

Having said all that, there are some additional concerns you simply have to address. In the wine business, we frequently find that our target consumers have little in common with some of our other key audiences. While wine drinkers might well love the idea of an exclusive reception at a modern art museum, it is pretty hard to use that same reception as an incentive for the distributor sales force. There have been some wonderful partnerships over the years with organizations that were perfectly positioned for the target consumer—only to find that the additional tickets given to the sales force were tossed away or, in one memorable case, scalped on the front steps of the museum by one of the distributor salespeople's girlfriend.

Another issue is the interest in building relationships with organizations well outside the normal arena of wine and culture. Wineries throughout the world have experimented with a wide range of activities and organizations, all seeking to find that unique niche that will give them direct and rewarding access to the perfect combination of wine consumers. NASCAR, sailboat races, the PGA, Major League Baseball, rock and roll concerts, and all sorts of other events have been tried. In most cases, they have not been wildly successful, often because those attending the events are not primarily wine drinkers— and support for these kinds of organizations ultimately fall into that wonderful no-man's land of Lord Leverhume. This is usually true when wineries support events that don't have a traditional link to wine. They know that *some* of the audience is interested, but it may well be that the rest of the audience is not even slightly interested... and that can distract from the overall image you create at the event.

Some of the wine industry's very best matches are ultimately so expensive that they simply do not make any financial sense. It would be wonderful to be the official wine sponsor of the Olympics, or to underwrite the National Football League, but that kind of money simply doesn't exist in the wine industry. The fashion industry, while not quite in that category, combines many of the classic demographic matches with wine. But it is also a very expensive game to play. If you want to have your wines at the top design shows, you will not only need to pay a pretty penny for the privilege, you will also have to spend a good deal more to create the kind of image and positioning at these events that will gain attention and admiration. It isn't enough to stand next to the star, you will have to get them to smile, shake your hand, and act as if they are happy to see you there. How will your winemaker look, standing next to Claudia Schiffer? Don't worry—the good news is that nobody will notice!

Do Support Your Local Charities

And we can never forget the local charities that really do need our support. Whatever national marketing goals you may have, every winery has a responsibility to the local community that cannot be ignored. And there is a basic element of goodwill that cannot be earned any other way. You should give to local charities, and you should do so for both commercial reasons as well as for social responsibility. And if you really want to make a difference, give more than wine. Give the time and energy of one of your employees a few hours a month. This will not only help the organization, but it will build the very thing that makes the world go round—good relationships with key audiences.

In the end, your donation budget needs to be as carefully considered as any campaign you manage, and it should undergo the same rigorous cost/benefit analysis that you use for all of your marketing communications. You and your winery management should agree on the goals of the program, the strategy and tactics to be used, and the results you expect to see. And you should all agree that the results you expect to generate are well worth the dollars they will cost to achieve. If they are not, why would you choose to spend the money this way?

If you do this right, wine donations can become a key factor in your marketing and sales success. Your donations budget can play a key role in developing positions and image for the winery, increase sales, and add visibility in the media. Or you can sit at your desk, and hope that the right letter happens to drop in your lap.

TRADE ASSOCIATIONS

We all belong to them, from regional wine associations to the local Chamber of Commerce. And it seems that every week we are invited to join another one. On the face of it, these organizations offer a number of benefits: economies of scale, larger budgets, moral support, and safety in numbers. But those benefits are often outweighed by other factors.

Some of these organizations seem to come and go on an annual basis, while others will seemingly live forever. What are the good ones? It may run counter to your first reaction, but sometimes the good organizations are not necessarily the best ones to join. And these decisions can often play a huge role in determining how successful your public relations efforts are going to be.

In the simplest of terms, what most wineries want from a trade association is strength in numbers. They feel that if enough wineries band together to promote a product, or region, that this increase in time, energy, creativity, and money will help them achieve goals that they could not achieve as a single winery. And the implication, at least, is that the benefits they reap from this association will outweigh their own contributions of time, energy, creativity and money. Sadly, that is not very often true.

The obvious advantage of any trade association is that it brings an already interested and focused audience to you. When you are trying to carefully target every marketing communications dollar, it's nice to know that the money you spend on Zinfandel Advocates and Producers (ZAP) is really going to reach people who are interested in Zinfandel. While *USA Today* or CNN reaches a vastly larger audience, most of the people in that audience are not interested in wine, let alone old vine Zinfandel. That's a solid target audience for your specialized product. Furthermore, if that organization is really energetic and dynamic, it can not only connect you with an existing audience interested in your specialized product, it can even play a role in increasing the overall market for that product.

Ultimately, then, a trade association can deliver two solid goals. It can put your message and product into the minds of a very targeted audience, and it may even be able to increase demand for a beverage category in your portfolio. Those are strong benefits.

So what are the costs? When your trade organization reaches out and grabs that nicely targeted audience, it will deliver that audience to every one of your competitors in the category, as well. There is no better example of this than the annual ZAP tasting in San Francisco. As a Zinfandel producer, wouldn't it be great to be able to pour your wines for a horde of wine drinkers who love Zinfandel? Of course it would. But it would be even better if you didn't have to share the attention of those wine lovers with 500 other producers of Zinfandel, all of whom are reaching out for the same kind of attention and recognition from that audience.

That's the pro and con in a nutshell—you get a beautifully targeted audience, but you have to share it with just about the entire category. And if the trade association does increase demand for the category, it is just as likely that it is also encouraging other companies and brands to enter into the category to compete with you. Does that make your life easier, or harder? As always, the answer to the situation is based on your positioning and your ability to do a better job of taking advantage of the opportunities. Better than whom? Better than your competitors in that very association.

Does that sound a bit mercenary? Good. Marketing communications is mercenary, and your job is not to take delight in being out on the field with the other players; it is to get the ball and score. You are not on the field to play around; you are on the field to win the game.

Setting Goals and Strategies for Participating in Trade Associations

It is important to develop specific goals for your participation in the organization. These should include goals for your company, as well as goals for the association as a whole. The goals should be both specific and measurable. For your own company, one goal might be that you are included in 50% of all of the stories written on the association or the category. If you are a major player, perhaps the goal should be 100% of the stories.

Now that you have defined the goal, the next step is pretty obvious. You need to develop a strategy to achieve that goal. You must first make sure that you are notified about all such stories before they are written. That may fall under the auspices of the trade association, but if not, then you need to find another source for this information. And you also need a very specific strategy to encourage the journalists writing that story to include you—often while excluding some of your category competitors.

How do you achieve that? You make sure that your story is better, that your information is more accurate, that your response is more timely, that your quotes are more memorable, and that your key individuals are more accessible to the media. It doesn't hurt if your wines taste better, either. Remember that journalists usually want news, and they want trends. If you can show that you are breaking new ground, or capturing the essence of a change in the way Americans are drinking, then you have a better chance of getting included in the story.

Journalists also want people. People are behind every story in every publication, and when it comes to wine categories, we can almost predict who will get quoted. There will be a quote from the largest producer in the category. There will also be a quote from the most interesting personality in the category. It pays to spend a little time thinking of ways to say what you want to say in a clever and memorable way—although most wineries completely ignore this advice.

There will also usually be a quote from the current president of the trade association. It is certainly in your best interests to spend the time and energy necessary to become the president for a year. Once in office, you should make every effort to use the visibility that the office provides to reach out to the media and promote the category with all your heart—especially if your last name also just happens to be on your wine label.

What other kinds of goals might you define? For an association, you might aim to have retail wine shops create a special area dedicated to the wines of your region or varietal—and then take very specific steps to achieve this goal in key markets across the US. Or you might simply aim to have every major wine magazine in the US publish a story about the category, complete with tasting notes on the leading wines.

In every case, the goal should be something that you can quantify—a final result that will translate into a real advantage in the marketplace. And as you do this, please don't forget to measure your success along the way. If you can identify a reason that your program is NOT working, that can be as valuable as achieving the goal. This is particularly true if you can do so early in the campaign. By identifying and eliminating a problem, you can then move ahead with a program that does work, and achieve the goals you have defined from the start. Without any such initial check, you can spend a lot of money on a campaign that is doomed to failure.

Of course, the other half of this equation has to do with money. It may be all well and good to achieve the kinds of goals we have identified in this chapter—but only if the cost of achieving those goals is within reason. Trade associations are not the only avenue to success, and every winery needs to evaluate the opportunity they present in relationship to all of the other possible strategies for achieving the same goals.

Don't overlook the economies of scale that trade associations can represent. By combining mailing lists and outreach programs, trade associations can help you distribute your message and build relationship with very interested members of the trade and consumers. A trade association website can help introduce your company and products to a larger audience that is already predisposed to buy within the category—and that should generate measurable results to your communications and sales goals. Even better, if your message is more memorable or effective than most of the other members' messages, then you will benefit more than they will. Your time and money will be well spent.

When should you participate in a trade association? Following is a quick checklist to help you decide:

- ✔ **When** the goals of the association are completely consistent with your own marketing and communications goals.
- ✔ **When** the association can offer a solid audience of interested consumers or trade.
- ✔ **When** the association may lack leadership or vision, opening the door for your own company to play a key and more visible role within the category.
- ✔ **When** the association offers the most cost-effective way to achieve the goals you have identified within your company.

And finally, when your own company is simply not large enough to make any legitimate noise on its own. But if that is the case, then you really can't expect the trade association to solve your problem. In that case, the trade association will offer you a wonderful opportunity to commiserate with a lot of other small wineries that aren't category leaders and don't know what to do about it.

TRADE SHOWS AND WINE FESTIVALS

Have you ever stopped to count all of the trade shows, wine festivals and tastings that wineries participate in every year? The number is mind-boggling. Virtually every major market hosts some kind of wine festival, and the state of Florida seems to have one every few weeks.

Considering the participation costs of most of these festivals and trade shows, it is critical to establish goals and develop cost-effective

Figure 4.3 Vinitaly—The World's Largest Wine trade Fair

strategies for this kind of event. What kinds of goals are realistic? Let's start with four goals often mentioned either singly or in combination by companies attending trade shows:

Goal 1: We want to find out what's going on in the industry, with customers, and with the competition. Taken alone, this is a poor reason to participate in a trade show. The same can be accomplished by simply attending the show, without the costs of exhibition space. And for that matter, if you don't know what's going on in the industry, by the time it's the talk of the trade show, it's way too late for you. You should be using market research, not industry gossip, in your decision-making process.

On the other hand, once your participation is indicated by one of the goals below, this becomes a legitimate secondary goal—one that takes advantage of the concentration of industry representatives and customers.

Goal 2: **We want to "show the flag."** This is a difficult goal to achieve because it is so hard to quantify. What is the benefit of "showing the flag"? Only very large companies wishing to maintain corporate image as important players (leaders in the category) should use this as a reason for participation in a trade show. For the rest, showing the flag is simply another way of saying, "We have no measurable goals for this event, but don't want to miss it if something important happens."

Goal 3: **We want to make sure our competition doesn't get an advantage.** This goal is often combined with "A" and "B" above in a very defensive approach to justify participation. In other words, "We can't leave the field open to our competition, so we must be there." Of course, this ignores a more obvious question: "If your competition isn't there, what do you expect to achieve?"

The sad truth about this approach is that it neglects more meaningful goals, and often leads to half-hearted efforts and poorly conceived plans. This is especially true when the axiomatic assumption is made that since we have low expectations we should invest little money, thought, or time into planning or strategy for the event.

Goal 4: **We really need to make more sales or media contacts.** This is by far the best reason to participate in industry trade shows. It is measurable, contributes directly to the bigger picture, and can have lasting impact. But if this is the goal, how many wineries actually develop a specific strategy to achieve it? And that means you have to answer the following questions.

Figure 4.4: An Exhibitor's Booth at Vinitaly

Important Questions To Answer When Deciding to Participate in a
Trade Show
• **How much will participation cost in terms of time, money, and
materials?** Don't forget to include product costs, travel and entertainment budgets, and all associated costs.

How big is the payoff? How many contacts (and of what importance) will we need to make to justify these expenses? This doesn't
mean that the sales contacts you make at the show have to place orders
large enough to pay for the costs of the show within three months.
That's not how marketing communication works. But you do need to
look at these events as investments—and you do need to understand
how they are going to pay off. If you don't have a way to track these
investments, how can you possibly make good decisions about them?

Clearly, the staff attending the trade show should agree on a
measurable goal for a specific number of sales contacts to be made, as

well as a target number of follow-up sales calls and orders placed. By tracking these numbers and the success of the attending staff, a much more refined sales plan can be developed that will make future decisions easier and more accurate.

By having a stated goal, your staff can focus on making sure those numbers are reached. Also, such an approach will encourage the sales and marketing team to explore other, more cost-effective methods of achieving these same goals. The result will be a professional and results-oriented approach to the often time-intensive process of sales calls. Trade shows are only one means to the end, and a good PR professional will explore a wide range of tactics to achieve any goal. Of course, as in all marketing communications, the secret here is to know your audience.

- **Who is the audience and what do they want?** This must be determined **before** the trade show. Your sales and marketing team should develop a profile of the contacts who plan on attending the show. These profiles should indicate special interests, products, or budgets that are of concern to those attending. This information should then be referenced against the marketing goals of the company to develop a plan for each trade show.

- **What can we do to get their attention?** Now that we know who they are and what they want, we can begin to develop a trade show booth and activities that will attract the target market and encourage them to spend time with us. We are not preparing for a party; we are designing a campaign—one that has a budget, objectives, and the potential for both failure and success.

Strategies for Successful Trade Show and Wine Festival Participation

So you've answered all of the questions above satisfactorily, and you've decided that it makes good business sense to pay the fees and devote the time to participate in the trade show or wine festival. What then are some of the strategies to make your participation successful? Following is a list of five helpful ideas:

1. **Use advance direct mail** to create interest in your booth, and to get a head start on making the key contacts. Most shows will offer to sell a list of those attending to any exhibitor. Such a list can often be used very effectively to encourage a visit to the company's booth, follow up on a marketing communication package presented at the show, or even pre-select attendees according to need or interest. If you know what you want to accomplish, then using this service to advertise your intentions, or to pre-screen visitors to your table, can be really effective.

   At every trade tasting or trade show, some of the participants are disappointed that they don't get to spend more time with the key trade visitors. Why does that happen? It often happens because they do not plan strategically. If the top industry leaders have done their homework, and invited most of the top attendees to meet with them about future business plans, the others will be left talking to the rest of the visitors, and not the key accounts.

2. **Host a hospitality suite** in the same hotel, or nearby, to give your key contacts a place to meet with you away from the distractions of the show. Often, the trade show floor itself is an overwhelming experience for potential customers. Offer these customers an interesting reason to leave the crowded floor and join you in a more relaxed and focused setting in a hospitality suite in the same hotel. This kind of participation can be done without the fees for exhibition booths, and will generate an environment that allows you the undivided attention of the sales contact. Offers of elegant food, a place

to meet with one's spouse, entertainment, or other incentives will draw the customers to your suite.

But this isn't as easy as it sounds. Drawing customers away from a wine festival to your suite requires a great deal of contact work by the company's sales staff to meet the potential customers and constantly remind them of the opportunity that awaits them in the hospitality suite.

3. **Organize interactive events** at the trade show to generate more attention for your company. These can be anything from "star attractions" to private dinners—anything that will give the sales contacts something to talk about and a reason to visit with you. The main drawback of most of these attempts is that they depend on borrowed interest—the contact is not interested in your company or products, but in the event. As a result, sales contacts are not always genuine, nor are they motivated.

On the other hand, the special dinners you organize should be planned well in advance, and executed against the stated goal. They are not just an excuse for your marketing team to spend its T&E budget by taking a bunch of colleagues to a nice restaurant—although that is what usually happens.

4. **The booth and its design must be symbolic of the quality and character of your company.** If you are making a claim to preemptive leadership, you must have a trade show booth that supports your position—both in content and in style. Thus if you want to be perceived as a major player, you must have a large, imposing booth. If you want to be seen as a cost-effective alternative, your booth must show the kind of clever, creative thinking that allows for cost-effective solutions without a loss of quality.

Finally, the staff and materials must be consistent with your corporate philosophy and your target audience. Do not use gorgeous teenage models to sell baby food, and » product.

5. **Give customers something to do at your booth.** Keep in mind that the average time spent at a trade show booth is fifteen seconds. At the end of that time, the viewer moves on to another booth unless he is given a reason to stay. Certainly, a discussion with your sales staff will accomplish that goal, but your sales staff can only speak to one person at a time. You must give other potential customers something to do while they wait.

At major wine festivals, it is often better to position the winemaker or principal out in front of the booth, where he/she can track down key contacts and interact with important industry leaders. The winery staff handles staffing the booth itself, so that the principal isn't trapped behind the table (and a crowd of consumers) when the most important journalist at the event walks on by—and doesn't stop to taste your wine.

6. **Make sure your staff is well trained**. In the final analysis, the results you achieve will depend on the efforts of your sales staff, and you should do all you can to give them training and the kinds of materials and environment that allow them to concentrate on selling your products. If there is one basic rule of trade show participation, it is that companies sitting down in chairs behind tables will never be successful. Your staff must be approachable, outgoing, and positioned in a way that places no barriers between them and the sales contacts. Your booth must be open, well-lighted, and must encourage contacts to enter your area and meet you, face to face.

Choose staff because they know the customers. Nothing can improve upon a salesman who has already established rapport with potential customers. This personal relationship can make contact easier, follow-up more effective, and closing more frequent.

Choose staff because they know the market. Knowledge and credibility should be chosen over a pretty face every time, because once you get a live sales prospect, the last thing you want to do is put him/her on hold while you go find someone who knows the business.

Choose your staff because of their ability to evaluate the trade show and make suggestions for future improvements in your booth, your participation, and your products. Make sure your staff has agreed to the goals for the trade show and hold them responsible for achieving them. Encourage them to suggest improvements in both the booth and their own efforts that will generate more success.

At every trade show you will meet a winery complaining about the quality of the show. "I just don't think there are any buyers here," they will say. Yet a neighbor at the next table will have sold containers of wine at the same show. Focus on these shows the same way you focus on a sales call: know the audience, bait the hook, and close the sale. Well-trained staff and advance preparation, born out of their focused strategy, give immediate and positive results.

7. **Follow up after the trade show**. The work does not stop when the doors close. After the show you have to follow up quickly and effectively with every sales contact. Without the proper execution of this single element, the world's most exciting booth and sales staff will fail to produce any results at all. And to make this even easier, it's a good idea to incorporate some kind of a promotion into your participa-

tion in the trade show itself—a reason to follow up on every contact—and a reason for them to look forward to that follow up. Whether it is a free gift or in-situ demonstrations, the reason for these follow up visits is to keep the door open for future contacts and future sales.

Most importantly, use the time after the show to evaluate your efforts. What can you improve? Was the show worthwhile? Why? What will you do next year to achieve your goals? And how will you adjust your expectations for next year?

A FINAL NOTE ON ADVERTISING & PROMOTION

All of the advertising and promotion practices described in this chapter are part of the larger picture—a marketing communications campaign that effectively positions your winery and brand in the marketplace and in relationship to your competitors.

The only way that you can legitimately evaluate that entire process is to measure the results you have generated against the costs to achieve them. As you look at your pipeline, and the way the product is moving through that pipeline, these programs are among your key tools in unblocking the problems and maximizing the flow. In the end, the flow through that pipeline will have to justify the costs of these programs, or they should be adjusted to fall into line with a reasonable return on investment.

REFERENCES

Kilburn, D. "How Auditing Has Transformed Advertising." *Advertising Insights.* 2004. Available at: http://www.japan.com/adventures/index.php

Phillips, M. & Rasberry, S. , *Marketing Without Advertising: Inspire Customers To Rave About Your Business & Create Lasting Success.* 5th ed. 2005. CA: Nolo Press.

Posert, H. & Franson, P. *Spinning the Bottle: Case Histories, Tactics and Stories of Wine Public Relation* Napa, CA: HPPR, 2004.

Kipling, R. *Just So Stories.* NY: Harper Collins, 1996.

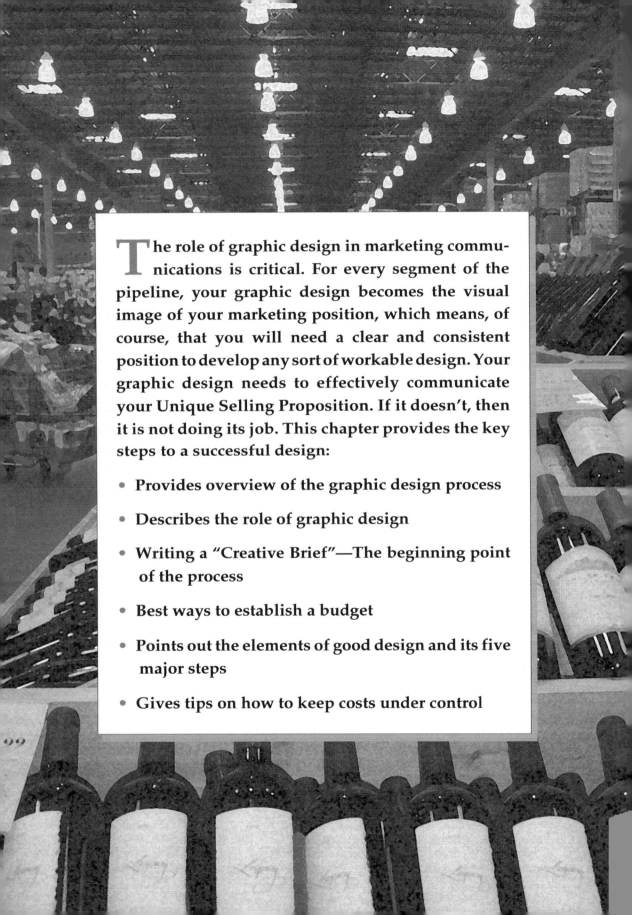

The role of graphic design in marketing communications is critical. For every segment of the pipeline, your graphic design becomes the visual image of your marketing position, which means, of course, that you will need a clear and consistent position to develop any sort of workable design. Your graphic design needs to effectively communicate your Unique Selling Proposition. If it doesn't, then it is not doing its job. This chapter provides the key steps to a successful design:

- Provides overview of the graphic design process

- Describes the role of graphic design

- Writing a "Creative Brief"—The beginning point of the process

- Best ways to establish a budget

- Points out the elements of good design and its five major steps

- Gives tips on how to keep costs under control

C H A P T E R

GRAPHIC DESIGN IN THE WINE INDUSTRY

T here is not enough room in this book to offer a complete course in graphic design, and that is probably a good thing. While it is helpful for wineries to understand the basic concepts of good graphic design, most designers would tell you that their worst clients are those who feel particularly expert in the subject. If there is a single caveat that we would like to place at the beginning of this discussion, it is that graphic design is best done by a professional. Leave the hard design work to the professionals, and focus your energy on managing them. Then the process should flow more smoothly, and you can reap the benefits of a successful marketing campaign.

THE ROLE OF GRAPHIC DESIGN

It is critical to understand the role of graphic design in marketing communications. For every segment of the pipeline, your graphic design becomes the visual image of your marketing position. If you do not have a clear and consistent positioning, then it will be impossible to develop graphic design concepts that capture that view. If your graphic design does not effectively communicate your Unique Selling Proposition, then it is not doing its job. This means you have not spent your money wisely.

Graphic design influences virtually every element of marketing, from its obvious role in the winery's packaging to the less obvious uses of letterhead, business cards, POS, sales and marketing materials, and websites. Just as every winery's key message should be consistent throughout all of its communications, so should the graphic design of its materials. Your ability to achieve this goal better than your competitors is one of the factors that will help you succeed in the market.

Preparing the Creative Brief

Whether you hire a graphic design firm, a freelancer, or try to do some of the work in-house, any graphic design project needs to begin with a creative brief. The creative brief is a simple outline of what you expect to achieve with the project. Ironically, most wineries do not use creative briefs, and far too many graphic design firms prefer to keep the client in the dark about them.

In the simplest sense, the creative brief is a series of questions that should be answered by winery management before any project is undertaken. It outlines the background of the situation, what you hope to change, and how much it will cost to effect that change. Why don't more wineries use creative briefs? Is it because they don't understand the process? The next few pages will make sure that you won't have that excuse. There are four process steps in preparing the creative brief.

Step 1: Define Your Current Situation and Audience

This step begins by asking the question: What is our current situation, and who is our audience? In order to answer this, you need to know your market positioning and your key messages. Make sure you give that information to the design firm in the beginning of the process. The corollary to that information is just as important: What is it about that situation that we must change? If there is nothing that needs to change, then there may be no need to consider creating a design project.

As you set about answering this first question, be brutally honest. The fact that you do not have a brochure is not a legitimate reason to create a brochure. The focus of your questions and answers must be as specific as possible and address an issue that is preventing the winery from achieving its marketing goals. In the end, that will almost always be defined in terms of a perception: what the market, or a segment of the market, thinks of your winery, brand, or wine. Defining this audience is critical, because most marketing communication work won't apply to all audiences or segments of the market equally. Define the issue as tightly as you can.

Your wines may be perceived as too expensive, or too inexpensive. You may have a strength in one varietal but not in others. You may be better positioned for chain store sales than for high-end restaurants. Your distributor may love your product, but find it hard to sell to his customers. Consumers may love your products, but can't find them in stores. Another possibility is that you may be stronger on the West Coast than the East Coast. Finally, you may want to extend the brand equity to include a new tier of wines at a new price point, or introduce a new series of varietals under the same label. All of these are legitimate marketing goals, but none of them can be solved by a new brochure.

It should not be a surprise to discover that the answer to your question is rarely something that can be captured in a single graphic design piece. The solution to your marketing challenge will almost certainly be a marketing campaign that combines many elements, from market visits and telephone calls to special promotions, pricing, or incentives. Of course, one of those elements may also be a printed piece that communicates the key brand message or supports a key strength. If so, proceed to the next step. If not, save the money for something that will do you some good.

Step 2: Determine How You Want
Consumer Perception to Change

This step will give added focus and direction to the process of preparing your creative brief. Ask yourself: How do we want consumer perception to change? The more you can narrow this answer down to the simplest possible language, the better you will be able to understand it and apply it to your marketing program. For example, the fact that consumers perceive your wines as too expensive is a problem. It will impede sales. However, the solution may not be to change the consumer perception of the wines. Instead it may be easier and more profitable to simply make less expensive wines, reduce the price, and match the product to the consumer's perception.

By the time you have completed the first two steps in this process, you have already done more to help your graphic design firm than most of your competitors. You have defined the current situation. You have defined the audience, and you have defined how you want to change the perceptions of that audience.

Step 3: Develop Your Message

Now the fun begins. The next part of the process can be quite creative, as you work to develop the message you want to deliver. Some wineries strongly believe that this part of the job is theirs, and that they are the only ones who can really develop the key message that will affect their customers. They will present the design firm with a specific message to deliver in text and images. Others prefer to involve the design firm at this point, taking advantage of the additional creative minds at the agency to help fine tune the message.

Whichever way you choose, focus on one result. There is only one best way to deliver your key message to the target audience in a way that is believable, effective, and feasible. Spend as much time as you need to get to this key message. As you do so, please try to remember that you are writing to the target audience, not to the winemaker, owner, or family friends of the winery. It doesn't matter if you like the key message, or if your winemaker finds it believable. It only matters that the key target audience believes it and acts on it.

If possible this is a good time to do some more market research. Do not try calling your friends to ask them what they think. Your friends don't buy enough wine. Ask people in the general market, and—if possible—ask them anonymously through surveys and focus group methodologies. Then listen to what they say. Even though this means an up-front investment in market research, in the long term it can save you a lot of money.

Step 4: Explore Message Delivery Mechanisms

Now the question you must ask is how you are going to deliver this piece in a way that will be effective. You can create the most beautiful website in the world, but unless people visit the site, it is worthless. You may create stunning brochures for your winery, but you may also find that most of them end up in the trashcans of trade shows because people aren't taking them home or reading them. You may end up creating a spectacular case card for retail display, but if they stay inside the distributor warehouse, you have spent your money foolishly.

How are you going to deliver the message? This is more than just a logistical question. It is also a question that affects the style and execution of the graphic design. If you want to mail something to 50,000 retailers, you will want to design something easy to mail—and don't forget to include postage costs in the overall budget! If you want to hand-deliver a personal invitation to fifteen of your top clients, that's a completely different project. It is important to tell the design firm about these decisions, or they won't be able to do their best work for you.

Other message-delivery mechanisms include an advertising campaign for consumers in targeted magazines and trade journals, posters and billboards; and even matching stationery, business cards, and other business communication tools that can extend your message. It is important to brainstorm the full range of message-delivery mechanisms with your design firm so you can determine the most effective choice for your business.

At this point, the outline for your creative brief should be complete, including the pros and cons of implementing each of the delivery mechanisms. The next phase in the process is to develop cost estimates, as well as to forecast expected return on investment. This is discussed in the following section on budget.

THE IMPORTANCE OF COSTS ESTIMATE FOR GRAPHIC DESIGN

At this point in your deliberations, you should be asking a very pointed series of questions about the cost of all of this. You know what message you want to deliver to your target audience. You explored the various delivery mechanisms, and now you need to examine costs in order to make a decision that will meet your budget and be effective.

For example, if you want to create an advertising campaign for consumers, you will need to estimate the costs of the media placement for the project. When you do, and you add up all the numbers, can you really justify the expenditure? If you cannot, now is the time to pull the plug. Don't design the ads, run them a few times, and then realize that your budget won't really allow you to achieve your goals. It would be far better to spend that money on a strategy and program that makes better use of your budget.

Do you really need a winery brochure? Some would argue that brochures are critical. But if the information and images are already on the website, and you print the URL on your label or wine corks, then is a brochure really your top priority? Or is it simply something to do—a placeholder instead of a real marketing communications program? In the final analysis, you must be able to justify your expenses by showing how they have improved the financial condition of the company. If you know that you really won't be able to do this, then it is hard to justify the fight for a major design project.

Figure 5.1: Sample Creative Brief

Date_____

Creative Brief for Roadkill Winery Brochure Project

Background

Roadkill Winery is a small, quality-oriented winery in Sonoma County that produces only two wines: Roadkill Red and Roadkill White. The wines are field blends of grapes, and owe their unique character to the century-old vineyard on the winery's property.

Total production is under 5,000 cases, evenly split between the two wines. The wines have received considerable critical acclaim and have won a number of medals and awards at wine competitions. Price point is $28 per bottle.

Over the past three years the winery has hosted a series of "Traveling Music" featuring top bands known for their "road trip" music. In addition, the winery sponsors a classic car rally every year in Sonoma County and regularly donates wines to Concours d'Elegance shows throughout the U.S.

The Problem

Despite the reviews and awards it has won, the winery has trouble convincing consumers and the trade that these are serious wines that belong on the table at fine restaurants and in consumers' houses.

The Proposal

Roadkill Winery is requesting proposals for the graphic design of a brochure that can be given out at the winery, at wine tastings, and during the various special events and sponsorhips that the winery organizes every year. The brochure should communicate the style and quality of the wines and give the readers a real impression that Roadkill Winery is not just another cute name in the wine business.

The brochure should be consistent with the existing wine label design and make use of the existing logo, logotype and colors.

Thematic Ideas and Points to Consider

- The style and production standards of the brochure must communicate quality and a serious committment to making great wine.
- The Roadkill name may work against us in this project—but that is a challenge we have to overcome.
- The use of animal skin, fur, or other products is **not** to be considered.

The Final Goal

This brochure will be successful if at least ten percent of the people who read it agree to sign up for the Roadkill Winery wine club.

When it comes to working with a graphic designer, it is a huge mistake to define your needs too tightly. Instead of explaining exactly what you need, it is better to explain exactly what you want to achieve. This gives the designer the opportunity to really be creative, and suggest solutions that might never have occurred to you.

Many wineries, particularly smaller ones, are hesitant to provide budgets to their graphic design firms. This is almost always a result of inexperience and insecurity. The wineries seem to sense that if they inform the design firm of the budget, then they will not get an honest estimate. While this may be true from time to time with less experienced design firms, the good firms always follow a strict pattern. They want to know how much money you have to spend. They need to know the whole amount, including printing, media placement, or postage. They also want to know the answers to those top few questions on the creative brief. If they have all of this information, then they can really put their creative minds to work, creating the best and most cost-effective solution to your marketing challenge.

It is important to give the design firm this opportunity. After all, they have a great deal more experience in this than you do. Give them the chance to show you what they can do. Give them the chance to exceed your expectations, and solve the problem in a way that will earn them awards, recognition, and many more jobs along the same lines—some of them from you.

WHAT ARE THE ELEMENTS OF GOOD DESIGN?

Among the most dreaded phrases to come out of the mouth of any graphic design client is, "We don't know what good design is, but we will tell you when we see it! " In general, it turns out that the first part of that sentence is true, whereas the second part is usually untrue. When this happens, the design firm fumes; the winery asks for more and more revisions; and the end result is not good design. Try to avoid this situation, and instead give the design firm good solid instructions up front, and then sit back and listen to what they say. You will be surprised at how successfully everything turns out.

When you do see something you like, take note of it, and try to get a copy to show to your design firm. Think of it as showing your hairdresser the style of haircut you want from a magazine. When talking to people who think in terms of images instead of words, a picture really is worth a thousand words. Most importantly, don't judge a design firm on the beauty of their work. Many beautiful design jobs fail to achieve their objectives, even while winning awards for use of photography or innovative use of color. Choose your designers for the results they achieve, not for the beauty of their work.

Here are a few simple rules for good graphic design. As in every field, there are designers and jobs that can absolutely violate these rules and still succeed. But at least you will be talking the same language.

Keep It Simple: If you want your audience to understand what you are saying, don't bury the message in a mosaic of design elements that make the reader embark on a scavenger hunt just to decipher it. Frankly, Scarlett, most readers aren't going to make that effort. Keep typefaces to a minimum unless you are printing a vaudeville poster. One or two typefaces are plenty. More than three typefaces can create unsavory results.

Pretty Pictures Are Nice—Make Sure They Communicate Something: Every designer loves to show off pieces that capture the essence of an Ansel Adams photograph of the Sierra Nevada, or Monet's memorable water lilies. When you are finished reviewing the portfolio of the designer, stop and try to remember the key message and client for each piece. If you can't remember those things, then what you have is a good artist. Look for a good graphic designer.

Think in Thirds: Don't divide your design into halves—it is too easy for the reader to choose one over the other. Instead, work with the way the eye flows over a new image, and work the message into that pattern. This is where your designer knows a lot more than you do. Listen. The eye is often drawn into designs where the elements are in three equal panels, while two panels often send the message of conflict rather than harmony.

White Space Is Elegant: Often, a major temptation is to fill every spare corner with text or an image. The rationale is: why waste all that space? Yet by leaving the space blank, you focus all of the attention on the main image, and the main text. Like an open, airy room, a design piece with a lot of white space conveys elegance, style, and focus. That's good.

Type Should Be Readable: Your key message will be communicated by a combination of the written word and images. Sometimes designers forget this. If you can't read the type without your glasses, make it larger, or make it clearer. If the type is obscured by graphics, or reversed out of a photograph, make it more legible. If you don't care that people can't read the type, then delete it. If you can live without it, so can they.

Make It Timeless: Too many brochures get thrown into the garbage because an image or text reference is out of date. Don't use the very latest in colors, because they often look dated after only a year or two. Do you remember Miami Vice? Earth-tones? Avoid using photos of people who may leave the company, and resist the temptation to show every bottle, every varietal that the winery makes. When you change your mind, it will be very costly to reprint all of the brochures. Focus the brochure on the key message, and it should last for a long time.

Make Sure It Works: A press kit folder should usually have a tab, so that it is easily found in a file drawer. A sales sheet with a tab may make it easier to find among those many pages in a distributor salesman's binder. An invitation should fit the postal service regulations for first class letters, or you may find yourself paying double the postage. A response card that includes the pre-printed address label of your addressee is an easy way to track who is responding to your direct mail, even when they don't fill in the card correctly. Think each piece through so that you really understand how it is going to be used, and how you can make it as effective as possible.

The Medium is the Message: As with all communications, how you say something is as important as what you say. Be sure that your materials really speak to the audience. Sometimes the result is something that makes the owner or marketing director feel good—and leaves the intended audience somewhere between befuddled and bored. It may be the best piece you have ever done, but it almost certainly won't be the best piece your audience has ever seen. If you really want to make an impression, make sure your delivery mechanism is the most appropriate one to deliver your key message to your audience.

Just as a non-profit organization should avoid very expensive-looking marketing materials, a small winery that prides itself on handcrafted wines should show a handcrafted style in the design of their materials. A winery that wants to be a major player in the market will need to match the quality, quantity and style of the marketing materials of their competition. Worst of all are those graphic design pieces in which the design actually works against the message of the text. A winery focusing on elegance and style should avoid crudely drawn illustrations unless they are drawn by Pablo Picasso. A winery that is emphasizing its leadership in sustainable or organic practices should certainly use recycled paper for its materials, or it will run the risk of being perceived as both clueless and dishonest.

Match The Images To The Message: A technical discussion of your new tank technology may be fascinating to those in the field of stainless steel construction, but if you can't get your customers to fall in love with it, leave it out of the marketing materials. Wine lovers are pretty predictable. They like the romance of handcrafted products.

They enjoy wines with personality, even when is quirky. They are not particularly receptive to the idea of marketing departments, brands, or corporate decision making. Given that information, your marketing materials should stress the elements that are attractive to wine consumers, and the design should capture a sense of your personality, complete with quirks.

Figure 5.2: Examples of Poor and Good Graphic Design

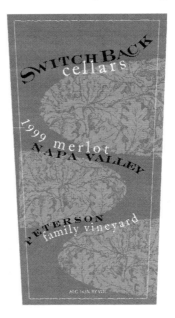

Poor Label Design

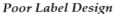

Good Label Design

THE FIVE STAGES OF THE DESIGN PROCESS

A design project is always approached in stages. Each stage is an opportunity to approve, reject, or fine tune the finished project. Yet each step is also an important achievement. Once the step is complete and approved, you cannot go back and change things without incurring additional costs. You will also incur the wrath of the designer, which may be even worse. A good designer will present a proof to you at each stage. Your signature on that proof indicates that you approve of the work done so far, and are ready to go to the next step. If you have specific things that you want changed, note those on the proof so that you and the designer can both reference them later. The paragraphs and Table 5.1 below describe the basic five stages most design projects follow.

Table 5.1: The Five Stages of the Graphic Design Process

1. Concept
2. Copy
3. Design
4. Illustrations and Photography
5. Printing

Stage 1: Concept

The first step in any design project is the initial concept. After you have presented the creative brief to the design team, they will take your information and come back with an overall concept or several concepts. Often, the number of concepts will be specified in the agreement. If it isn't, it should be. A concept should not be judged on the quality of the artwork or the selection of the colors. A concept is simply the design firm's suggestions as to how to solve the communications challenge you have identified.

A good concept should capture the essence of your positioning, and it should also be clear in how it will achieve the goal you have established for the project. It should address such critical issues as how the piece will be used, how it will be distributed or shipped, and how it will encourage further interaction between you and the audience. While it will usually include a headline or tagline, it will not include either final copy or final artwork. That comes later, after you have selected the concept you think hits the nail on the head.

When the Lodi-Woodbridge WineGrape Commission wanted to create a simple concept that would capture the organization's leadership in the whole field of sustainable agriculture and its regulations, they considered many different ideas: clever acronyms, visual images incorporating icons and symbols, and official-sounding language. In the end, they agreed that the simplest concept was the best one: *Lodi Rules.* This captured the region's extensive work on developing regulations and certifications for sustainable agriculture, but it also created a simple and easy-to-understand, positive image for Lodi as the region who had succeeded where so many others were struggling. Live Oak Cellars (an imaginary winery at the time of this writing) might consider a number of concepts for its marketing image, from a carefully created, accurate etching of an oak tree, to a more dramatic, freestyle icon of that oak tree, to an image of the winery itself, with an oak tree carved on the cellar door. All are different concepts, and should be judged on how well they communicate the primary marketing message of the brand, and how well they can be adapted to capture the goals and dreams of future plans.

When you review concepts, don't get too involved in any of the smaller decisions. If you like the general idea, assume that you can work out the other details in the later stages of the design. Do not reject a concept because you don't like the artwork, size, or color. Look for what works, and identify that for the designer. Of course, if there are details that you dislike, now is a good time to point them out. Details can always be fixed, but you will give yourself a better chance of getting a great design piece if you can share those early on in the process.

Stage 2: Copy

Once you have determined what the concept looks and feels like, the next step is to write the copy. It is important to do this before you begin the design work, because the length of the copy will play a huge role in the look, feel, and even the size of the finished piece. As with a print advertisement, the goal of your headline should be to capture the imagination and interest of the reader, while still communicating your brand message and positioning. And the body copy should provide the reassurance and documentation to support that headline.

When it comes to copy, most companies don't know when to stop. They somehow think that more copy is better, and that more information is more interesting. It is not. Only interesting information is interesting. The rest is simply wasted effort. We have all seen ads that had so much copy that we simply turned the page. Make sure that doesn't happen with your materials. Look for ways to reduce copy in every sentence, every paragraph, and every page. Your designer will thank you, and your audience may actually read it.

Stage 3: Design

This is where you finally get into the details. The design stage is where the designer presents the whole layout, complete with colors, suggested illustrations, and the text blocked in as well. When you look at the design, you should have a pretty strong sense of how the whole thing will look, and how it will work.

In the old days, there was an intermediate step between design and printing, called the mechanical. This was the absolute, drop dead, final version of the piece, complete with every single "i" dotted and "t" crossed: illustrations, text, foils, and die cuts. However, computers have changed all of that. Now the final version that goes to print will evolve out of the computer files used for the design stage. That makes this stage even more critical.

As your designers work on this stage, please make sure that the input you give them is accurate. It is too late to change the overall concept—you approved that long ago. Focus on the very specific elements of the design. Is the copy legible? Are the photos or illustrations exactly right for what you want to say? Does the piece really convey your key messages? Do those key messages stand out clearly? Is the piece consistent with the rest of your marketing communications efforts?

Because this version will become the final printed piece, this is also the time to take a close look at how it all works. Does the response card have enough room to write the required information? Give a copy of the piece to a few people who don't know much about the project. Ask them for their feedback, and ask them to fill out any forms. You may be surprised what you have forgotten to ask, or what is not clear to someone who hasn't worked on the project for months.

It is also critical at this point to proofread the copy. Do not rely on someone who has worked long and hard on the project to proofread it. A fresh pair of eyes, eager to find mistakes, is always better. Make sure you check the big words and letters, too. Headlines, phone numbers, and address blocks are frequently the site of unnoticed typographical errors.

The final stage in all of this will include color swatches for each of the inks used in the piece, as well as examples of how the piece folds together. It should include paper samples so that you can get a sense of not only how the piece looks, but also how it feels in your hand. It should include final versions of all illustrations, photos, and text. When you sign this proof, you are signing an approval for the final piece, and no further changes can be made without creating additional costs at the printer.

Stage 4: Illustrations and Photography

Many clients believe that artwork somehow springs forth from the internet free of charge. It doesn't. Every illustration or photograph that you use in your materials will either have to be created for you, or purchased from a stock supplier who sells such images. While custom illustrations or photographs can be more costly, they also give a unique look to your piece that can't be copied by anyone else. If you commission an illustration or a photo shoot, it is usually a good idea to negotiate a price for the full use of the materials forever. Those images can become part of your overall brand image, and it can be frustrating to go back to the artist or photographer every time you want to print something new, just to negotiate another fee for another use.

Beware the designer who uses a nice simple black and white photograph to "give you an idea of what we will have here." That photo may come from Ansel Adams, and the use fee would be steep. Understand what *design* is and what *illustration* is.

A Note About Approvals

Whenever you are tackling a large job, try to include the winery's top executives in the major decisions. If the executive is going to have a strong opinion of the finished piece, then it only makes sense to get that opinion up front, rather than later. All too often, design projects are managed by middle managers at the winery until this last approval. Then, when it is too late to change much, the project is shown to top-level executives, who suggest a series of changes to the very nature of the job. This is bad management. It is not the fault of the design firm, and they should bill you for any changes made to an already approved stage.

Stage 5: Printing

The final stage in your graphic design project is putting ink to paper, and printing out the finished piece. In most cases, your designer will attend the initial part of the printing process, to make sure that all is going according to plan. Printing is not an exact science, and requires both scientific and artistic sensibilities. It may seem that printing is a straightforward replication process, but it is not.

Printing presses create colors by blending primary colors, and the blending process can be adjusted at the press to get the best possible look for your piece. The way the colors looked on your designer's computer monitor or on the color proof that was printed out on a computer printer may vary. The colors that come from the printing press are what really matters. You can't change it once it comes off the press, so it is important to make sure the colors are correct in the first run.

If the specific color you want is really critical, you can use a special ink that is created exactly in that color, and add that ink as an additional color to the press. This usually involves the Pantone Matching System (PMS), and is something that your designer can specify to the printer.

TIPS ON MANAGING COSTS

Creating collateral materials is always an adventure, and part of the excitement comes from the fact that every change in design does imply some kind of change in the budget. What began as a simple two color postcard can quickly become a major project with multiple colors and a glossy finish, along with costs that are ten times the original estimate.

How does this happen? Often, clients do not understand what costs money and what does not. Changes in the early stages of a project are fairly easy to make, but changes later on cannot only be much more complicated, they can also be expensive.

The first place you can save money, or spend more of it, is in the selection of the paper. Sadly, cheap paper looks cheap, and this is usually a false economy. Nothing communicates quality quite so effectively as nice paper stock.

Printing presses are the second place that money can be saved or spent. As a general rule, it costs a lot of money to turn on the press—after that, the individual pieces cost relatively little. That's why it can cost $135 a piece to print 73 brochures, but when you decide to print ten thousand of them, the unit price drops to less than a dollar. When you begin planning the project in the creative brief stage, make sure you understand this, and plan the print run accordingly. Then make sure it gets included in the budget.

The more colors on the job, the more you will pay. A simple one or two color job can often be printed on a simple press with little supervision. Once you add a third or fourth color, the press job is more complicated, and the price goes up. By the time you add two gold foils, a matte varnish, and two PMS colors, you can expect to be on the most sophisticated of presses. You will pay much more for this. Don't try to second guess the printer—they know which press is best suited for your job, and will make the decision accordingly. Keep in mind that foils, which are very thin layer of metal and can give an intense and rich look to any piece, are expensive to buy and complicated to apply.

Another element of the printing process that can increase costs is the layout itself. Designs that require the printer to print two colors very close to each other (close registration) or that require the ink to "bleed" off the edges of the page are always more expensive. Careful color matching, including delicately tinted photos, is always hard to get exactly right, and will cost more to print.

Sadly, many designers don't explain these details in advance. Then when the "small" design modifications add up, the printing price slowly rises beyond the limits of the budget. For this reason it is hard to get an accurate print price before the piece is in its final design stages. As a result, clients often feel that they are being taken to the cleaners, not the printers. However, this is a chicken and egg problem—you can't budget the printing before you do the design, and you can't do the design without knowing the budget.

Die cuts, where the design is something other than a simple rectangle, also add to the cost, and must be done separately after the printing. While many printers may have an existing die for some winery applications, a custom die also adds to your costs. This is also true of folds, especially those clever, involved origami designs that designers love. Most of those cannot be done by machine, and so you have to pay for the handwork involved. This makes a lot of sense when you are producing only a few hundred, but when the numbers reach into the thousands, it can be prohibitively expensive.

Embossing, where a design is pressed into the paper, and debossing, where it is pushed out from the back, also involved additional costs. These are created via a special metal die, and you can expect to pay a subcontractor to create the die, as well as the printer to put the piece through the machine.

Finally, once the piece is printed and folded you may also have to pay for binding the pages together, via any number of different methods. Each one has its advantages, and each one has costs. Packaging the finished pieces is yet another cost, as is shipping them to various points around the USA.

In conclusion, if all of this sounds complicated, then the reason is because it often is. That's why it is hard to do on your own. Therefore, try to work with a design firm that makes things seem simple, and isn't afraid to put things in writing. Then read the writing, and make sure you understand what you are getting, including all of the costs.

Most design contracts will be written so that you pay them at the approval of each stage. This way the designer gets paid for the work, and you continue to have the opportunity to approve the next stage. Pay your designers promptly. Just as it is a bad idea to eat at a restaurant where the cook is angry, you won't get good design from a designer who isn't getting paid on time.

In the end, if you understand the intricacies of the graphic design process, and are familiar with the terms and stages, then you should be able to work in partnership with a design firm to produce a compelling project. Ideally, the finished project will meet your initial goals, and have the positive impact on sales and brand recognition that you are seeking.

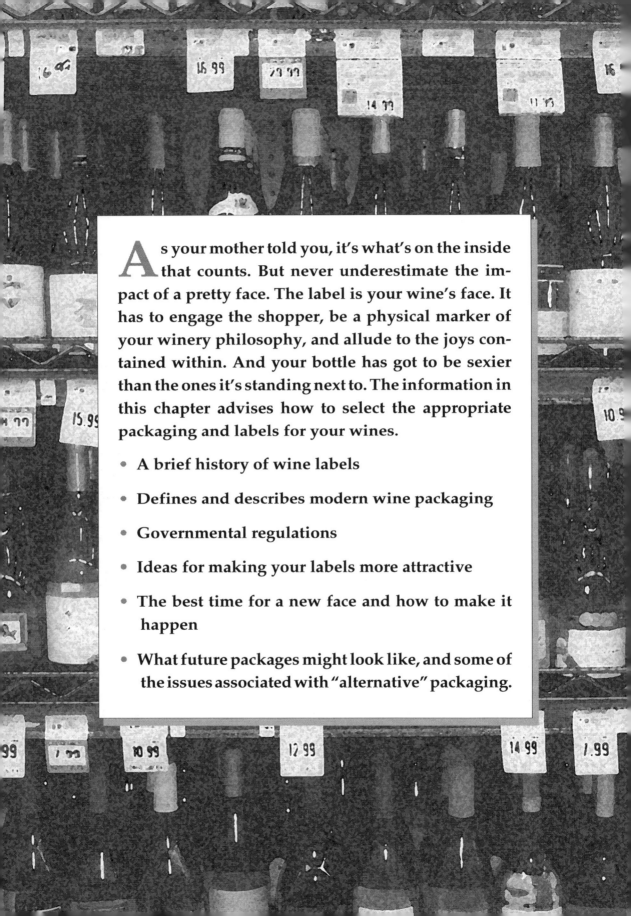

As your mother told you, it's what's on the inside that counts. But never underestimate the impact of a pretty face. The label is your wine's face. It has to engage the shopper, be a physical marker of your winery philosophy, and allude to the joys contained within. And your bottle has got to be sexier than the ones it's standing next to. The information in this chapter advises how to select the appropriate packaging and labels for your wines.

- **A brief history of wine labels**

- **Defines and describes modern wine packaging**

- **Governmental regulations**

- **Ideas for making your labels more attractive**

- **The best time for a new face and how to make it happen**

- **What future packages might look like, and some of the issues associated with "alternative" packaging.**

C H A P T E R **6**

WINE PACKAGING
AND LABELS

W ine industry insiders often speak of brands in terms of "labels" because the impact of a label is so important in the wine business. It is so important that many wine marketers add a sixth "P" to the traditional five "Ps" of marketing (Product, Price, Placement, Promotion, and Position). Of course, in traditional marketing, packaging is included in the concepts of product and promotion, but in wine it is so important that it really deserves its own "P," and its own chapter.

When a consumer faces a wall of wine in a wine shop or super-market, most of the other "Ps" will fall off to the side. The products will seem remarkably similar, whether they are Chardonnays or Merlots. The pricing on them may also be similar, with the majority of the wines falling into popular price categories. By definition, the placement of these wines is similar: they are in the same store, on the same shelf! If there is much promotion at all, it is in the form of the ubiquitous shelf-talker. For the average American wine consumer, there is no way to distinguish one bottle from the next—unless we talk about the label.

The wine label is the ultimate expression of the positioning of the brand. It must somehow capture the essence of your key message, and deliver it in a space smaller than the average postcard. It must serve as a billboard for your brand, attracting the attention of your customers as they stare at that wall of competing brands. It must also reassure those customers who pick up the bottle—making them feel comfortable that the wine is of good quality, suitable for their table.

It is for all these reasons that this chapter presents information to help you select the most appropriate packaging and labels for your wines. It begins with a brief history of wine labels, and then moves forward to define and describe wine packaging today. Next, information on the required components of the wine label are covered, including government regulations and ideas to make your labels more attractive to your target audience. This is followed by some advice on when and how to change your wine label. The chapter concludes with a section on potential future packaging, such as tetra-packs and six-packs, as well as some of the issues associated with these alternative packaging concepts.

A Brief History of Wine Packaging and Labels

In the beginning, wine containers were necessarily primitive. The goatskin bag, still in use today as the Bota bag, has been used for thousands of years. The first archeological evidence we have of any wine is sediment left in ancient ceramic vessels from more than 7,000 years ago. Amphorae were used throughout the ancient world, and sometimes included a clay seal that listed the region, vintage date, and producer of the wine inside—the ancient version of a modern wine label. These amphorae were a major trading cargo for Roman sailing vessels. Once the Romans conquered Britain, the use of the wooden barrel became more prevalent. While all of these were effective shipping containers, none of them protected the wine from air or spoilage bacteria.

Throughout the Middle Ages and the Renaissance, wine was shipped in wooden barrels, and then decanted into bottles for wine service—both at inns and in private homes. This job was performed by a specific servant, called the "Bottler." The title continues in usage today as the "butler."

In the 1600's wine was first put into bottles with corks. This process sealed the wine, and allowed it to age without the negative impact of oxygen or spoilage. However, as it became apparent that more powerful wines could actually improve in this sealed bottle, wine styles were changed forever. Wineries began to make rich, powerful wines that took years to mature, and delivered the elegant, complex flavors of the wines we love today.

As the use of glass bottles became more common, different regions in the world began to use distinctive bottles to identify their products. German wines were often found in the tall, elegant hock bottle, while Burgundy and Bordeaux each had their own distinctive shape. Franken wines came in short, rounded bottles, and Vintage Port in tall, black glass. Even today, we use those bottle shapes in the New World to indicate wine style or varietal, even when the wines are really quite different from their European antecedents.

DEFINING WINE PACKAGING TODAY

In the past few years, a whole new world of wine packaging has come into play, from screw cap bottles, aluminum cans, to bag-in-the-box containers—the modern equivalent of the goatskin bag. These are exciting times for wine packaging. As such, there are great risks, and great opportunities.

Each container today offers a different modern technological solution to that age-old challenge of wine packaging: protecting the wine from its traditional enemies of oxygen, ultraviolet light, spoilage bacteria, shipping damage, and overeager butlers. The package must serve as a shipping container for the wine as well as a serving container. It must protect the wine from tampering, and must convey some guarantee of quality. Finally, it must be an attractive sales and merchandising presentation—one that will sell the wine more effectively than its competition. Table 6.1 lists the majority of packaging components for wine today. Each of these is described in more detail in the remainder of this chapter.

Table 6.1: Packaging Components for Wine

Container	Closures	Bottle Info	ShippingCases
• Bottle • Box • Bota-Bag • Tetra-Pak • Plastic • Multi-packs	• Natural Cork • Synthetic Cork •Constructed Cork • Screw Cap	• Front Label • Back Label • Micro Labels • Capsules • Printed corks and neck labels • Bar Codes & Numbered Bottles	• Quality of materials • Inserts • Cases form design when placed together

PACKAGING FOR QUALITY CONTROL—
THE ISSUE OF CLOSURES

The revolution in wine packaging today is the culmination of millennia of experimentation with wine containers and closures. Ancient wines were sealed into pottery amphorae with a wooden plug, wrapped in cloth, and then covered with wax. The seal did not eliminate oxygen, but it did limit the number of larger insects in the wine.

How your winery packages its wine should not only address the obvious issues of appearance, but also insure quality control and purity. While consumers may occasionally express concern over a bad cork, the bottles rejected in a restaurant can become a major source of irritation, as well as financial loss. Some wineries have used this to create a perceived advantage in the marketplace. Their screw cap wines, while perhaps less attractive to some consumers, will never suffer from cork taint. Today winemakers have a large variety of closures they can use.

Natural Cork: The traditional natural cork is still the choice of most of the top wineries in the world. It makes an excellent seal with the bottle, and there is some evidence that the cork interacts with the wine over time, adding to the complexity and richness of the wine's flavors. Consumers, on the whole, prefer it.

Cork also has its problems. As a natural product, it is not as consistent as winemakers would like, not only containing occasional structural defects, but also can become "tainted" with a moldy smell that ruins the wine. At most wineries, the quality control program for corks is comprehensive, and is a major focus for the winemaking team. (However, as any wine marketer will tell you, wine is still the only consumer product sold that requires consumers to purchase a separate specialized tool just to open the package.)

While the cork industry has proposed and developed treatments and processes to remove or reduce concerns about tainted cork, none is widely accepted as perfectly effective. In response, a number of other solutions have come into use.

Synthetic Corks: Some companies have started to use synthetic corks of varying types. Made from plastic, these synthetics eliminate the concerns about moldy flavors, but don't always seal as well as natural corks.

Constructed Corks: Some cork companies have introduced a series of "constructed" corks, molded from smaller pieces of cork, to compete with some of the new alternatives.

Screw Caps: While some winemakers cheer loudly for the simplicity and consistent predictability of the screw cap, that enthusiasm isn't yet shared by the general U.S. public. Recent studies show that the vast majority of consumers currently believe that a screw cap on a bottle of wine indicates a wine of lower value and lower quality. Aluminum screw caps seem to offer excellent and predicable results, but consumers usually find these less attractive. There is also some evidence that wines age differently without the contact of cork.

Box and Plastic Containers: At the furthest end of the spectrum, newer plastic containers use food-grade bags or envelopes to seal the wine, very much like a modern goatskin bag, but again, these are usually associated with lower-priced wines. These are often contained within a box or plastic container instead of the traditional glass bottle.

Packaging to Attract Consumers

After concerns with product quality and integrity have been resolved, the next major issue is designing packaging that is attractive to consumers. This, of course, is done with an eye to meeting the specific needs of your target consumer group.

The challenge, however, is designing a unique package that isn't quickly copied by your competitors. For example, over the years we have seen wine labels introduced with a delicately torn edge, as if each label were created by hand. Within a couple of years, major wine labels were replicating this look on an industrial basis. Wax capsules, once used exclusively on very small production wines, can now be applied much more easily. Proprietary glass bottle shapes quickly become the target of endless replicas. Every time you find a dramatic element of artwork on a successful label, you will quickly find six or more labels with similar images, almost always at lower price points.

In the wine market, that wonderful and dramatic label that gives you a real Strength "S" from your SWOT analysis is an almost instantaneous invitation for a "T" as well. That threat comes from any number of other wineries willing to mimic some of the successful "quality cues" that you have created for your packaging.

What Is a Quality Cue?

It turns out that many consumers see certain elements of packaging as clear indications that the wine is of higher quality. The natural cork closure is one of these clues. So are ivory colored paper and gold foil. Just about any kind of seal, medal, or indicia is seen as a guarantee of quality, even if they refer to awards won 100 years ago, or are simply a winery logo in that format. When you add in the concepts of neck labels, back labels, bottle shapes, bottle colors and the other variables, it is easy to see why some designers prefer to talk about a package as opposed to just a label.

When it comes to designing the package, every element should be addressed, and the pros and cons assessed with your customer in mind. Following are some considerations.

Bottle shape: Unusual or proprietary bottle shapes can often give a unique look to your package. Twenty years ago, there were only a few shapes and colors available to wineries on a commercial basis. Now there are hundreds. Yet these bottles do not always serve the winery effectively. (e.g., their sides are not cylindrical, so they won't stack in a wine rack; the taller shapes don't fit well in a refrigerator.) What at first seems attractive to consumers can often turn them away from the brand after they have struggled with these issues. Waiters in restaurants actively dislike the very heavy bottles now in vogue because they are harder to pour.

Capsules: Restaurants also try to avoid wines with wax capsules. Those may seem very attractive in a store, but after trying to get some of that wax out of the carpet, restaurateurs have a different opinion entirely. Capsules have fought a number of battles over the past twenty years. The traditional lead capsules were ideal in terms of consumer perceptions, but once they were outlawed (for reasons pertaining to the potential of lead poisoning) the industry has explored many of the alternatives.

Various alloys and multi-ply solutions have attempted to approximate the feel and look of lead with differing levels of success. Other wineries have eschewed the capsule altogether, choosing to go with a bare neck, or a simple adhesive sticker on the top of the cork. Do these make the bottles seem more hand-finished and elegant, or simply unfinished and cheap? Only your customers know for sure.

Printed corks and neck labels: Each change you make in one element of the packaging has implications for the rest of your package. The bare neck look does show off your cork in a way that is quite revealing, and many wineries using this approach have chosen to print their corks with strong graphics to compensate. This has the additional advantage of hiding, to a certain extent, the quality of the corks you are using. Often this look also seems to need a neck label of some kind to add a touch of elegance.

Micro labels: Additional labels can really create a completely different look to your package, and they can also convey a lot of information that consumers want or like. In the most traditional manner, some wineries use a standard label for many vintages, and only identify the vintage on much smaller labels, such as a neck label or snipe. This has the advantage of reducing printing costs over the years. Other micro labels can provide vineyard designations, awards won, or just a note of style to an otherwise less impressive package.

Back labels: The back label is a subject worthy of its own discussion. Because the federal Alcohol and Tobacco Tax Board regulations require that certain elements appear on the front label of every wine bottle, some wineries choose to put all of the required information on a small and undistinguished "front label." They then create a visually dramatic back label with no regulatory constraints. When the bottle is put on the shelf, the graphic back label is facing front.

Shipping cases: The shipping case is another area where wine packaging is beginning to move into modern times. While the traditional wooden case box is still the shipper of choice for the very best wines, there are lots of interesting uses of graphics on wines that are intended to be stacked at the retail level. No longer content with brown boxes and rough stamped information, these have now expanded to include cases that form a large graphic when stacked together. Beautiful graphics, higher quality paper stock, and even better internal dividers all send a message of quality to both the consumer and the distribution network. Along the same lines, cheaper cases, scuffed or peeling labels, lightweight papers, bad graphics, and bad closures also send a message to the consumer.

Barcodes and individualized bottles: For years, every bottle of Châteauneuf-du-Pape has come in a specially branded bottle with a debossed "cartouche" identifying the region. Even more sophisticated is the new bar code system for use on Italian DOCG wines. Each bottle now includes a numerical code that allows the producer to trace the roots of the bottle back to the winery, the bottling date, and even the individual vineyard or lot of grapes. Most major US wineries now print some kind of bottling code on the bottle so that they can trace individual bottling lots through any quality control concerns. A few wineries, like Imagery, actually number their bottles like great works of art, so that the consumer feels they are buying something very special.

Appealing front labels: As mentioned previously, the label on a bottle of wine is incredibly important, because in many cases it is the only reference point for consumers. Numerous studies show that the design, color, graphics, and font on a wine label are determining factors in whether or not a consumer will purchase your wine.

LABEL DESIGN ISSUES AND SUCCESS FACTORS
In designing your wine label, there are some givens, such as the U.S. government requirements that must be included on all labels. If not, they will not be approved to use in wine sales. However, once these requirements are met, much creativity can be unleashed to design labels that are attractive and appealing to your target audience.

Required Government Components of Wine Labels in the U.S.
In the United States, the Federal Bureau of Tax and Trade (TTB—

formerly called the BATF) requires that your wine label contain certain information. They pre-approve all labels for wine containing more than 7% alcohol. Following is a summary list of the required wine label components; however, you should still consult the full text of the Federal Regulations to make sure that you are in compliance.

Brand name: The name under which the wine is marketed OR the name of the bottler or importer, if there is no brand name.

Class or type designation: Gives the specific identity of the wine. An approved grape varietal name, a semi-generic name or name of geographic significance may be used if an appellation of origin is also stated. "Table Wine" may be used if the wine is not over 14% alcohol by volume.

Alcohol content: Must be stated as "Alcohol ___% by volume" or "Alc ___% by Vol." or "Alcohol ___% to ___% by volume."

Percentage of foreign wine: For blends of American and foreign wine, the percentage and origin of the foreign wine must be shown, if reference is made to the presence of foreign wine on the label.

Bottler's name and address (American wine); importer's name and address (imported wine): If the wine is bottled or packed after importation, the name and address of the bottler or packer must also be stated.

Net contents: Must be stated in the same manner as the metric standard of fill for wine (for example, "750 ml" but not "75 cl") and may be blown or etched into the glass. For imported wine, a sample bottle must be submitted with label application if the net content is not shown on the label.

Sulfite declaration: Required for wine containing 10 or more parts per million sulfur dioxide. Must read "Contains Sulfites" or "Contains (a) Sulfiting Agent(s)." If this is omitted, evidence of analysis is submitted with label application that the wine contains less than 10 pm.

Health warning statement: Must appear on all alcohol beverages for sale or distribution in the U.S. containing more than 1% alcohol by volume.

Country of origin of imported wine: The U.S. Customs Service requires the label must state the country in which the wine was produced.

That's what the U.S. Government wants from your packaging. It's hard to imagine another consumer product with this kind of regulatory labeling, but this is the wine industry in a nation that is still recovering from the effects of Prohibition.

Figure 6.1: Example of Government Requirements on a Wine Label

FRONT LABEL

1. BRAND

2. VINTAGE DATE

3. CLASS, TYPE OR VARIETAL DESIGNATION

4. APPELLATION OF ORIGIN OR VITICULTURAL AREA

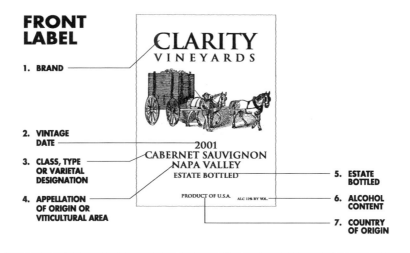

CLARITY
V I N E Y A R D S

2001
CABERNET SAUVIGNON
NAPA VALLEY
ESTATE BOTTLED

PRODUCT OF U.S.A.   ALC 12% BY VOL.

5. ESTATE BOTTLED

6. ALCOHOL CONTENT

7. COUNTRY OF ORIGIN

FRONT, BACK OR SIDE LABEL

8. NAME AND ADDRESS

9. GOVERNMENT WARNING/HEALTH STATEMENT

10. DECLARATION OF SULFITES

11. NET CONTENTS

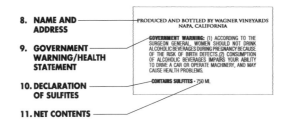

PRODUCED AND BOTTLED BY WAGNER VINEYARDS
NAPA, CALIFORNIA

GOVERNMENT WARNING: (1) ACCORDING TO THE SURGEON GENERAL, WOMEN SHOULD NOT DRINK ALCOHOLIC BEVERAGES DURING PREGNANCY BECAUSE OF THE RISK OF BIRTH DEFECTS.(2) CONSUMPTION OF ALCOHOLIC BEVERAGES IMPAIRS YOUR ABILITY TO DRIVE A CAR OR OPERATE MACHINERY, AND MAY CAUSE HEALTH PROBLEMS.

CONTAINS SULFITES - 750 ML.

DESIGNING LABELS TO ATTRACT YOUR TARGET AUDIENCE

As with all other marketing communications programs, it is critical to define your target audiences and define what they want. It would be really easy if they all wanted the same thing. They don't. Always keep in mind that your packaging will not only attract customers; it will also play a role in deterring other customers from trying your wines.

Going back to the concept of "label as billboard," this is easy to understand. Some billboards work well with some audiences, but as Abraham Lincoln once said (and we paraphrase here), "You can't use one billboard for all the people all the time."

What does a billboard do? It creates an immediate impression. When a consumer sees your label on the shelf, you only get a second or two to make a good impression. It must stand out from the competition. It must grab the eye and steal attention from the rest of the products on the shelf. This is not the place for discreet wallflowers.

That part sounds easy. Why not just make a really big, bold, bright label that can be picked out at twenty paces? Because the kind of impression consumers want from their wines isn't loud and flashy. Most consumers think of wine as a stylish, elegant, sophisticated purchase. Your job, then, is to create a label that is big, bright, stylish, bold, elegant, loud, sophisticated, flashy...

This is getting harder, isn't it? In some ways, the perfect label is like the perfect date. Yes, there are those dates that are really attractive in a loud and glamorous way, but your wine should be like the date you want to bring home to meet your parents. Your label must be absolutely attractive, but it also must stand for something more than just a good time. Wine, for many consumers, is more important than that.

The danger, of course, is that all consumers are not like minded. While traditional wine consumers seem to like the traditional label styles, complete with ivory-colored paper and gold foil, there is a new generation of wine drinkers that is attracted to fun, innovative, and irreverent labels. A few years ago, names such as Starved Dog Lane, Fat Bastard, and Cat's Pee on a Gooseberry Bush would have been unthinkable. Now they reach out to a new generation of wine drinkers—or at least their producers hope they do!

Beware. Those labels may well attract new and younger wine drinkers, but many traditional wine consumers see them as an abomination. Be careful that in attracting one group of consumers, you don't drive away an even larger group. Your label will not only define your positioning; it will also define your target market in a way that was not foreseen a few years ago. Figures 6.3 and 6.4 illustrate the difference between traditional and trendy wine labels. Both are fine—just as long as they are designed to target specific audiences.

Figure 6.3: Example of a Traditional Wine Label

Figure 6.4: Example of a Trendy Wine Label

This trend to be more creative with wine label design is predicted by classical marketing theory. As a category gets saturated, producers look for ways to stand out, and consumers look for new and interesting things. Pushing the envelope becomes more than just an expression; it becomes an economic necessity.

All of this may seem quite innovative and exciting to those of us in the wine business, but compared to other beverages, wine packaging is still as conservative as it gets. To get a much better idea of what is possible, go to the local liquor store and look at the shelves of liqueurs and aperitifs. You will see a panorama of wild and wonderful bottle shapes, each one a work of art. The colors range from bright yellow and blue to gold and silver. They do not need to fit in a refrigerator door or stack neatly in a wine rack, and therefore these packages are not constrained by many of the limitations of the wine business.

Now look at the shelves of wine. The wine industry has a long way to go before it can call itself innovative when it comes to packaging. Until recently, wine bottles were usually limited to a few very traditional and somber colors. The shapes of the bottles were usually one of three or four that can trace their roots back to the European wine regions of two hundred years ago. Now we are seeing a few new shapes, and many new colors. Most importantly, there is a whole new sense of making wine approachable.

WHEN SHOULD YOU CHANGE YOUR PACKAGING?

This is one of the great questions in wine marketing. Classic marketing teaches that your message must be timeless. You should have a package that effectively communicates your brand message, and will continue to do so for the long term. After all, it takes years for these messages to work their way into the mind of the consumer, and your packaging is the single most important interface with the consumer. With that in mind, one suggestion is that you develop a perfect packaging solution, use it for all of your products, and never change it. This is basically the philosophy of the great Château Lafitte Rothschild in Bordeaux.

On the other hand, there is ample evidence from the fashion and automotive industry that each year is a new opportunity to develop a new relationship with your customers, and each year should be the occasion of a new package that correctly conveys how perfectly your brand fits into the latest lifestyles of your target customers. New colors, new typefaces, and new looks are all the rage, and your winery will want to stay on top of the latest trends. Bear in mind that these trends change every year, so by definition such an approach will be out of style within months. Therefore, in the wine industry, where labeling and bottling must take place months (and in some cases years) before the wine is released, this would seem to be a very difficult process to manage, not to mention an expensive one.

With that in mind, another recommendation is that you develop a standard wine label design, but change one element on it each year as you make the announcement of a new vintage, complete with a press release party and event. This is essentially the philosophy of the great Château Mouton Rothschild in Bordeaux, who maintains the same label design, but replaces the painting on it each year. In the U.S., Imagery Winery in Sonoma Valley has followed suit.

This is where marketing becomes more of an art, and less of a science. Market research on labels is fascinating stuff, but all too often, the research doesn't lead to easily understood conclusions. If you are looking for one label that will make everyone happy, you are going to be disappointed. However, it is difficult to bring yourself to go to market with a label that you know will drive some customers away. Therefore some wineries hem and haw, fiddle and poke, and drive their designers crazy. In the end, wine packaging still continues to be far too traditional for good marketing implementation.

If you ask your sales team about your label, the answer is always simple. When sales of your wines slow, it is time to change the packaging. Most of them would argue that the time to change is before sales start to slow, as a pre-emptive measure. This is because when sales people often have no news to share with customers about a wine, they look to the label as a way to generate interest in a brand that has nothing else to offer. In this situation, the solution is not to change the label, but to give the sales force the kind of news they need to effectively position and sell your wine.

Figure 6.5: Example of Redesigned Wine Label

Before   *After*

WHAT'S NEXT—WINE IN TETRA-PACKS OR SIX PACKS?

The American market seems to be considerably less eager to try new packaging trends than some other wine-producing countries. Australian wineries have been able to sell top quality wines in bag-in-the-box packaging for a generation now, but many American wine drinkers still resist this idea. The concept is really quite simple: Because the bag contracts as the wine is removed, the remaining wine is not exposed to oxygen. For those who like to drink a glass or two a day, this makes a lot of sense.

Smaller versions of bag-in-the-box mirror the containers used for fruit juices, and are enormously convenient for use by everyone from backpackers and sailors to swimmers and tennis players. These so-called Tetra-Paks are yet another packaging innovation that offers convenience and efficiency, rather than the traditional cork and bottle complications.

However wine in America is less about convenience, more about style. A few producers, such as the Black Box from Napa Valley, have had some moderate success with more expensive wines in bag-in-the-box packages in the US, but they are still a long way from being major players in the market. Much of that has to do with one of the great challenges of wine packaging in America: When a packaging element is adopted by inexpensive wines, it becomes less attractive to more expensive wines.

Figure 6.6: Examples of Non-Traditional Packaging

Of course, the minute that a packaging element is recognized as a "quality cue," every inexpensive wine tries to adopt that packaging as part of their brand. Then once a packaging element has been used extensively by inexpensive wines and brands, it loses all consumer appeal as a quality cue. It becomes, instead, a quality detractor. This cause and effect relationship quickly forces most packaging innovations off the table for higher-quality and higher-priced wines. It has prevented more widespread use of screw caps, bag-in-the-boxes, aluminum cans, or other interesting, approachable, and fun ways to package wine.

For at least a generation, the American wine industry has bemoaned the fact that wine is perceived as a formal and intimidating beverage. Many industry executives have given hours of speeches about the need to make wine more approachable, easier to understand, and easier to use. They have begged for help in demystifying wine, and suggested ways to do it. They plead for affordable, well-made varietal wines in simple, consumer-friendly packaging.

However when the issue is packaging for their own wines, they draw the line. It is all well and good to talk about these issues, but every wine marketer knows that brands are affected by extensions in both directions. An affordable, well-made varietal wine in simple, consumer-friendly packaging is a wonderful idea for consumers, but it will not help establish the prestige and perception of quality for a top-level brand. It may, in fact, drag that prestigious brand down a notch in the eyes of consumers and the trade.

The irony of all of this is that there are already affordable, well-made varietal wines in simple, consumer-friendly packaging. They are in every supermarket, and they sell reasonably well, but they are not elegant or expensive. Those in the wine business often look down on these wines, and very few wine marketers have a strategic plan for moving the customers of those wines into their higher price categories.

There is a delicate balance to the wine industry's marketing efforts. For every attempt to make wine more approachable, more consumer-friendly, there is an almost immediate plan to take those consumers and try to convert them to more complicated and higher priced wines. These more expensive wines usually are much more profitable for the winery, so the desire to move consumers up the price point ladder is understandable. Also, the wine industry, from producers through the distributors and retailers, has consistently sent the message that these inexpensive wines are somehow not only bad, but embarrassing.

Where other industries encourage consumers to learn about their products and explore what they like, the wine industry all too often discourages consumers from the beginning. It tells them that their first choices are wrong, that the wines they like, such as white zinfandel, are bad, and that they really should take the whole thing far more seriously. Given that, it is amazing that the U.S. wine industry continues to grow. It is a testament to the remarkable character of wine itself.

There is significant room for improvement. Wineries looking to distinguish themselves from a vast wall of competitive brands should explore new packaging options, and take the kinds of risks that offer great marketing rewards. New categories remain undiscovered, new consumers await just the right product or campaign, and new marketing approaches will succeed where less innovative ones have failed in the past.

IN SUMMARY

There are no hard and fast rules for label design. Labels must be an expression of the vision of the brand, and that requires two key elements. You must have a clear vision for the brand, one that you can explain, discuss and present to everyone from your sales team to your graphic designer. You also must have at least one individual who can determine which graphic image successfully captures that vision and communicates it to the target markets.

For most small wineries, the idea of creating a massive market research budget to achieve the second goal is beyond their means. They will have to depend on their designer and their marketing team to make that determination. This means they will ultimately invest the future of the brand in those decisions.

If the design is good, and the decision-making is sound, then your packaging will give you a solid advantage over your competitors in the market. If not, then your sales team was right. It is time to re-design the label.

Nothing captures so many of the inherent conflicts in wine marketing better than packaging. The challenge, as always, is to come up with a combination of ingredients in your packaging that defines your position, attracts potential customers, and does not give others a reason to reject your product on face value. It should be unique and different, yet attractive to consumers in a very traditional industry.

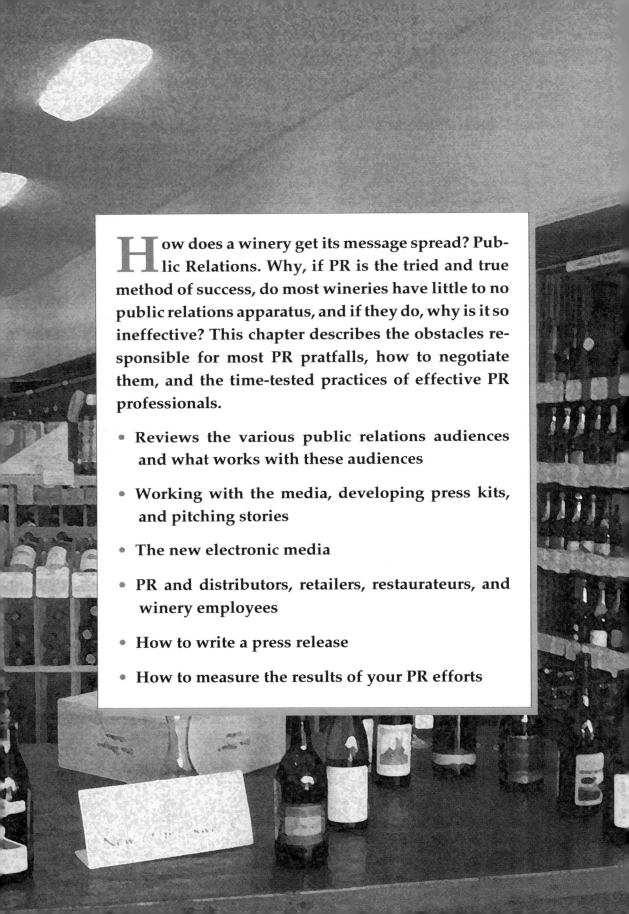

How does a winery get its message spread? Public Relations. Why, if PR is the tried and true method of success, do most wineries have little to no public relations apparatus, and if they do, why is it so ineffective? This chapter describes the obstacles responsible for most PR pratfalls, how to negotiate them, and the time-tested practices of effective PR professionals.

- Reviews the various public relations audiences and what works with these audiences

- Working with the media, developing press kits, and pitching stories

- The new electronic media

- PR and distributors, retailers, restaurateurs, and winery employees

- How to write a press release

- How to measure the results of your PR efforts

C H A P T E R

WINE PUBLIC
RELATIONS

Every winery knows that public relations is a cost-effective way to reach large numbers of people. For many wineries, including some of the most famous in the world, public relations, or PR, is the key to success. However, most wineries do not take full advantage of the opportunities that PR presents. Furthermore, donations, sponsorships, and strategic alliances can eat up huge portions of the budget and of your time without producing any appreciable results.

WINE PUBLIC RELATIONS AUDIENCES

Wine Public Relations is concerned with providing positive news about the winery and its wine brands to the media and other audiences. In the simplest of terms, **public relations** is the art and science of managing your company's relationships with the various "publics" or audiences that are important to your success. This is a very broad definition, but it is a particularly valid one for the wine business. Especially for smaller companies that do not have the budget for advertising or national promotions, public relations is usually the single largest element in marketing efforts.

This definition automatically implies that there are a number of audiences, or publics, that should be addressed. The most obvious of these is **the media**. When most people think of public relations, they think of creating and pitching stories to the key trade and lifestyle media—stories that will put a brand on the map, create demand for the wines, or generate attention for the winery itself. However, there are many other audiences that are important—neglect them at your peril. Some require constant attention, others only an occasional meeting or message, but all have the potential to significantly affect the success of your business.

Table 7.1: The Major Audiences for Winery Public Relations

Key Audiences
The Media
The Distribution Network
Retailers and Restaurateurs
Wine Organizations: professional, educational, appreciation
Winery ownership
Local, regional, and national regulatory agencies
Winery staff
Consumers

The various parts of the **distribution network** are obviously a critical audience, and every successful winery needs a program to reach out to this network and build a closer working relationship with it.

The **retail and restaurant trade** are another obvious public that requires thought and attention from any winery. Each segment of this market has specific requirements and requests from any winery, and a good public relations program will make an effort to address these specific interests.

Wine professional, educational and appreciation organizations serve as gatekeepers to many other audiences, including both consumers and many members of the trade. How a winery uses these organizations to build better relationships throughout the industry will have an impact on the long-term success of the winery and its brands.

For any marketing executive or manager, the **winery ownership** (and shareholders, if it is publicly held) is an audience that cannot be ignored. Often this audience is well understood, but not included in the planning and execution of Public Relations efforts.

Local, regional, and national government and regulatory agencies will certainly have an impact on your business. While these are often addressed through trade organizations and lobbying groups, it is important for individual wineries to know who the key players are, and how to contact them concerning issues of importance.

Perhaps the most frequently overlooked public is that of the **winery staff** itself. All too often, the employees are seen as foot soldiers, to be ordered about on one important mission after another. However, an effective public relations program aimed at motivating and involving the employees more enthusiastically in their jobs will pay dividends many times over.

The remainder of this chapter describes how to deal with each of these respective public "audiences," beginning with the media. In addition specific information on how to write a press release is provided.

THE MEDIA

For the purposes of this book, the media will be broken out into four primary categories: 1) general interest media; 2) wine trade media; 3) electronic media; and 4) the internet. While each of these categories has its own approach to its business, all of the categories will share a general approach based on news and entertainment. The techniques for effectively dealing with all media will be addressed first.

There is no secret to successfully pitching a story to the media. It is a simple matter of understanding exactly what the media want, and then delivering it. The real challenge for most wine companies is that the media is not very interested in wine, and wineries don't have the kinds of stories that end up on the front page of the newspaper. We all know what these stories are. In fact, there is an old saying in the PR business. If you ask people what they want to read about in the news, they always give the same answer: "Sex, Money, and Me."

Sadly, most wineries cannot create stories that capture this kind of sensational news. And if they did, those stories might not reflect well on their brand image. The most challenging element of public relations is exactly this dilemma: How do we balance the need for sensationalism to attract the media with the need to effectively tell the winery's own story in the messaging?

In the end, the media are really best understood as "purchasing agents for their readers." They are looking for the best possible story for their readers, and they want to tell it in the most effective way. Good public relations professionals understand this, and help these writers find the best possible stories. Coincidentally, these stories often involve the PR agency's clients.

The analogy can even be expanded when we discuss the various professional roles in the media. The editor is the most obvious purchasing agent. It is the editor's job to get the best story, make it as effective as possible, and make it fit into the space available. Also editors, not writers, write the headlines we all love to criticize.

Editors are the ones who often have a blank page to fill, and not enough staff to write all the stories they need. A well-constructed story that is not too overtly commercial can often find a home in a newspaper, or even a magazine, given this situation. Many public relations agencies spend a huge amount of time cultivating relationships with these editors so that they can create stories that feature their clients. In that situation, the editor will almost always pick the story that best meets the goals of his or her publication, not the one that best promotes your winery.

Staff writers work for editors, and often receive assignments from their editors. They frequently need help with facts, quotes, images, or simply information on the stories they write. These writers can also help pitch a story. If you get the writer interested in the story, he or she can often convince the editor it is a good idea, and get the assignment. Again, the easiest stories to pitch are the ones that appeal the most to the publication's readership. Don't forget about sex, money, and me.

Freelance writers are the hired guns of the media world. They do not have regular jobs, and as a result, they do not get regular paychecks. When pitching a story to a freelance writer, the first thing to address is where that story might be sold. If the freelancer can't sell the story, then it is unlikely it will ever get written. These writers often have good relationships with editors, and can pave the way for a good story.

Freelancers are also always looking for ways to re-package a story so that they can resell it for additional income. When working with freelancers, it pays to understand how they make their living. Don't expect many freelancers to join you for a weeklong rafting trip with your winery president. Freelance writers only get paid for writing, not traveling, and every day spent on the river is a day that cannot be spent writing a story. Often a freelancer will decline to participate in longer events simply because of this concern. The solution? Offer more than just one story. If the trip can give the writer material for three or four different stories to sell, then it will be a much more efficient use of his or her time.

How is the Wine Media Different?

It is very important to understand that most writers consider themselves to be journalists first, and wine experts second. This is the case even in the area of food and wine journalism. Therefore, wine writers seek the same kinds of stories that the general media wants: trends, new developments, and exciting news. However, wine and food writers also write many stories simply to review the products available in the marketplace. These are not really news stories, and though they often deal with new releases, they are better characterized as buying guides for consumers.

Wine journalists live by the same general rules as the rest of the media. They are looking for good stories. Editors, staff writers, and freelancers all play the same kinds of roles in the wine media as they play in media which focuses on other industries. All too often, those in the wine business overlook this fact, and the results are less than successful.

Wine journalists are likely to have some real expertise in the field, and they are also likely to have good relationships with other producers. Chances are, they have seen many of the standard Public Relations pitches before. Furthermore, they know that their readers are interested in the same kinds of stories that other readers want: sexy packages and producers, expensive wines, and stories about wine consumers just like me.

HOW TO WORK WITH THE MEDIA

The media is a critical audience: a key market for your stories. As with any good marketing campaign, there are several steps you should follow.

Conduct Market Research on the Media

The first step is to do a little market research. If you really want to know what kinds of stories appeal to an editor or writer, all you have to do is read what they have written. This is important, because the single most common complaint by journalists is that they are often pitched stories that have nothing to do with their interests or areas of expertise. As you develop your list of key media, be sure that you compile a selection of stories from each writer, so that you can effectively target your stories to the right people and the right publications.

Develop a Media Kit

A good public relations program should also provide a complete media or press kit to any journalist who is working on a story that could be related to the company. This kit must address two concerns. First, it must define the identity of the company and its services, and secondly, it must supply any press or media with information about the company. It can only accomplish these goals if it is successfully targeted to the audiences we need to attract — top- flight journalists.

The first goal can only be achieved through a series of meetings with the management team. It is crucial that any story told in the press kit be completely consistent and compatible with the marketing goals and strategies developed for the company. The most obvious need here is for educational materials that can be used to provide the media with more "meat" for their stories.

Table 7.2: Press Kit Components

Press Kit Components
Backgrounder
Biographies of key personnel
Wine fact sheets for each wine
History of the winery
Appellation information
Recipes to pair with the wines
Photos to illustrate all of the above
Special interest articles to support the winery positioning

The second goal is in some ways more complex. The press kit must hold a series of background articles that will serve as reference materials to any writer working on a story about the company. As such it should include a history of the company, biographies of key company personnel, a history of the appropriate growing region and the winery's role in the industry. A complete media kit will also include an article on wine and food pairing, the role terroir and appellation play in that philosophy, and other similar background information. Because the media often lacks the time or funding for top quality art and photos, a successful media kit will provide these as well.

Most importantly, the media kit must communicate the vision and dreams of the winery —it must position the winery in terms of its goals and its visions for the future. However, it is critical to note that each representative of the media will be working on an individual story and want specific information. Generalized media kits with lots of inserts, sales and distribution sheets, and information unrelated to the writer's topic, are actually counterproductive.

Finally, the media kit should **never** include articles written about the company by other journalists. This is particularly true of media kits developed to accompany a press release or major news announcement. All information in these kits must be specifically targeted to the story at hand. The inclusion of other materials in such kits simply distracts the media from the importance of the announcement.

Develop Relationships to Target Press Releases

As noted above, food and wine writers consider themselves journalists first; and gastronomic experts second. Because there is little substantial news at most wineries over the course of a year, planning a series of press releases without the correspondingly interesting news is self-defeating, and often send exactly the wrong message to the media. Instead of mass mailings of generically commercial information, most wineries will be more successful developing long-term relationships with various writers and offer them inside looks at the operation on a regular basis. These writers can then be tipped off to major developments and industry trends as they happen.

At the same time, well-written releases that bring real news to the attention of the media, or which put trends and major issues in perspective are always welcome, and will find their way into print. Major business news stories can be distributed to the business news press, but such stories will live or die by the newsworthy nature of the story itself. In the business section of any paper, the story that gets the most ink is usually the one with the most zeroes in the number. Guidelines for writing press releases are provided at the end of this chapter.

Determine the Type of Story You Want to Pitch

What kinds of stories can you pitch to the media? Every winery would like to be the focus of an in-depth feature story—one that baldly declares it the greatest winery in the world. Sadly, that just isn't very likely. Instead, you should look for the classic kinds of stories that journalists write, and find ways to include the winery in such stories. Following is a list of five different types of stories you may want to consider:

1. **The feature story** is an in-depth look at the winery and its products, usually written by a single journalist. These are the Holy Grail for public relations campaigns, and are very hard to achieve. You must have all the elements, from great wines and great reviews to interesting people and great stories, to make these happen on a regular basis.

2. **The round-up story** doesn't focus on a single producer, but instead tries to give readers a good idea of the general category. Such stories might focus on top producers of a single varietal, leading women winemakers, new wineries

making an impact, or an overview of a region or style. While these can generate attention for the winery, that attention will, by definition, be shared among all of the profiled subjects.

3. The **Sidebar** story is named for how it appears in the publication: as a solid bar down the side of a page. Here is where publications often explore an element of the larger story in more detail, or select a single example for more coverage. A larger story on hot new varietals might include a sidebar on a single producer who specializes in these varietals.

4. The **Profile** can range in impact from a smaller sidebar story to a major feature length article. It always focuses on a key individual, and the role that individual plays in the industry. Not surprisingly, these are often written about top executives at major companies, or elected leaders of trade organizations.

5. The **Laundry list** is all too familiar to those of us in the wine industry. This is simply a listing of wines, with reviews, points, or comments in small print alongside. A great score in such an article is always welcome, but most wineries get lost in the middle of the pack. The only thing worse is not being included at all.

Decide Who Should Deliver the Message and Provide Training

In the best of all possible worlds, the owner of your winery should also be the winemaker, and should be as photogenic as Brad Pitt and as cleverly entertaining as Robin Williams. And did we mention the wine knowledge of Hugh Johnson? Luckily, none of your competitor wineries has a spokesperson like that, either!

The first goal of any winery spokesperson must be to establish credibility. While public relations specialists are often very effective communicators they are also viewed with suspicion by many in the media. The media wants to talk to the person who writes the checks or who makes the day-to-day decisions about the winery and its wines. Speaking to the media is a specialized technique. That is why you should always provide media training for all the company spokespeople.

Your company spokespeople should fully understand your company's copy points, and also understand the need to stick to them without variation. A good spokesperson should know how to read the media, and understand what the media hopes to get out of an interview. He or she should be able to give a solid representation of the winery and its vision in both an intimate interview setting and to a large group at a conference or dinner.

Luckily, there is training available for all of these skills. Take advantage of that training, always remembering that your spokesperson must not only be good; he or she must be better than your competitors' spokespeople. That is how you play the game to win.

If you are lucky enough to have a really likable, articulate, and charismatic spokesperson for the winery, the other issue you must face is availability. Time on the road is time away from the winery, and many top winery executives cannot or will not dedicate the time to make such a spokesperson program effective. However, keep in mind that if the spokesperson cannot travel, then you are not playing the game with the same number of cards as some of your competitors.

How important is a good spokesperson? He or she can change not only the future of your winery, but of the wine industry as a whole. Robert Mondavi certainly did that. He is the most famous winemaker in America—and yet he was never a winemaker. His role was that of the visionary and spokesperson for his brand. He left the winemaking to others. Instead he focused on the message, and he did it with enormous success.

ELECTRONIC MEDIA—HOW IS IT DIFFERENT?

To understand the electronic media, you must understand that most electronic media has a far more generalized audience than most print media. Electronic media includes television, radio, and the internet. While there are magazines about wines, even wines from specific regions or particular varietals, most electronic media is directed at the general public. Why is this important? Because most news directors for electronic media will tell you that 35% of all consumers in America never drink wine. That makes it tough to pitch a story, when the news directors know that it won't be of interest to a third of their audience.

Certainly there are ways around this, but they require creativity and often significant funding. Taking wine out of the realm of the wine drinker and into the realm of the general consumer is often done with borrowed interest from celebrities, cultural activities, or special events. As a result, the wines in the limelight will also share the attention with these other elements in the story.

Table 7.3: The Four Types of E-Media

Broadcast Television	Cable Television	Radio	Internet

The **national television media** will always do a story about sparkling wine around the holidays, and will often cover wine as part of their gift suggestions for Valentine's Day. How to become one of the only two or three wineries (out of ten thousand wines on the market) that receive that attention is well beyond the scope of this book. Successful pitches usually involve great spokespeople or celebrities, innovative products or packaging, and excellent press contacts.

More targeted shows on **cable television** deliver a focused audience, but those shows are usually funded by sponsors who benefit from most of the press coverage. In the world of public relations, this is called "Pay to Play." Wineries should not underestimate the funding these kinds of program require. It is substantial. Nor should they overlook the need for an additional budget to promote the show and take advantage of their sponsorship. A good campaign like this will require a huge amount of time and energy, not to mention the product used for tasting and events. In the end, this kind of program must be judged by the same criteria as all marketing communications programs—a careful analysis of the costs must be measured against the specific goals the program is expected to achieve.

On the other hand, there are various **radio shows** on wine and food that are currently broadcasting in markets around the country. These offer an excellent opportunity for coverage when a winemaker is visiting that market. Thanks to modern technology, these shows can also interview guests via telephone. These are a much more likely target for winery public relations programs, but of course cannot deliver the same kind of impact as national television.

Many radio stations or radio shows also place their content on the internet, so that the shows reach far beyond the rather meager local market share that radio can deliver. This is very helpful, because in major markets, it is rare to find a radio station that can deliver ten percent of the market share—due to the large number of competing radio stations in the same market. Therefore, the additional internet element is beneficial.

Insert Table 7.4: Examples of Wine Internet Sites

The Wine Spectator
e-Robert Parker
Wine Lover Discussion Group
Vinocellar
America on-line wine
All-experts.com

The internet can be a very important outlet for public relations stories. It is an extremely active media, and new developments occur weekly. Furthermore, internet stories can have a large impact on television news media. Following are three types of internet sites to consider:

1. **Websites from print and electronic media sources**, which offer additional markets for their information, and also can provide additional information beyond that appearing in the mainstream press.

2. **Specialized wine and food websites** that have built a strong community of readers and users. These are frequently quite influential in some markets or with some consumers and trade. Some of them even attract participation from journalists in the field.

3. **Web logs, or Blogs**, are independent websites produced by individuals who share their interests, experiences, and expertise on the internet. There are now several important ones focusing on wine and wine consumers. Some of these are now achieving the kind of respect and consumer following that traditional media sources enjoy.

Six Tips For Successful Media Relations

In every case, from print to electronic media, your public relations communication should be governed by the same rules. You must be clear in what you say; it must capture what is interesting and newsworthy about your winery; and you must provide reference materials and support for those writing the stories.

Here are six basic rules for working with the media on every level:

1. **Treat them as partners** in the effort to get your story told. They know how to tell a story better than you do. Listen to them.

2. **Don't let them put words into your mouth**. They know how to tell a story better than you do—but the story they want to tell may not be in your best interests. Talk to them, and only tell them what you are comfortable seeing in print. There is no such thing as "off the record."

3. **Understand that stories are almost always written about people**, not things. A new winery, wine, or marketing effort will not be nearly so interesting without the background story of the person who made it happen.

4. **Be cautious with samples**. Journalists get hundreds, even thousands, of free samples. If there is no real reason for them to write about your products, those samples may well be donated to a local charity, or recycled as gifts. Some publications will not allow their staff to accept any free samples of any kind. Plan accordingly.

5. **Share good quality wine**. Wine journalists will not write stories about wineries unless they can taste the wines. If the wines don't taste good, the rest of the story may well be immaterial. Many wine writers and publications taste all wines blind. A good public relations professional can be successful at getting a journalist to taste your wines, but in the end, it is the quality of the wine and your winemaker's expertise that will determine if the journalist likes the wines.

6. **Focus on your unique story**. Journalists only like to visit companies that have great stories. In most cases, a journalist would gladly pass up an elegant four-hour lunch for a one-hour in-depth interview with someone important. While you may believe that your winery is something really spe-

cial, most wine writers have seen hundreds of crush pads, stainless tanks, and barrel rooms. Only show them what makes you different.

BEYOND THE MEDIA: THE CONSUMER AUDIENCE

The end user is always a critical part of any marketing program, and the wine industry is no different. The media is often regarded as the most critical audience by far, and this is accurate. But the importance of the media can be traced to the specific fact that the media influences both consumers and the trade. There are wineries that avoid dealing with the media, and work directly with consumers, but these wineries generally have small budgets, small goals, and no real brand presence.

With this in mind, the single most cost-effective way to communicate your message to large groups of consumers is via the media. A single story in a major newspaper or magazine will not only sell a lot of wine, it can establish the reputation of a brand in a very positive way.

On the other hand, the media is only one way to communicate with consumers. Particularly in this era of changing regulations, no winery can afford to ignore the need to talk directly to its consumers in a number of ways. While many of these topics are addressed as separate topics in other chapters of this book, it is important to summarize them briefly from a public relations context.

Consumers will learn about your winery from one of three possible sources: the media, the distribution and sales network, or a special event of some kind. In every case, the most tangible evidence of your winery is the wine bottle itself. If you are truly interested in developing relationships with your customers, then the bottle must provide the contact information they need to reach you. A toll-free phone number and website address should be on every bottle. Thus every bottle becomes an invitation for the consumer to contact the winery and become part of your marketing communications family.

How you respond to these consumers is just as important as attracting them. You will need to create a team to manage customer interaction, one that is trained, competent, and has goals and objectives for their work. While you may look at these interactions with consumers as time-consuming chores, please remember that your competitors are using these same interactions to sell wines and build brand loyalty. Your ability to take advantage of these consumer contacts will have an impact on your ability to survive and excel in a competitive and saturated marketplace.

Outside of the tasting room itself, the most likely venue for wineries and consumers to meet is at an event of some kind, from expensive wine weekends to small events at local charities or restaurants. Each of these events is an opportunity to do more than just pour your wine and meet consumers. It is a chance to build relationships with new consumers, and to enhance the relationships you have with existing customers. It may seem obvious that you should provide them with information about your wines and winery, but many producers do not. Providing information must be considered the bare minimum activity for a wine event, and will often leave your company far behind others who are more effective at maximizing the potential of the event.

Every event should be seen as an opportunity to effectively position your winery in relationship to the competition. How will consumers be drawn to your table or booth? How will they remember you out of the many other wineries that are in attendance? What will they remember about you and your wines? Each event should be the focus of a strategic discussion, including costs, goals, and measurable objectives. Not only will this make your events more rewarding, but it will also help you determine which events are most cost-effective, and which should be eliminated from the budget.

The most successful wineries market their participation in events to their extensive consumer mailing lists. A winemaker dinner in Toledo or a charity wine tasting in Alabama will generate a series of emails to consumers in that area, inviting them to the event and encouraging them to say hello. Donations to wine auctions will be promoted to this key audience in the hopes that they will be motivated to bid on the items in question. All of these tactics encourage consumers to become more closely affiliated with the winery, to become a closer part of the winery family. In every case, you should give these customers a reason to follow up, a reason to contact the winery again, and become more involved in the wines and activities of your company.

THE DISTRIBUTION NETWORK

If public relations is the science of how to keep people happy, then this potential audience is an easy one to understand. They want help selling your wine. They want to see great reviews from top publications, and they want to have access to all the sales support information as conveniently as possible. In that sense, the campaigns you organize for the media and the information you provide to consumers should be enough to keep this audience satisfied.

The first element to this effort should be an easily accessible website that offers all of the background information your distributor network could ever want about your winery and its wines. History, key people, wine styles, wine fact sheets, wine and food pairings, and all of the articles that you would normally create for a press kit should be included in the website. Some wineries even create a special part of their website for this purpose, which provides up-to-date information just for their distributors.

You should consider the distribution network as part of your team, and provide it with all the information you can. Not every salesperson will want this information, but when they are challenged by an account to provide it, your work here will create its own rewards.

Every winery should have a very active program to achieve great press—but it should also have an equally efficient program to collect the positive press it garners and distribute it out to the national sales network as quickly as possible. A great review from a major journalist is a real coup for the PR department of any winery, but that is only half the job. The other half of the job is getting that review into the hands of the distributors, salespeople, retailers and restaurateurs who buy and sell your wines.

The old-school method was to copy these reviews into an attractive format, reprint them, and send them out on a weekly, monthly or as-needed basis. It was slow and ineffective. Today these top reviews need to be formatted and placed on an accessible website within 24 hours of publication. They should be emailed to your sales force as well as those in the distribution network who are interested in selling your wines. Finally, they should be catalogued on a website so that any salesperson can access both current reviews and older vintages whenever needed.

In the best of all possible systems, your salesperson should be able to hear about a hot new review via cell-phone on the way to a sales call, and use a local internet access point to print out the review in time for his or her presentation. Ideally, the printed version should include both a full-page layout and a small layout suitable for use as a shelf-talker or restaurant table tent.

There is one area in which the distribution network deserves special attention. Many wine companies send out press releases to the media, but never send copies to their distributor network. This is a mistake. Your distributors are part of your team, and they should be notified every time you send something out. They will not read it, as a rule. However, if it appears in print in their local paper, they will absolutely call you and ask you why you didn't tell them first. Will you have a good answer for that question?

In the end, your communications program to the distributor network needs to accomplish three goals. It must give the distributors all the background information they need to effectively represent your wines. It must provide this information in a timely manner, and in a format that is easy to understand and easy to use. Finally, it should include a means for you to make sure your distributors know about this information, and how best to access it. A regular part of your presentations should always include a quick primer on how to access your winery's information.

RETAILERS AND RESTAURATEURS

Your customers have much in common with the distribution network, and should be treated with the same basic philosophy: they want sales support, and you should give it to them. Your retailers and restaurateurs also want your support with sales, but in a slightly different manner.

The main method to support your retailers from a public relations standpoint is to involve your other PR audiences. For example, when you arrange to undertake a promotional event at any retailer or restaurant, it is strongly recommended that you reach out to your consumer base in that market and give them the information they need to attend the event. This not only supports your sales goals for the area, but also shows the retailer or restaurateur that you have an active fan base, and one that can respond to the offers these partners have made. It is a classic case of using all of the information at your command to bring your consumers and distribution network together in a way that makes sense, and profits, for everyone.

WINE ORGANIZATIONS

Wine professional, educational, and appreciation organizations play a key role in the wine industry by reaching out to consumers in a way that wineries cannot, and serving as gate-keepers for large groups of the wine drinking public. With this in mind, your company should have an active program to reach out to these organizations and develop programs that not only support the members, but also provide the members with the information and positioning to effectively represent your wines and winery to their audiences as well.

In developing the positioning for your winery, you should develop a few key messages that stress a particular focus of your winery: a region, grape varietal, winemaking style, or other topic. These topics should form the basis of your interaction with these professional wine organizations. You should become the primary source of information and training about the topic, as a way of claiming your preeminent leadership in the category. Once again, your success in this endeavor is a good way to judge your ability to take that leadership role.

In addition, it is recommended that you take an active role in soliciting opportunities to make presentations at national conventions and conferences. Furthermore, you should consider working with one or two of these organizations to fund or develop training materials on your area of focus. These efforts will not usually generate immediate results (although such presentations can result in media attention rather quickly), but the long-term commitment to this work will absolutely position your winery and wines in the market.

COMPANY OWNERSHIP AND/OR SHAREHOLDERS

It is a rare employee who can forget the critical audience of your company: owners and shareholders. But sometimes, in the heat of battle, they get overlooked. Never forget that every program, every campaign, and every element of marketing communications will be reviewed by this audience, either before or after it appears in public!

It is our recommendation that every element of any program be presented to this audience with a complete explanation of strategy, goals, and expected (and measurable) results. Involving the top levels of the company in this way should pave the way for your efforts, and gain their trust over time. Most importantly, by making these individuals aware of your plans and strategies, you can then expect them to adopt both the language and the philosophy behind these programs, giving them added support and credibility.

WINERY EMPLOYEES

Unfortunately, winery employees are the major public relations audience that is most often forgotten. Yet every communications program depends on these individuals to make it true. Therefore, it is strongly recommended that you provide regular briefings with all winery employees on the key communications initiatives for the next sales season. These briefings should include a question and answer period to discuss the various ways the employees can help make these programs a success.

Some of the implications of this are obvious. A tasting room employee should know about advertising or sales promotions in the local market because questions about those programs are certain to come up. Consumers who read a press release about the winery would expect that the tasting room staff also know about the subject, and be able to shed more light on it. But it is just as important that a cellar worker understand the commitment to a particular technique or philosophy. When these workers have a chance to meet the public, the media, or other winery employees in a social situation, their understanding and support of your programs will go a long way towards making them and you more credible. Sadly, very few wineries follow this approach.

HOW TO MEASURE YOUR PR RESULTS

There are many different tracking systems to measure the effectiveness of a public relations campaign. Some wineries opt for a basic clipping service and an analysis of total impressions by program and brand on a quarterly and yearly basis. The clips arrive by mail and are photocopied, logged and analyzed. The results can be compared to previous periods or even against competitors' success in this area to establish some realistic goals and objectives for your programs.

More sophisticated wineries will add additional value to the media clipping service by creating a value-based criteria that rewards placements in key markets, with key messages, or in key publications. The criteria may include circulation, target market, publication, content, focus brands, etc. Some clipping services now offer an electronic delivery clipping option, which allows you to view coverage instantly, manage articles using online search, sort and select, save and store clips by brand, subject, date and most important create a system to tag, assign tonality and favorability to each article for qualitative purposes.

Media coverage is relatively easy to track with the system above, but the costs of doing true consumer market research based on public relations efforts are quite expensive. Various market research firms can produce questionnaires to track such information at events, as well as inexpensive internet research and tracking programs, but sometimes such data is inaccurate. There is no such thing as good, cheap, accurate research.

In the final analysis, the single best way to evaluate any public relations or marketing communications program is to track the regional spikes in sales after a consumer-related program. This method, while grossly simplistic, does include all audiences, from media through the distribution network to the consumer, in its analysis! In judging the results, you should always be guided by the simplest of philosophies: Your programs, both in concept and execution, must be better than your competition.

HOW TO WRITE A PRESS RELEASE
It may seem obvious, but start with the news. If you do not have news, do not send out a press release—it will only convince the media that

you really don't value their time, and really don't understand their business. To make sure, ask yourself if the story could wait another week, or if it really should be printed today? If it can wait, it isn't news.

Every press release should have a contact name, phone number, and email address right at the top. This makes it easy for the media to find out more. Please make sure that the contact listed is someone who will be available once the story goes out, for obvious reasons.

It is generally recommended that the top line on any press release read: **For Immediate Release.** If you would like to try to manage the media's timing, you can try to send a release that says, "Hold Until 6 a.m. on May 17," and hope that they will wait. Good luck!

The headline should come immediately after the contact information. This is your chance to summarize the story and capture the interest of the media. Do not expect to see the headline in print, because the publication's editors will insist on their own headline. Next, start the first line with a dateline, including the place of the release. This information will appear on the story as it is printed.

The first paragraph is really the only one that matters. Never forget the advice of Rudyard Kipling (1902), who wrote the motto of all journalists: "I keep six honest serving-men, (They taught me all I knew); Their names are What and Why and When, And How and Where and Who." You will need to answer all six questions in the first paragraph, and you will need to do that in two or three sentences. Keep re-writing it until you have succeeded.

The rest of the first page should include as much detail as is appropriate. It is preferable to provide at least two quotes from a key figure in the story, as well as some information to put the story into context. Good reporters will know a good story when they see one, and follow up for more information. Please have that information prepared in advance.

Figure 7.1: Sample Press Release, Page 1

CONTACT
Mary Ann Vangrin, Balzac Communications
800.709.7667; mvangrin@balzac.com

For Release 6:15 p.m. P.D.T.: August 13, 1996

**Napa Valley Wineries Participate with Microsoft in the
Global Launch of Internet Explorer 3.0**

Sterling Vineyards and Mumm Cuvée Napa offer a sneak preview of www.aboutwines.com.

San Francisco, California--Sterling Vineyards and Mumm Cuvée Napa announced a strategic working relationship with Microsoft Corporation yesterday in San Francisco at the launch event for the Microsoft® Internet Explorer 3.0 Web Browser. The companies have been working together over the past months on a dramatic redesign of the winery website using Internet Explorer 3.0 technology.

"Internet Explorer 3.0 and ActiveX™ enable a huge leap forward in terms of sensory quality, interactivity and just plain fun on the Internet," said Brad Chase, vice president in the Internet platform and tools division. "A toast to Sterling Vineyards and Mumm Cuvée Napa for their choice of Internet 3.0 as the foundation for their new web site."

Although these wineries were among the first on the Web, this site has a completely new look created by Grey Direct e.marketing, New York, one of the country's premier Interactive agencies. The team, headed by Grey Direct e.marketing President Steve Carbone, took full advantage of the latest Microsoft Internet Explorer 3.0 technology to fashion a sophisticated, dynamic insider's look at the world of wine. Packed with information and fun to read, the site will appeal to everyone from the seasoned wine expert to someone who isn't sure what wine to serve with dinner. On the menu are virtual tours, tasting notes, and news about Sterling Vineyards and Mumm Cuvée Napa, two top Napa Valley wineries. But there's also general information on wine culture, including cellar management, q & a's, virtual wine tastings, interviews with celebrities in the world of food and wine, live on-line events and more.

A special feature of interest to those in the media is the Press Box. This revolutionary digital image server allows access to digital photos of the wineries, winemakers and product images on request.

-more-

Figure 7.1: Sample Press Release, Page 2

Sterling Vineyards/Mumm Cuvée Napa on Internet Explorer page 2

What makes this site come alive? Microsoft Internet Explorer 3.0 features ActiveX technology, a Microsoft delivery system that has allowed Sterling Vineyards and Mumm Cuvée Napa to incorporate these design innovations into their site:

"Floating" frames: frames that appear on the web page without gray borders, cleaning up the appearance of the design.
No-tiled backgrounds: background images that are used instead of the usual repeating tiles used in most sites.
Real Audio: With the RealAudio player, all you have to do is click on a RealAudio link from your Web browser and audio begins playing instantly, without download delays. It's like a CD player—you can pause, rewind, fast forward, stop and start
"Rollovers": buttons and similar page elements now animate the position when you position the mouse over them.
HTML Layout Control: The position of the page elements can now be described based on the exact position on the page, allowing image overlaps and tighter control over page design.

"We wanted to create a site that provided high-quality content and real value to the consumer interested in learning about and buying wine," says Gary Glass, Group Product Director for the Sterling Vineyards. "The beauty of the new Internet Explorer 3.0 technology is that it allows for creative design that is still compatible with the delivery systems most people use." Access to the site will be quick and easy, without the long wait to download images that can be an issue for some users.

Those interested in the new website are invited to take a sneak preview starting August 12, 1996 at 6:00 p.m. P.D.T. As the site comes up, you will be able to scan several new pages, and are encouraged to leave an E-Mail address in the Guest Book for notification when the site is fully operational, sometime in September of 1996.

The Seagram Classics Wine Company, a division of Joseph E. Seagram and Sons, Inc., is headquartered in San Mateo, California. The company produces, markets and exports the wines of Sterling Vineyards, Mumm Cuvée Napa and the Monterey Vineyard. Seagram Classics is also the exclusive importer of Champagne Mumm, and Barton & Guestier wines. Microsoft and ActiveX are either registered trademarks or trademarks of Microsoft Corporation in the United States and/or other countries.

#

Press releases should usually fit on one page, and be double-spaced. These are guidelines that were developed a long time ago, when press releases went out on real paper. This format allowed editors and writers to hand-write notes on the release. The format is still observed, even though most releases today go out via an electronic format.

Finally, end the release with a simple ###, centered at the bottom of the page. This tells the media that the story is over, and they don't have to look for further pages or attachments.

Once the press release is written and has been approved by your owners and/or shareholders, you can either fax or email it to the appropriate audiences. Ideally, you will already have a list with contact information of your key media contacts, as well as your distributors, consumers, retailers, and other target organizations. Another option is to use the professional wire services of companies such as Business Wire and PR Newswire. For a fee, they will email the release directly into the newsrooms of up to 1,500 publications. Also don't forget to share the press release with your employees by either posting it, sharing the information in a meeting, or emailing it to them.

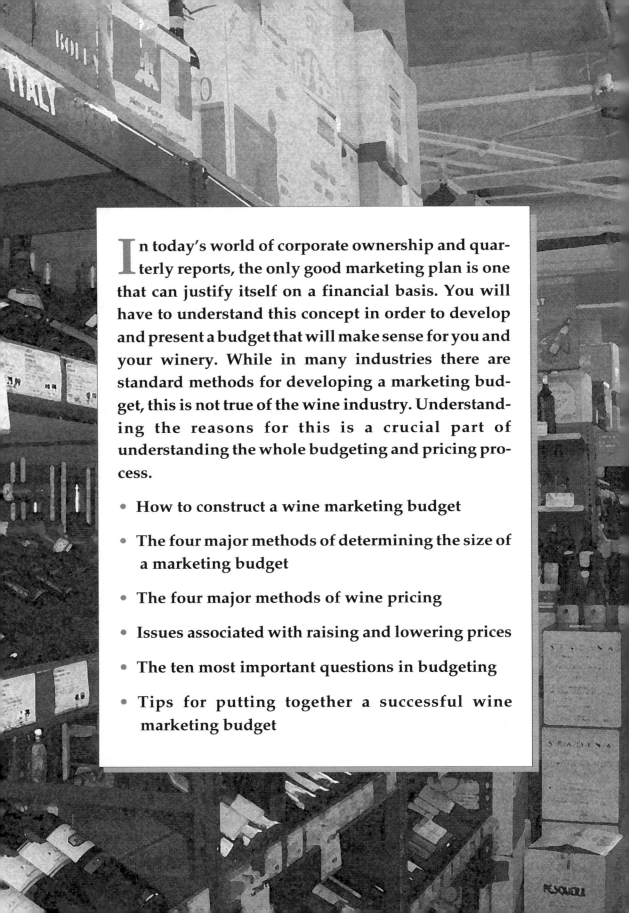

In today's world of corporate ownership and quarterly reports, the only good marketing plan is one that can justify itself on a financial basis. You will have to understand this concept in order to develop and present a budget that will make sense for you and your winery. While in many industries there are standard methods for developing a marketing budget, this is not true of the wine industry. Understanding the reasons for this is a crucial part of understanding the whole budgeting and pricing process.

- How to construct a wine marketing budget

- The four major methods of determining the size of a marketing budget

- The four major methods of wine pricing

- Issues associated with raising and lowering prices

- The ten most important questions in budgeting

- Tips for putting together a successful wine marketing budget

C H A P T E R

8

WINE BUDGETS AND PRICING

I t would seem that budgeting, like accounting, is a very nuts-and-bolts kind of science, where every column adds up correctly, and the answer is in black and white for all to see. Unfortunately this is not so, because developing a marketing and sales budget is an art form, requiring not only a firm grasp of the technicalities, but also the vision to take those numbers and create something that will convey real meaning.

The enormous range of winery size in our business makes standardization very difficult. There is simply no way to compare the methods a small producer making 2,500 cases uses to develop a marketing and sales budget to the way that budget is developed for a one million case brand. At the larger end of the spectrum there is some agreement on a rough estimate for marketing dollars. With smaller wineries, the issue is so complicated and tied to so many variables, that it is very difficult to reach any conclusions.

CHALLENGES OF WINE MARKETING BUDGETS AND PRICING

For a marketing and sales budget to be effective, it must justify the costs of the programs with corresponding increases in sales or image enhancement. That much should seem obvious. The difficulty, as always, comes when we examine the fine print. If you spend part of your budget to increase sales, then you should be able to see an appropriate increase in sales as a response. If the revenue (or even better, the profit!) from that increase exceeds the budget for the program, you can congratulate yourself on a successful product.

In the wine business, such conclusions are hard to find. This is due to the time lag in the pipeline, where it is often found that sales increases are hard to tie directly to sales and marketing programs. A marketing program that convinces distributors may show up as increases in your depletions. However, unless those depletions work their way through the distribution channels, which includes selling inventory out of the retailers and into the hands of consumers, you won't really see a long term gain.

Many winery incentive programs overlook this simple problem. They reward the distributor sales force for filling up the pipeline, but don't move the product through the retailer. An initial and exciting jump in depletions slowly evolves into a year-long problem, as the retailers slowly sell through their overstocked inventory, and resist ordering anything new until they need more product.

On the other hand, a program that is aimed primarily at retailers or restaurateurs may sell much wine, but that doesn't always translate into new orders from the distributor. Your supermarket data shows that your sales are up, but your depletions are still stagnant.

It is also possible to develop a program that lowers the retail price and increases sales volume over a specific time period. Such programs are easy to justify in terms of inventory movement and depletions, but they often have a very negative effect on the image of the brand. Buying market share may increase volume, but over the long run it can also damage the prestige of the brand, and reduce profits significantly.

Finally, many marketing programs can increase or enhance brand image, and such programs often are attractive to winery owners because of the prestige they deliver. However, unless that prestige can ultimately be translated into higher sales volumes or high prices, the results are largely illusory. Illusory results are a good way to end up looking for a new marketing job.

DETERMINING HOW MUCH SHOULD BE BUDGETED ON MARKETING AND SALES

There are four standard measurements in the wine industry to determine how much money should be spent on marketing and sales, as illustrated in Table 8.1. The actual amounts are completely open to debate, but the measurement systems themselves are quite simple. The selection of the best measurement system for your winery depends on the size of your production and the philosophy of the owners and management team. There are advantages and disadvantages to all four measurement systems.

Table 8.1: Measurement Systems for Marketing Budget

Budget as Percentage of Revenue
Budget as Percentage of Profit
Budget as A Dollars Per Case Ratio
Budget Based on Marketing Program Goals

Measurement 1: Budget as Percentage of Revenue

As in other industries, many wineries calculate their marketing budgets in terms of a percentage of their revenue. This has the advantage of being adjustable over the course of the year. If your sales volume is exceeding your projections, then you can revise your marketing budgets upwards for the second half of the year. Conversely, you can scale down your efforts if sales are falling short of your plan.

The irony of this latter strategy is obvious. When sales begin to lag behind projections, it is all too common for companies to reduce their marketing and sales budgets. A better philosophy would be to increase those budgets to attempt to solve the problem. Spending less money isn't a solution, it's a reaction. Spending more money, more effectively, certainly is a solution.

There is also the question of what percentage of revenues you should use. Sadly, there is no single answer to the question. In a recent research project which attempted to establish some kind of industry average for marketing and sales budgets, the winery response varied so wildly in both amounts and accounting systems that the results led to more questions than answers. The charts at the end of this chapter show some of the results of this project, and illustrate percentages that range from 6% to 55%. It must be noted that for the higher percentages, these wineries were small, developing brands, and were not only building sales, but establishing image in the marketplace.

One disadvantage of the percentage of revenue system is that it does not do a very good job of accounting for price reductions, discounts, or distributor incentives. All of those activities may increase sales and generate higher sales revenues, but they won't generate higher profits. Spending money to increase sales without increasing profits can lead to the disastrous situation of Milo Minderbinder in Joseph Heller's *Catch-22*, who was losing a dollar on every sale, but making it up in volume!

Measurement 2: Budget as Percentage of Profit

A more effective way of monitoring marketing and sales budgets against profits is to calculate those budgets as percentage of profit. As a sales management tool, this is perhaps the best system, because it takes into account all of the costs of doing business, and then provides a marketing budget that will stay within the parameters of profit. This system results in a more consistent range of figures, with many wineries investing between 15 and 35% of the before-tax profits in marketing budgets.

The challenge with this measurement system has to do with brand introductions and product launches. These kinds of activities almost always require an investment beyond that which can be justified by a percentage of the profits. Without that investment, the brand or product launch will almost certainly fail to take off. In these types of cases, a smaller budget is virtually wasted, where a larger budget might well be successful.

On the other hand, a small and newer winery might choose to invest all of its profits, and more, into building the brand image. In the end, the return on the investment would be realized when the winery is sold, and the appreciation in value recoups the dollars invested in the brand. This is obviously long-term thinking, and requires a stable market. Any winery sold under economic duress will not come close to achieving this goal.

Measurement 3: Budget as A Dollars Per Case Ratio

For smaller wineries, in particular, the marketing budget is often calculated on a simple dollars per case ratio. The beauty of this system is its simplicity. The marketing costs can be easily calculated in advance, and can fit into the budget almost as if they are a production cost, to provide a baseline above which everything is profit.

The drawbacks to this system become apparent when you start applying it to very small production lots. A ten dollars per case budget might work out well for a winery producing 5,000 cases of wine, but once you get below 500 cases, this all can become a bit silly. It is also more difficult if the winery produces a number of different wines with wildly varying price points. A reserve Cabernet that sells for $65 a bottle may well support a nice marketing budget. A Grenache rosé selling for $6.99 a bottle will have a hard time generating any marketing budget to support it.

Measurement 4: Budget Based on Marketing Program Goals

All of the above methods are designed to provide a "top down" budget number from which to work. However, the fourth measurement system is based on marketing program goals. If you have developed a carefully conceived marketing plan, you should know exactly what your goals are. You should know exactly what you need to achieve, and with a little hard work and a bit of luck, you will have determined how you are going to measure the success of your efforts. Your marketing budget process then becomes a very different exercise altogether.

You will begin with a chart of your goals and objectives, each carefully defined, and each quantified in a meaningful way. It is then your job to develop a marketing plan that addresses each goal and objective. You will have to design the strategy and tactics for each program, and demonstrate how it will achieve the goals and objectives. Each element of the marketing plan will have costs associated with its execution, and it will be a relatively simple process to compare those costs with your goals.

Those elements of your marketing campaign that achieve your goals in a cost-effective manner will be approved. Those that fall short of the goal will need to be re-worked, or they will be rejected. During the course of the year, each program will be evaluated against the measurable goals and objectives, and revised or eliminated based on the results. Those that are really working can be given additional funding, or additional attention.

Much like farming a vineyard, those programs that do well are expanded, and those that do not are removed, to be replaced with newer ideas and better executions. The first year, you can expect a number of failures, and some frustration. However, after five years or more developing your marketing campaigns and budgets this way, you should have a very solid group of programs that can be justified both financially and through the objectives they are achieving.

The Issue of Winery Size

One aspect of budgeting that makes industry standards difficult to cite is the variety of ways that wineries of different sizes account for their staff and management time. Smaller wineries often combine budget items, roles and salaries. This makes a strict accounting quite difficult.

If the winery is small enough that the owners also manage the business, do most of the traveling, and condense most of the marketing activities into their travel schedule, it is almost impossible to develop sound comparative budget analyses. There may be tax advantages to writing off a trip to visit a city where you can sell wine and also see your daughter, but that kind of accounting plays havoc with the budget comparisons to other wineries.

Medium-sized wineries face a very different dilemma. While smaller wineries must accept the fact that they cannot justify a national or even regional sales force, medium-sized wineries must consider this more seriously. The expense of having a full-time employee working a specific market certainly takes money away from the bottom line. However, unless the winery has the star power to demand attention from the distributor, the alternative is almost certainly going to result in far lower sales figures. As the winery grows, it will not be able to endure these lower sales figures.

Larger wineries and brands have the benefit of much larger sales volumes, and correspondingly larger marketing budgets. While smaller wineries may expect to hand sell much of their product, the challenge for larger brands is that they have to live on the crowded shelves of supermarkets and discount stores, where hand selling is non-existent and every brand is playing hardball for shelf space. These larger brands must learn to leverage their size and power to get attention from distributors, retailers, and restaurateurs.

The tables at the end of this chapter illustrate the marketing and sales budgets for eleven small to medium-sized wineries. The case production of these wineries ranges from 1,000 cases to 400,000 cases. In a review of the figures, it is obvious that a variety of different measurement systems are being employed.

WINE PRICING

No discussion of budgets would be complete without touching upon that most complicated of all wine marketing issues: wine pricing. Whatever other elements impact the perceptions and profits of a brand, pricing is of paramount importance. In fact, when blind tastings are conducted, consumers usually assume that a more expensive wine will be of better quality. Even when the prices are falsely ascribed, the tasters rate the wines with the highest apparent price as better. "You get what you pay for" is more than just a saying in the wine business—it is a firmly held belief by almost all consumers. How you price your wine will immediately tell consumers how good you think the wine is.

Wine marketing research has identified a common thread regarding wine price points and consumer perception. That is the perception that consumers believe—regardless of whether they are buying wines for $3 a bottle or $35 a bottle—the wine they are buying is of better quality than anything less expensive. In fact, they are usually quite convinced that less expensive wines are easily rejected on taste alone. At the same time, those very same consumers, at every price point, take the position that wines above their usual price point are a poor value and/or a waste of money. In focus group language, consumers are saying: "I can tell the difference between what I drink and that cheap stuff. But anyone who spends more than I do on a bottle of wine is wasting money."

At face value this makes a great deal of sense. The consumer is willing to pay for quality, but will not overpay for suspect glamour. However, the irony of the situation is lost on most consumers because there is little consensus among consumers about price and quality. Each holds true their own personal beliefs about wine value and quality—regardless of the price point they purchase. They can't all be correct, can they?

Among the five "P"s of marketing (described in Chapter 1), price holds pride of place in the minds of wine consumers. Given that most consumers buy wine based on specific price points, pricing is the very first consideration when defining the category of a brand or wine.

So how do wineries determine the pricing for their products? There are four common methods in use today (see Table 8.2), but each method has its advantages and disadvantages. Each of these are described below, beginning with the oldest and simplest method, and ending with the most sophisticated method.

Table 8.2: Four Methods of Wine Pricing

Production-Cost Pricing Method
Wine Expert Pricing Method
Strategy and Consumer-Driven Pricing Method
Combination of Methods

Production-Cost Pricing Method

The oldest method taught in viticulture and enology programs is to base the bottle price on the price per ton you pay for the grapes. In many ways, this makes good sense as the more expensive the grapes, the more expensive the bottle of wine. The standard rule of thumb is to divide the tonnage price by $100. Therefore, if the grapes were $2000 per ton, then the wine should be priced around $20 per bottle. Likewise, if the grapes were only $700 per ton, the bottle cost would be closer to $7.

The obvious advantage of this pricing method is its simplicity. However, that is also its downfall, as there are so many other variables that must be considered in pricing wine. Therefore, though this method is still discussed today, it is generally considered outdated by most, and some of the more sophisticated pricing methods described below are used in its place.

Wine Expert Pricing Method

The second method is to identify a set of wine experts to taste and compare a series of blind tastings against a competitive set of wines. The traditional competitive set tasting at a winery places a group of eight to twelve wines, all from the same basic price and varietal category, in front of a group of tasters that is normally composed of winemakers, marketers, and an occasional retailer or distributor account. The total number of tasters usually ranges from four to eight. These tasters are then asked to rate the wines, and a summary of the scores is produced, and the results analyzed.

If the winery's wine finishes in the top third of this grouping, the winery is pleased, and the pricing is considered to be effectively competitive. If the wine finishes in the middle of the group, the pricing is competitive, but the winery may not be so pleased. If the wine finishes lower in the pack, then some kind of mitigation is in order regarding the wine's price.

The advantage of this method is that many consumers regard the opinion of wine experts to be fair and valid. Indeed, many wine consumers seek out wine expert ratings and feel comfortable paying the suggested retail price based on the ratings. After all, what could be fairer than a blind tasting of competitive wines? Another advantage of this method is that it is relatively quick to implement and is not that costly to set up.

Unfortunately, this method has more disadvantages than advantages, however. To begin, in many cases, the judges are almost always affiliated with the winery. They not only know the house style, they presumably like it. They have heard their winemaker or owner describe repeatedly the kind of wine they are trying to make, and why it is preferable. So the judges in this scenario are usually not impartial. A second problem with this system also lies in the selection of the judges. While wine consumers don't know as much about wine as winemakers do, they know a lot more about wine consumers. Your winemaker isn't going to buy a lot of your wine, so his or her opinion is in some ways irrelevant. Consumers may not know about malolactic fermentation or anthocyanins, but they know what tastes good to them. If you want to know what consumers think of your wine, you should put consumers on the panel, not winemakers or marketing managers.

Additionally, any statistician will tell you that the results from a panel of four to six judges tasting ten wines will usually produce very little statistically significant data. Decisions on pricing should not be made based on this kind of poor statistical analysis. If you really want to see how weak the conclusions from such panels are, delete the scores from one of the judges selected at random, and observe how this changes the final result. If one judge's scores can make that much difference, your results are statistically flawed. In general, unless there is a massive difference between the scores in such a tasting, there is no statistically significant difference between the wines.

The competitive set policy is also a false premise. If you really want to know how your wine compares in a blind tasting to the rest of the market, include wines from much lower or higher price points as well. Just as your wine might well finish in the middle of the pack of a group of wines from their projected price point, it might also finish in very much the same position when tasted against wines that are much less expensive. This is particularly true when the tasting panel is composed of true wine consumers, not winemakers. Why don't wineries do this? Because they don't want to know the answer.

For all of the above reasons, the methodology of these tastings is fatally flawed. But methodology is not the only problem with this system. There is another, even more obvious problem with this procedure for determining wine pricing: consumers in a retail store almost never engage in a blind tasting of competitive wines before making their buying decisions. While wine quality is certainly a factor in any purchase, consumers' perceptions of quality are tied to many factors that have nothing to do with the taste of the wine.

The most expensive wines in the world usually have long and elegant heritages. They have earned their pricing with generations of high quality wine and marketing to match. To throw your new brand into that mix and somehow claim that a "middle of the pack" finish justifies a pricing policy on a par with the First Growths of Bordeaux shows a complete lack of understanding of the market.

Consumers make their purchasing decisions based on a wide range of quality clues, most having to do with the packaging and merchandising of the wine. Only when they get the wine home and open it does wine quality affect their perceptions. At that point it will only affect future buying decisions. Since brand loyalty is almost non-existent in the wine industry, this is of little help to wine companies. The fact that consumers liked your wine means that they will not eliminate it from future purchase considerations. It doesn't mean that they will buy it to the exclusion of other wines or brands.

Strategy and Consumer-Driven Pricing Method

The third pricing method, then, is one that is obviously consumer-driven. This begins, however, with your wine business strategy, because your strategy describes your target consumer segment. There-fore, if your wine strategy is to focus on the high-end luxury niche of Napa Cabernet Sauvignons and Merlots, then you need to find con-sumers who match this segment. On the other hand, if you are pursuing a low-cost niche strategy that focuses on sweet whites and rosés, then you need to consult consumers who match that market segmentation.

The next step is to assemble a group of wine consumers from your price category, and ask them to comment on the wines as they appear on the retail shelf next to competitor wines. It is generally best to identify a market research firm to set up and implement an objective focus group or panel. Once the consumers are convened, the market research firm will ask them a series of questions regarding what they find attractive about the wines—what looks cheap, what reassures them, and other relevant issues. Consumers may then be asked to taste the wine and comment how much they would be willing to pay for each of the wines.

If you don't have the budget to hire a professional market research firm to assist you in pricing your wine competitively, you can also use informal methods. An ideal format is the wine cocktail party. Convene a group of consumers, and present them with a table full of competitive wines. Watch to see which ones they open first—those are the ones that have done successful work in packaging and positioning. That's good marketing. Then count up the empty bottles at the end of the day. The winery with the most empty bottles did the best job on wine quality. Their wines appealed to the palate of the consumer. Then, if those wines are competitively priced, they are the ones who will win the battle.

Once you've gathered data from your consumers, you can then compare how your wine did with the competitive set. From here you have information on how to set your pricing. If your wine performed better that the rest, then you are justified at setting your pricing a bit higher. However, if you were rated in the middle of the pack or lower, this informs you of where your pricing should be. If you are not pleased with the results, you can take actions to improve the quality perceptions of your wine.

A good marketing research firm should be able to assist you in making modifications to your packaging and perceived quality so you can achieve the competitive price point you are targeting. In most cases they will also identify other data regarding your pricing competitiveness, including Nielsen scan data, distribution depletion reports, and other retailer sales data to see how well your particular price segment is doing against other segments, as well as specific sales data on your wine brands versus your competitive set.

The advantage of using the consumer-driven method is that you are gathering feedback from the real marketplace. The feedback is not being diluted by distributor and retailer channels. You also receive a good amount of data on potential improvements you can make. The downsides of this method are the cost of implementing, and the concern that the consumers you are dealing with may not be the correct samples.

Combination of Methods

Many of the larger wineries use a combination of the above methods when setting prices. Obviously the production costs of the wine must be considered in setting the price, and since many consumers are swayed by wine expert ratings and medals, this method is still used as a contributing factor in wine pricing. This information is then combined with consumer perceptions of wine quality and pricing, as well as competitive pricing data, to identify a price range that will sell well and generate decent margins.

In the end, regardless of which pricing method or combination of methods you use, the main consideration is to compete effectively in the marketplace in order to maximize profits. If your production costs are out of line with the perceived value and price of your wine in the market, then adjustments will have to be made. The most important aspect of wine pricing is to be clear on your strategy and the consumer segment you are targeting. Then focus on understanding your consumers VERY well so that you can provide the packaging, wine quality, and brand image they perceive as being worth your price.

ISSUES WITH RAISING AND LOWERING PRICES

If you happen to be a winery with a limited production, and you sell out of every vintage, then it is only natural that you increase your pricing as a way of building brand image. Should you take this step, you must be mindful of the dangers that lurk ahead. True, the wine industry is full of wines that might sell better if they were placed in a slightly higher price category. It is also true that there are many brands that raised prices prematurely, watched their sales lag far behind projections, and now languish at a point that gives them neither prestige nor profit.

In the opposite situation, the classic response from every sales-person is to suggest a price reduction as a way of increasing sales. But such a price reduction carries with it the perception that wine quality is lower. Can your brand withstand that kind of damage? Probably not. Pricing your wine should not be some kind of arcane ritual that has huge importance, but gives you little confidence. With this in mind, here are a few rules for pricing strategies.

What goes up sometimes comes right back down. In 1999 and 2000, the wine industry saw prices (and profits) soaring to unheard-of levels. Within a few years, most of those prices had come back down again in the face of a declining economy and intense marketing competition from overseas. That process has led some consumers and many connoisseurs to conclude that pricing on American wines is still too high. If large amounts of expensive American wine go unsold, they will have been proven correct. The wineries that have prospered during this time are those that have been able to keep their prices competitive and their market share strong.

What goes down doesn't always come back up. Once you reduce price as a way to increase sales or decrease inventories, you will find it very difficult to raise the price back up again. The wines of Chile were introduced in the American market as an exceptional value, and were priced well below wines of comparable quality. The strategy was successful. The wines of Chile are still priced well below wines of comparable quality, much to the chagrin of Chilean producers.

For wines of limited production, high scores are money in the bank. If you are fortunate enough to make a wine that earns a 98-point rating from a reputable wine critic, your prices and profits should be in great shape. As you contemplate reaping the rewards from such an event, be careful that you don't alienate your long-time customers. They are the ones who may stand by you when your next wine is rated only 69.

A good rating is money in the bank. A bad rating isn't the kiss of death. There are many wines in the market that sell consistently well, despite the fact that one or two critics have lambasted their quality, integrity or style. Don't take a bad rating as a reason for suicide; just get out your marketing manuals and get to work.

For wines sold in supermarkets, a floor-stack is worth more than a gold medal. There are lots of wines in America that have won gold medals. The wines that sell are the ones that consumers can find—preferably floor-stacked in their local retailers.

In the end, the perfect pricing for your wine is one that will allow the wine to sell out over the course of the year, and position the next vintage as something that can take a price increase and still be perceived as an excellent value.

Ten Important Budgeting Questions

Once the issues of marketing budget allocations and wine pricing have been agreed upon, there are still a number of other questions that you should ask as you build your marketing and sales budget. If you can answer these effectively, then you will certainly develop the kind of budget and marketing campaigns that really work. Furthermore, if you can get your management team to adopt these questions as a way of evaluating your work as wine marketing professionals, you will be even farther ahead in the game:

1. **What percentage of your marketing budget is spent on long-term, image enhancement/brand building?**
   This is a critical question, because sales, revenues, and profits are easier to measure than image enhancement. To measure image enhancement effectively, you will need to do extensive before-and-after market research. For a small winery, that's a huge cost. For larger wineries, it should be a part of doing business. Understanding this question, and

understanding the implications of the answer, are the perfect way for you to put a limit on expenditures aimed at achieving image enhancement. That is the first step in getting your marketing budget under control.

2. **How do you measure the success of each part of your budget?**

If you can develop measurable goals and objectives for each part of the marketing budget, then you have built a foundation for years to come. Developing and executing marketing programs to achieve these goals is usually far easier than developing the goals themselves. As you work with these measurable goals over time, you will fine tune your marketing campaigns to be really effective.

3. **What goals do you have for consumer tastings? How do you measure your success?**

Consumer and trade tastings can eat up huge amounts of product and staff time. If you don't have specific and measurable goals for these tastings, they can consume far more than their share of the budget. Be brutally honest about these evaluations, and really work hard to define exactly what each tasting should accomplish. Then make sure you do the follow-up work that will take advantage of the connections you made at the tasting. Keep a catalog of these tastings, and update it each year. At the beginning of the next budget cycle, review the catalog, and ruthlessly eliminate those tastings that did not live up to your expectations. There will always be opportunities to give away wine. What you want are opportunities to build your brand and sell your wine.

4. **What is the best investment in marketing you made this year?**

This may seem like an obvious question, but many wineries

really don't address this issue effectively. All too often, they want to keep doing everything they are doing, rather than focusing on what was the best program. Identify the best investment you made, and then develop plans for doubling, tripling or quadrupling that investment. If you can't multiply the program in a way that makes sense for a much larger audience, then move on to something else. Your ability to do this will give you a huge advantage over your competitors. They are still doing everything on their list, and trying to do *more* things ineffectively. You will be doing a few things very effectively. You will win.

5. **What is the worst investment in marketing you made?**
You know the answer to this one. When you see that something isn't working, there are only three possible outcomes. The first is to fix the problem so that it is much more effective the next time around. This will take time, money, and expertise. It may be easier to eliminate the program and focus on things that really do work. Remember that every minute you spend fixing something that is broken is a minute that you are not executing a program that works. The third possible outcome is that you continue to invest in this program, and get fired.

6. **If youhad to define your budget in terms of the three major audiences, consumers, distributors, and retailer/restauranteurs, what percentage of your budget would go to each category, and why?**
In previous chapters of this book, we have outlined the reasons you may want to focus on one or the other of these audiences. Distributors control your national market presence. Restaurants often introduce new customers to a brand. Retailers are the secret to large sales volume, whereas direct sales to consumers are the most profitable avenue

for wineries. A sensible and carefully designed approach to the answer to this question will define where your winery is going in the next few years. It is an answer that should be shared with all of the audiences mentioned (with a certain amount of discretion to avoid utter disappointment by one group or the other) so that everyone in the pipeline understands what you are doing and why. That, on its own, is a goal for every winery. Once you have the answer, and can begin to develop programs that successfully spend against each of the audiences, you will begin to feel in charge of the situation, instead of fighting off the alligators in the swamp.

7. **What goals do you have for your tasting room and winery newsletter programs? How do you meaure their success?** For most wineries, the tasting room and newsletter program are separate marketing campaigns, and they should be. Marketing a tasting room is much more like marketing a destination than a brand. Your customers want different things from you, and your competitors are different as well. If you understand this, you will be ahead of the game. Do not confuse generating traffic with generating sales. There are wineries that refuse to accept bus tours at their visitors center, because the tourists on the buses are not likely to be serious wine buyers. Other wineries welcome them for the incidental merchandise sales they can generate.

Newsletters can be the most expensive single item that wineries take on—and sometimes those very expensive newsletters do not generate sales. Be very honest about your goals for these projects. If you could triple the newsletter audience, would you want to? If not, why are you sending it out at all?

8. How much do positive reviews affect your sales?

Almost every winery will tell you that a great score from a prestigious publication makes their sales projections much easier to meet. If this is the case, is your winery doing everything it can to get the kinds of high scores that make selling wine easy? If not, why not? If you are getting some good scores, are you doing everything you can to take advantage of those scores in the marketplace? You need to go beyond an email to your sales force and a shelf-talker. Look at placing major advertisements, case cards, and other promotion efforts to really get the word out quickly. Your competitors will do that when they get a good score. They may even do it when you get a low rating. When it is your turn to boast, do it loudly.

9. How do you measure the success of your media contact?

You will rarely get more than one story from any one journalist in the course of a year, so it is crucial that you make every effort to maximize the results of each media contact you make. Measuring success by press clippings and impressions is a long way from an exact science, but it gives you something to measure. Your media contact program should be as carefully designed as the rest of your marketing outreach, and you should measure its success against some specific objectives.

It's a good idea to begin each year with a couple of target media that you want to meet, get to know, and eventually pitch a story. You will also want to follow up with those who have written about you in the past, to make sure they haven't forgotten about you—or think that you have forgotten about them. It also helps to have a series of key phrases that you want to see in any media story about your winery. That helps everyone on your team stay on message, and deliver the most important communication clearly.

10. Do you advertise? To whom? And how do you measure success?

Please don't just show the flag as a matter of routine. Each advertising campaign should have a specific objective, and be measured against some standard for success. If the ads don't increase sales at the consumer level, win more placements at the retail or restaurant level, or generate more depletions at the distributor, then you are probably wasting your time and money. Put the goals down in writing, and be scrupulously honest about how your ads are faring. It is better to pull a campaign that isn't working than to leave it up and running while you try to come up with something better.

SPECIAL MARKETING BUDGET TIPS IN THE WINE INDUSTRY

As previously discussed, the wine industry is quite different from other industries in that there are thousands of winery brands playing amidst global moguls. This creates some unique marketing challenges, but it also creates wonderful opportunities as well. Following are a few budgeting tips that can help you.

Maximize Your Dollars

Wineries have one advantage that is not available to many industries. Wineries are glamorous. That glamour can often help a winery get special pricing, special consideration for sponsorships, and better value for their marketing dollars. Whether you offer product in trade for radio advertising, or simply convince an organization that your participation in a dinner is payment enough, wine marketing dollars often go further than the marketing dollars of other industries.

That's a good thing, because wine companies generally have very small marketing budgets compared to other industries. If you were to tell a soft drink company executive that he has a budget of $250,000 to develop a national marketing campaign for a product, he would laugh at you. Yet many wineries are faced with creating a national brand image for their wine with a budget far smaller than this.

To make it work, you have to be creative, and talk fast. You have to work hard to develop personal relationships with your partners that will pay dividends when the budgets run dry. Also, look for ways to piggyback programs and brands on the backs of much larger, but perhaps less prestigious companies in other industries. Their funding, with your prestige, can be a marriage made in heaven.

What wineries have to offer their strategic partners is often little more than a presence on the shelf and an image of quality. Your ability to turn these two assets into something that can be leveraged against national advertising dollars will have a lot to do with how successful your marketing is.

Make Sure it All Adds Up

The costs of doing marketing in America are not always easy to capture. Initial budgets often start with a single figure that is intended to cover every element of the program. However, as the program is expanded, and marketing teams begin to look for ways to maximize the program, they often fail to increase the budget to cover these additional activities. The result is a budget that is too small to do the job right.

Sponsorships or other budget areas that include wine donations should include a figure for the cost of the wine as well. While wineries may arrive at the cost per case for this figure in a number of ways, the impact on the bottom line of the winery is still the same: wine costs money. It is often tempting to conclude that a sponsorship that only cost wine, and not cash, is somehow a great deal. It is a great deal only if the marketing benefits you received in return for the cost of the wine exceeded the results you could generate with the same amount of cash in another program. Do the math.

Shipping costs or other kinds of fulfillment are another area frequently overlooked in the initial budgeting process, only to raise their ugly heads further down the line. Wineries sometimes hide these budget items by assigning them to the tasting room staff, and asking that department to cover the expenses. That's not good management, and it obscures the true financial results of the tasting room, as well.

Finally, staff time is valuable. For every special event, tasting, or sponsorship that requires you to provide staff, make sure that you budget against these hours. When those events require a top-level executive to deliver a speech, accept an award, or make a presentation, that costs money. If that executive were visiting a distributor in a key market instead of attending the dinner, would the end result be more beneficial to the winery? If the answer is yes, then spend the money where it will do the most good.

Return on Investment

Describing return on investment is the key to presenting any marketing budget to management. You are not suggesting ways to spend money. You are offering investment opportunities that will pay dividends over time. Some are short-term investments, and others are long-term investments, but all should demonstrate to your management team a solid return on those dollars.

The presentation should begin with an analysis of where the winery stands in terms of marketing, sales, and brand building. Then define how you want that picture to change, and why. In every case, the rationale should be short term sales growth, price increases, or enhancing prestige over the long term.

Then present your budget. Explain that this is the most cost-effective way to achieve the goals you have identified, and why this is so. For each program, explain how you will measure success, and how you will know if it is working. Ideally, you would like to be able to do this before the end of the year, so that you can revise and refine a budget mid-year.

Finally, add up the figures. Explain how each program will impact sales, pricing, and long-term brand building. Show where that investment will provide the highest returns. If you do this well, you have only one more thing to do—sit back and enjoy the compliments, then go make it all happen.

One last tip—that party that the winery owner's wife wants to hold this summer for her anniversary? Put that one at the end of the budget, where it will really stand out. That way the executive team will approve the budget, and they will be able to demonstrate that the reason you went over budget this year... was that anniversary party!

Table 8.3: Small to Medium-Sized Winery Marketing Budgets Ranging from 42,000–400,000 Cases

	Winery 1		Winery 2		Winery 3		Winery 4		Winery 5	
Cases	44,320		127,868		126,500		42,000		401,075	
		Per Cases		Per Cases		Per Cases		Per Cases		Per Cases
Revenue	6,440k	145.31	9,441k	73.83	9,963k	78.76	4,146k	98.71	14,545k	46.28
Commissions	0	0	0	0	0	0	0	0	0	0
SBA/DA	0	0	0	0	0	0	0	0	0	0
Excise Tax	39,000	0.88	322,760	2.52	269,715	2.13	40,000	0.96	1,022,741	2.55
NET REVENUE	6,401k	144.43	9,118k	71.31	9,693k	76.63	4,106k	97.75	13,527k	33.73
Sales Expenses (salaries, T&E, phone)	943,370	21.29	1,745k	13.65	2,055k	16.24	464,100	11.06	3,025k	7.14
Marketing Expenses (ads, materials)	421,536	9.51	234,000	1.83	331,238	2.62	139,069	3.30	244,892	0.61
TOTAL MARKETING AND SALES EXPENSES	1,365k	30.80	1,980k	15.48	2,386k	18.86	603,169	14.36	3,270k	8.06
NET REVENUE LESS EXPENSES	5,036k	113.63	7,138k	55.83	7,307k	57.76	3,502k	83.39	10,257k	26.07

Table 8.4: Small Winery Marketing Budgets Ranging from 1000–45,000 Cases

	Winery 1	Winery 2	Winery 3	Winery 4	Winery 5	Winery 6
Production	45,000	3,600	33,000	1,000	10,000	1,700
Budget Costs						
Commissions	380,000	0	0	0	0	3,000
%	12%				20%	
SBA/DA		0	0	0	0	0
%						
Excise Tax	35,000	1,500	100,000			1,000
%	1%	0.5%		1%	5%	
Sales Expenses (salaries, phone/fax, etc.)	205,000	120,000	10,000			18,000
%	6%	40%		5%	30%	
Marketing Expenses (ads, materials)	39,000	22,000				3,000
%	1%	7.3%		5%	10%	
Public Relations	130,000					
%	4%			2%		
Visitors/Tasting Room	206,000	22,000				700
%	6%	7.3%		2%		
% of Total Marketing and Sales Costs of Revenue	30%	55.1%		15%	65%	43%
Prioritize Top Goals						
1	Nat. Brand Image	New Markets Distribution	Nat. Brand Image	Increase Direct Sales/Tasting Room Activity	Nat. Brand Image	Liquidating Inventory
2	New Markets Distribution	Improving Image/Justify Price Increases	New Markets Distribution	New Markets Distribution	New Markets Distribution	Increase Direct Sales/Tasting Room Activity
3	Improving Image to Justify Price Increases	Increase Direct Sales/Tasting Room Activity	Improving Image to Justify Price Increases	Changing On/Off Premise Mix	Improving Image to Justify Price Increases	New Markets Distribution
4	Increase Direct Sales/Tasting Room Activities	Changing On/Off Premise Mix			Liquidating Inventory	

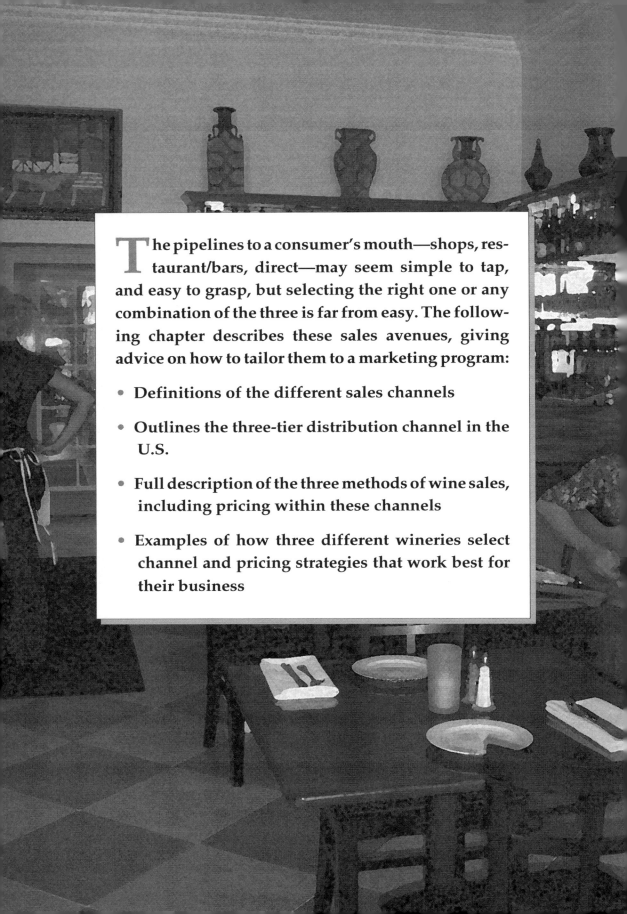

The pipelines to a consumer's mouth—shops, restaurant/bars, direct—may seem simple to tap, and easy to grasp, but selecting the right one or any combination of the three is far from easy. The following chapter describes these sales avenues, giving advice on how to tailor them to a marketing program:

- Definitions of the different sales channels

- Outlines the three-tier distribution channel in the U.S.

- Full description of the three methods of wine sales, including pricing within these channels

- Examples of how three different wineries select channel and pricing strategies that work best for their business

C H A P T E R

THREE AVENUES
TO SALES

ine marketers have three major options when it comes to choosing the ways they will get their product into the mouths of consumers. They can: 1) sell in a store where consumers can take the wine to another location to consume, 2) sell wine to be consumed at the point of sale, for example at a bar or restaurant, and/or 3) sell wine directly to consumers without the participation of intermediary companies.

The key question for wine marketers is which of these three options, or combination of options, is most appropriate for their wine business. Therefore, the purpose of this chapter is to describe these avenues to sales and discuss how they can best fit into your marketing plan. To begin, a definition of sales channel is provided, as well as an overview of the three-tier distribution system in the United States. Then each of the three methods of selling wine is described in detail, including basic information on pricing within the channels. Finally, three examples are provided which illustrate how three different wineries select channel and pricing strategies that work best for their businesses.

DEFINING SALES CHANNELS

A **sales channel** refers to the network of firms that perform the tasks to link producers with their final consumers. In wine, these options include using brokers and distributors who then sell to retailers, restaurants and bars, and other businesses who sell wine to final consumers, and selling directly to final consumers themselves. There is not one single choice of channel that works best for everyone. Some wineries may choose to concentrate on just one channel while others use a combination of channels to distribute their wine. Ultimately, the best channel or channels to use will depend on the size of the winery and the marketing goals as specified in the marketing plan. One of the most important decisions a winery will make is which avenue of sales to use.

THE THREE-TIER DISTRIBUTION SYSTEM

One of the aspects of wine marketing that is unique to the wine industry in the United States is its distribution system. This distribution system is referred to as the three-tier distribution system, and it is necessary for anyone trying to sell wine in the U.S. to understand the important role it plays in wine sales. There are many complex rules and restrictions that govern wine distribution, and the rules vary state by state. These legal requirements were implemented after Prohibition was ended and give each state control over the sale and distribution of alcohol. The result has been a myriad of laws and regulations affecting the sale of alcohol.

Some of the most influential restrictions imposed on wineries have been the laws mandating the use of distributors in most situations. Because of the requirement to use distributors, as well as retailers, before the wine is sold to the end consumer, the channel of distribution in wine in the U.S. is known as the "three-tier system." The three-tier system is found in some form in all states and is currently required by law in 24 states (Gross, 2004). The winery and other suppliers of wine are considered the first tier in the system.

Distributors are the second tier, and the third tier is made up of retailers (see Figure 9.1 below).

Figure 9.1: Diagram of the Three-Tier Distribution System

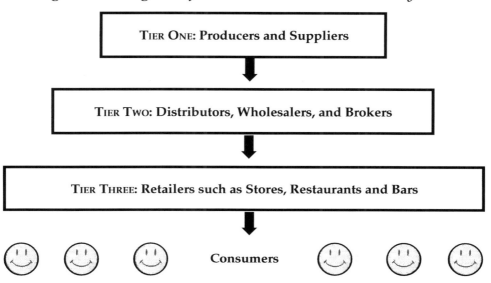

The retail tier includes stores, restaurants and bars, hotels, airlines, cruise lines and other firms that resell wine to the final consumers. In some states, called **control states** or **monopoly states**, we find that the distributor tier, and in some cases even the retail tier are operated by the state. In other states, the wholesalers and retailers that handle wine are private companies, although they usually have many state regulations that they, and the wineries they work with, must follow.

Note that in the three-tier system, the consumer level is not counted as one of the tiers, although some marketers speak of them as the fourth tier in the distribution system. Others, however, use the term "fourth tier" to refer to national sales and marketing companies who are independent companies that provide marketing support for wineries. Their purpose is to operate within the channel of distribution providing marketing and sales support, and to work with distributors to see that wine is placed with customers. They are often employed by smaller wineries that cannot afford to operate a full marketing department themselves. In any event, the traditional three-tier system refers to the producers-distributor-retailer network used to sell wine.

THE WHOLESALE/DISTRIBUTOR TIER

The second tier of the system is comprised of wholesalers/distributors and brokers. The distributor system is one which has been undergoing a lot of changes in the last decade. There has been consolidation in the number of distributors that are available to wineries. During the last decade, the number of wine wholesalers has decreased from 450 to 170 (Wine Institute, 2003). At the same time, as the distributors have become larger, they have become more influential in the distribution of wine. Selecting and managing distributors is perhaps one of the most critical elements of marketing of wine and will be discussed in much more detail in Chapter 10.

Although there has been a lot of attention given lately to the avenues of sales that by-pass the use of traditional distributors, the three-tier system is still one of the most important channels of distribution in reaching consumers, and it is not likely to disappear any time soon. One way to think of this channel is as a pipeline, as depicted in Figure 9.2.

Figure 9.2: The Pipeline

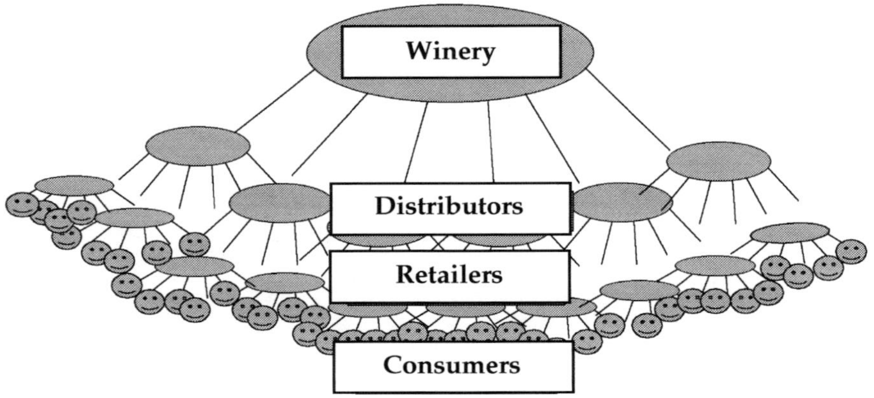

For this simple example, assume that this winery sells its wine to nine different distributors across the US. Each of these distributors might sell the wine to 50 to 70 different retail accounts, and of course, hundreds or thousands of consumers may purchase the wine from these accounts, depending on the size of each retailer's clientele. Therefore it is imperative that wine marketers have an appreciation and understanding of the role distributors play in wine sales.

Distributors provide a number of important services in wine channels. They provide sales staff to visit accounts and give sales presentations and take orders. The distributor sales force is often responsible for monitoring shelf space and seeing that point of purchase materials are used properly by retailers. They may provide training to the retail and restaurant staff on how best to sell wine to their customers. There are many ways that winery salespeople can help the distributor sales staff reach their goals, but ultimately it is usually the distributor sales force who visits accounts on a regular basis.

Distributors also provide many logistic services in the channel of distribution. They arrange deliveries, often for the next day, to retail customers. Distributors can also arrange transportation of wine from the winery to the warehouse where the wine is stored. Distributors provide storage services in temperature-controlled warehouses so that when the wine is sold, it is in good condition. This service is especially valuable for smaller wineries that would find it economically impossible to maintain storage and delivery capabilities throughout the country.

Distributors are able to provide timely information to wineries in the form of depletion reports indicating the removal of wine from their warehouses and sales reports on where the wine is selling. Because the distributor sales force is in direct contact with customers, they often can spot trends, identify new opportunities, and discover marketing problems before the winery is aware of the changes taking place in the market. In this respect, distributors can be viewed as a marketing research provider.

Distributors also provide financial services in that they pay wineries for the wines they purchase, usually on a thirty-day term basis, and then they are responsible for collecting payment from the various accounts to whom they sell the wine. In doing so, they provide a form of financing that saves wineries money in inventory carrying costs. The distributors also assume the risk that the accounts may not be paid.

At this point, it is useful to differentiate **wine wholesalers** from **wine brokers**. Wine wholesalers purchase wine for resale, whereas brokers represent wineries to retail accounts, but usually do not purchase the wines first. Brokers do provide many of the same services that wholesalers do, but the wineries bill the accounts directly for purchases and pay the brokers a commission of the sale. Brokers are often most interested in handling wines that move quickly so that they can earn sufficient commissions.

THE RETAIL TIER

The third tier of the three-tier system is the retail level. There are many different types of retail establishments in which wine is sold. The terms **on-premise** or **on-sale** are used to refer to places where wine is consumed at the retail location, such as restaurants, hotels, bars, clubs and similar settings. The terms **off-premise** or **off-sale** refer to retail stores where wine is sold. This category includes wine stores, liquor stores, discount stores, grocery stores, drug stores, convenience stores and all other types of retail outlets where wine may legally be sold.

All retail accounts other than large chain stores are referred to as the broad market. Chains refer to retailers, restaurants and hotels that have more than one location and therefore tend to purchase in larger quantities. Some national chains may have their wine buying centralized into just one or two locations. Many wineries and distributors have salespeople who focus specifically on large chain accounts.

Wineries should have a clear strategy for the types of retail accounts that are the best fit for the brand. Many factors should be taken into consideration in determining the right mix of retail accounts. Because wine is often sold at higher prices in restaurants than in retail stores, many restaurants prefer to purchase wines that are not widely distributed in stores. This makes it difficult for customers to compare prices and more willing to pay the prices the restaurant charges. Some wineries have even developed brands specifically for restaurants. For example, Gallo has several brands that are sold only to restaurants.

Many wineries with more expensive wines would like to find their wines on the wine lists of highly rated restaurants. Besides the sales that might occur, there is also the prestige of being on their wine lists, a factor that can be used to encourage other restaurants to consider putting the wine on their wine lists as well. However, the downside is that with so many wineries targeting the same select group of restaurants, it is very competitive to get a listing, and even if you do, the wine list is likely to be so extensive that not a lot of your wine will be sold. Many wineries have instead targeted restaurants that focus on a specific type of cuisine, or have chosen less competitive markets within the country. The key is to find a mix of retail accounts that fit the brand image that the winery is trying to create.

One high-end winery in Sonoma County has a strategy in which they place 60% of their wine in expensive and highly rated restaurants, and the other 30% is sold in fine wine shops. They save 10% to be sold directly from the winery or to their wine club members.

Wine by the glass (BTG) programs are offered at restaurants and are very popular, as many customers prefer to order just a glass or two of wine instead of the entire bottle. Marketers often consider selling their wines for BTG programs because of the volume of wine sold and exposure they receive among buyers. On the downside, wineries often are required to discount their prices substantially to be considered for BTG programs. Most restaurants will try to recover the cost they paid for the bottle on the first glass of wine they sell.

Several years ago, Opus One used the BTG process as the method to launch their wine by offering it only in very fine, high-end restaurants. They worked with their distributors and the restaurateurs to create a special promotion in which customers were offered a small glass of Opus One for $10. The wine was served in a special Opus One glass, and arrived at the table on a small silver platter with a card on heavy parchment paper describing why the wine was so special. This promotion effectively introduced Opus One to thousands of customers who frequented high-end restaurants, but perhaps did not want to take a chance on ordering a $160 bottle of wine they had never tasted. After tasting the wine, they felt comfortable ordering it in the future.

Another important point is that the average price points of wines sold in the retail tier differ by the type of retail establishment. For example, the price of wines sold in the grocery store is not the same as the average price point of wine sold in a fine wine shop. Here again, the type of consumer the winery is trying to reach should dictate the retail accounts that are chosen. Also important is the quantity of wine available. Most large retail chains are not interested in carrying wine that comes in small production lots as they require a steady source of supply.

PRICING IN THE DISTRIBUTION CHANNEL

Wineries are not allowed by law to dictate what the final price to a customer will be in the retail store or restaurant. They can make a suggested selling price, but ultimately, the distributor and retailer can discount or deviate from the amount the winery suggests. The suggested retail price is typically determined by doubling the winery's FOB (freight-on-board) price. The FOB price is the total cost the winery spends to make the wine, plus their profit. This assumes that the distributor would mark up the price by 33.3% and the retailer mark-up would be another 50%. This allows for a 25% distributor margin and a 33.3% retail margin. Keep in mind though, that these computations are just a starting point in coming up with the suggested selling price. Often wineries provide different types of discounts, such as lower prices for customers who buy in large quantities or for wine by-the-glass programs. Discounts will be discussed further in Chapter 10.

DIRECT SALES OF WINE

At this point, it might be tempting to ask why wine marketers even use distributors. Wouldn't it be better to sell to the retailers directly and avoid having to pay the margin they require to handle to sales aspect? There is not an easy answer to that question as there are both advantages and disadvantages to selling wine directly to consumers. The easy answer, of course, is that in many states, using distributors is the only way to legally sell wine to consumers. These states have chosen to make direct sales illegal.

Secondly, as we have just covered, distributors provide many useful services to wine marketers. It would be very costly and time consuming for wineries to perform these services in every instance. It often makes economic sense to have distributors provide the services in which they are proficient. This is especially the case if the marketing plan calls for a wine to be widely distributed and to be sold at price points that are under $10. But the reality remains that there are far more wineries today than ever before, and they are bringing many more brands to the marketplace. At the same time, due to consolidation in the wholesale level, there are far fewer distributors who are looking for new products to add to their portfolios. This has created a bottleneck in wine distribution that frustrates many wine marketers.

In order to reach consumers and sell the wine that is made, many wineries have found that they must rely on direct sales. If they are to find customers for their wine at all, direct sales are the only option open to them, since distributors are overwhelmed by the number of brands available. The good news is that more wine is being sold directly to consumers. A recent study estimated that consumer direct sales in 2004 were $2 billion (*Wine Business Monthly*, 2005).

Direct sales include sales through the tasting room, over the internet, through the mail and telephone. Wine club sales are one rapidly growing method of direct sales. Fortunately for the winery, there are many advantages to direct sales, as we will see in Chapter 11. The most easily recognized advantage to selling direct is that the winery is able to capture the profit margin that would otherwise go to both the wholesaler and retailer under the three-tier system.

There are other less tangible benefits as well. First, the winery can maintain better control of the pricing strategies so that prices fit the brand image they are attempting to create. Wine clubs allow wineries to plan their sales more accurately as they have a better idea how many wines will be shipped in the next shipment. Tasting room sales require a personal selling approach that is often better at establishing brand loyalty among consumers. Customers may purchase more wine when they are able to taste the wine first as they feel less fear of purchasing a wine that they won't like. Even when customers do not choose to purchase wine while at the visitor center, when favorable impressions are created the customers may choose to purchase the wine at a later time. Visitors who have had enjoyable visits often share their experience with others, in essence becoming brand ambassadors for the winery.

But wine marketers must realize that direct sales bring with them their own expenses that must be covered if direct sales are to make sense. Tasting rooms can be expensive to build and operate. Internet and direct mail sales require the creation of promotional materials to encourage customers to purchase. For wine clubs to be an option, databases of members' addresses and credit card information must be created and constantly updated. Packaging and shipping costs must be covered to send wine to customers. Unless all of these activities are done efficiently, direct sales may not turn out to be any more profitable than selling wine through the traditional three-tier system.

EXAMPLES OF WINERY CHANNEL STRATEGIES

If you are a new winery, and just starting out, it can be difficult to find a distributor to carry your wine in their portfolio. Table 9.1 on the following page illustrates an example of a new winery producing 6,000 cases, called Winery A. In this situation, since the winery is new and has not received much positive press, high ratings, or medals, the owner selects a strategy of selling 80% direct to consumer and 20% through brokers in surrounding states who can get the wine placed in local restaurants and wine shops.

The second example, Winery B, illustrates a 15,000 case winery that has been in business for a while and has elected a channel strategy of 30% direct through tasting room and wine club sales and 70% through brokers. The third example, Winery C, illustrates an established 20,000 case winery that is selling 10% direct and 90% through brokers.

In the first scenario, the winery decides to price the wine at $25 a bottle, in the second scenario, the wine is priced at $15 a bottle and in the third, the wine is priced at $12. Notice that the largest winery may be selling the most cases, but because they are using distributors, they do not have the highest gross profit of the three wineries. In this case it is Winery B, with 15,000 cases, that is making more money than the other two wineries.

Tables 9.1: Three Channels with a $25 Price

Winery A	Per case	Total cases	% in Channel	Total Cost of Goods $
Cost of goods	$120	6000		$720,000
Retail Price $/Btl	25			
Direct	300	4800	80%	$1,440,000
Brokers	200	1200	20%	$240,000
Distributors	150	0	0%	$0
Total sales		6000		$1,680,000
Gross Profit				$960,000

Winery B	Per case	Total cases	% in Channel	Total Cost of Goods $
Cost of goods	$120	15000		$1,800,000
Retail Price $/Btl	25			
Direct	300	4500	30%	$1,350,000
Brokers	200	10500	70%	$2,100,000
Distributors	150	0		$0
Total sales		15000		$3,450,000
Gross Profit				$1,650,000

Winery C	Per case	Total cases	% in Channel	Total Cost of Goods $
Cost of goods	$120	20000		$2,400,000
Retail Price $/Btl	25			
Direct	300	2000	10%	$600,000
Brokers	200	0	0%	$0
Distributors	150	18000	90%	$2,700,000
Total sales		20000		$3,300,000
Gross Profit				$900,000

Tables 9.2: Three Channels with a $15 Price

Winery A	Per case	Total cases	% in Channel	Total Cost of Goods $
Cost of goods	$80	6000		$480,000
Retail Price $/Btl	15			
Direct	180	4800	80%	$864,000
Brokers	120	1200	20%	$240,000
Distributors	90	0	0%	$0
Total sales		6000		$1,008,000
Gross Profit				$528,000

Winery B	Per case	Total cases	% in Channel	Total Cost of Goods $
Cost of goods	$80	15000		$1,200,000
Retail Price $/Btl	15			
Direct	180	4500	30%	$810,000
Brokers	120	10500	70%	$1,260000
Distributors	90	0		
Total sales		15000		$2,070,000
Gross Profit				$870,000

Winery C	Per case	Total cases	% in Channel	Total Cost of Goods $
Cost of goods	$120	20000		$1,600,000
Retail Price $/Btl	15			
Direct	180	2000	10%	$360,000
Brokers	120	0	0%	$0
Distributors	90	18000	90%	$1,620,000
Total sales		20000		$1,980,000
Gross Profit				$380,000

Tables 9.3: Three Channels with a $12 Price

Winery A	Per case	Total cases	% in Channel	Total Cost of Goods $
Cost of goods	$60	6000		$360,000
Retail Price $/Btl	12			
Direct	144	4800	80%	$691,200
Brokers	96	1200	20%	$115,000
Distributors	72	0	0%	$0
Total sales		6000		$806,400
Gross Profit				$446,400

Winery B	Per case	Total cases	% in Channel	Total Cost of Goods $
Cost of goods	$60	15000		$900,000
Retail Price $/Btl	12			
Direct	144	4500	30%	$648,200
Brokers	96	10500	70%	$1,008,000
Distributors	72	0	0%	$0
Total sales		15,000		$1,656,000
Gross Profit				$756,000

Winery C	Per case	Total cases	% in Channel	Total Cost of Goods $
Cost of goods	$60	20000		$1,200,000
Retail Price $/Btl	12			
Direct	144	2000	10%	$288,000
Brokers	96	0	0%	
Distributors	72	18,000	90%	$1,296,000
Total sales		20,000		$1,584,000
Gross Profit				$384,000

These three examples illustrate the various types of channel strategies that wineries can elect to implement, as well as the resulting gross profit. Though it may not be possible for a new winery to immediately find a broker or distributor to carry them in their portfolio, they can still choose this option as part of their channel strategy, and implement an interim plan while they are developing their brand image and reputation. Once this has been achieved through positive press, good ratings, and awards, then they will have a better chance of attracting the attention of major distributors. But just because their wines are carried by distributors, it does not necessarily mean they will be the most profitable choice. On the other hand, a winery may elect to stay with a channel strategy that is focused primarily on direct to consumer. It just depends on their overall business strategy.

REFERENCES

"E-Commerce: The Case of Online Wine Sales and Direct Shipment" Wine Institute, Oct. 29, 2003. Available at: www.wineinstitute.org.

Gross, S. (2004). Direct wine shipments. *The Wine Institute*. Available at: http://www.wineinstitute.org/shipwine.

"U.S. Direct Wine Sales Reach $2 Billion." *Wine Business Monthly*. March 21, 2005. Available at: www.winebusiness.com,

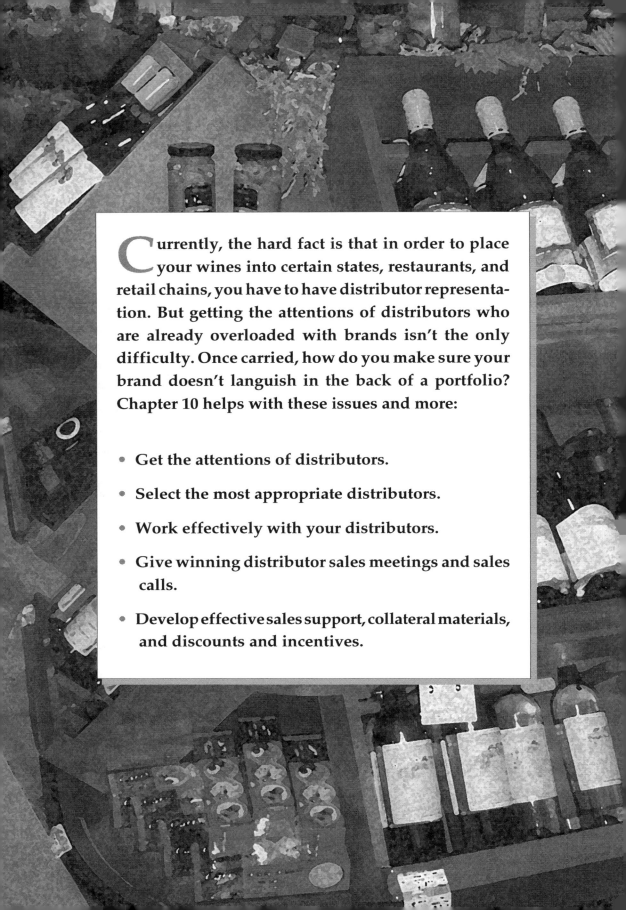

Currently, the hard fact is that in order to place your wines into certain states, restaurants, and retail chains, you have to have distributor representation. But getting the attentions of distributors who are already overloaded with brands isn't the only difficulty. Once carried, how do you make sure your brand doesn't languish in the back of a portfolio? Chapter 10 helps with these issues and more:

- Get the attentions of distributors.

- Select the most appropriate distributors.

- Work effectively with your distributors.

- Give winning distributor sales meetings and sales calls.

- Develop effective sales support, collateral materials, and discounts and incentives.

CHAPTER

10

C H A P T E R

SALES AND DISTRIBUTION MANAGEMENT

Years ago, a winery could approach distributors with a basic business proposition. The winery provided a new and interesting product, and the distributor helped build the market for it. Together, the two companies grew the brand, increased sales volume, and made a profit. It is a model that created many of the top wine brands in the 1960's and 1970's.

Today it is rare to find this model in operation, because distributors find themselves weighed down with portfolios filled with thousands of brands, and, in turn, wineries are almost forced to beg distributors to carry their products. Distributor consolidation has meant that in many markets there are only two or three major distributors, each representing vast numbers of wineries, and even vaster numbers of individual products. Distributors who represent more than one thousand SKUs are hard pressed to find a reason to add yet another wine to their portfolio. To complicate matters, many wineries offer the same types of wine as their competitors, and usually do not present it in a way that is new and intriguing to consumers.

So what are the secrets of gaining the attention of a distributor and developing a win-win relationship? Currently, the hard fact is that in order to get your wines into certain states, restaurants, and retail chain, you have to have distributor representation. However, if you can't find a distributor to carry your wine, how can you achieve your goals?

GETTING THE ATTENTION OF DISTRIBUTORS

In many cases, small wineries find that distributors are little more than delivery agencies for their wines. With more than 1,000 or even 5,000 SKUs in their sales book, and the average sales call lasting only a few minutes, it is hard to imagine how a distributor salesperson can effectively represent all of the wines in their book. The simple truth is they can't. Instead, the distributor will focus on a few products that have received extra emphasis from management; a few that capture their personal fancy, and a few that they know will sell with a minimum of effort. The other thousands of wines will be glossed over quickly and only sold when the retailer or restaurateur requests them.

The last thing a distributor salesperson needs is another line of wines in their portfolio. The sales book is already so thick that he or she keeps fit just by lugging it around from account to account. From the distributor's perspective, a new product simply adds to the workload of the sales force, without any corresponding increase in volume or profits. In many cases, the new product may achieve some basic sales volume goals, but only by cannibalizing other products within the distributor's existing portfolio. Therefore there is no incentive for the distributor in this type of situation—he or she is simply chasing the same rabbit down more rabbit holes. Why then would a distributor agree to carry a new line of wines? There are a few reasons.

Reasons Distributors Are Interested in Carrying A New Wine
1. **Sheer muscle:** The new line of wines comes from a major supplier, one that already does a significant sales volume with the distributor. If the supplier already represents 15% (or 45%!) of the distributor's total sales, then that supplier

will enjoy considerable attention from the distributor. The new wines will get everyone's attention. That may not help you, though, because this option is usually only in the hands of a few very large wine companies.

2. *A competitive advantage*: The new line of wine gives the distributor a key advantage in the market. For a distributor, this means that the wines must provide a way for them to take market share away from their competition. Note that this does not mean that the new wines will be cannibalizing from the existing portfolio, but will be stealing market share away from a specific product or category in the competition's portfolio. For a producer, this is marketing strategy—pure and simple. It requires you to identify a target product and category that your distributor does not carry, and then develop a product and campaign that will successfully drive sales volume away from that product and category and towards your own wines and distributor.

3. *Easy Pickings*: The new lines will sell themselves—the winery has done such a good job of marketing, public relations, and sales support that the distributor salespeople can increase their sales volume and profits with the same amount of effort. These wines simply make everyone at the distributor look good, by making it easy to sell them. In this case, the wines will often cannibalize other products, but the increase in total volume justifies the distributor support. The good news is that this plays nicely into any well-designed marketing campaign, including the kinds of strategies mentioned under #2 above. However it may require a huge amount of effort.

For any but the largest wineries, the best solution is the strategic approach described in #2, supported by an exemplary marketing communications and promotions campaign mentioned in #3. Every year, there are a few wineries that successfully achieve these goals, while hundreds of others fall short. The reason is that those less successful wineries did not provide their distributors with fully realized answers to both #2 and #3. Your competition is fighting this battle against you. Your chances of success are directly proportional to your ability to achieve these goals better than your competition.

Since strategic marketing elements were already covered in earlier chapters, it is useful to focus on the kinds of marketing support that distributors and their salespeople want and need. They want materials that sell the wine as quickly and effectively as possible. While almost everyone in the wine industry decries the importance placed on numerical ratings from wine publications, the simple fact remains that those ratings sell more wine quickly than just about anything else.

As good marketers, we should not criticize the ratings or resent their impact. We should understand how and why they have such an impact: a saturated market, a confused and often intimidated customer base, and a sales team that has far too many wines and not nearly enough time to talk about them.

Given that, the wineries that will get attention from distributors are those that have huge sales volumes already, have great strategic plans, have great marketing support, and sell themselves. The rest of the wines in that portfolio will just be hanging on for the ride. As the market goes up, their sales will improve a bit. As it goes down, they will suffer. Every producer must fight against this fate.

How To Select a Distributor

Selecting a distributor to represent your wines is a classic marketing dilemma. Do you want to be with the largest, most powerful distributor, and struggle to get any attention? Or do you want to be represented by a small distributor who has plenty of time to talk to you, but has little leverage in the marketplace? There is no easy answer to that question.

In the best of all possible worlds, you would like to be with a distributor who has a clear void in their portfolio which you can fill, and who will work hard to take advantage of this new asset by selling your wine aggressively against the competition. In the worst-case scenario, you would be the sixth Chilean wine brand in a market with only two distributors. The Chilean category is not growing vigorously, and your wines will have to fight with wines within your own distributor's portfolio for even a small piece of the category pie.

Your own positioning, combined with a careful analysis of the portfolios of each distributor in the market, will give you an idea of where you stand between these two extremes. The exercise should be completed in every market, but the results and corresponding strategies will vary widely. This first step gives you a critical foundation from which to pursue the most likely distributor suspects in every market.

There is more to selecting a distributor than just analyzing the portfolio of each company. The wine business is one of relationships between people, and certainly these play a key role in selecting a distributor. The right combination of producer and distributor can overcome strategic challenges. Therefore don't overlook your gut feeling when it comes to whom to believe. Ask yourself if you will be able to work with the distributor salespeople for the long run. Is there a good culture match between your company philosophy, values and goals and theirs?

This relationship is more than just a psychological feeling of comfort. Some distributors have a more successful on-premise focus, while others are more effective in chain stores. Your goals for your wines will need to find a corresponding resonance with the philosophy of the distributor to achieve the sales goals you have developed.

A distributor who really understands the subtle differences between the various appellations of the Côtes de Nuits will have a different approach to selling wine from one whose biggest success stories involve national sales and merchandising promotions at major retailers. Also the sales forces of those two companies will have very different kinds of expertise as well.

Finally, you should look for a distributor who wants to work with you. This means more than just someone who wants to sell your wine. It also means someone who has the time to talk to you on the phone, will take the time to meet with you when you are in town, and who will assign sales staff time and energy to support your efforts when you come to work the market. The best way to judge that is to meet the team, ask questions, and really spend some time checking references with other producers who are your approximate size and price point.

Selecting a distributor is not an easy task, but it is a critical one. Mistakes made here will have long term implications for your brand — not just in this market, but in neighboring markets as well. Take the time to do your homework, and recognize, that like a marriage, a good distributor relationship can begin with a honeymoon, but the next thirty years will take a lot of hard work from both sides.

Table 10.1: Questions to Ask Distributors

1.	What are your long range plans for your business?
2.	What do you think the future will be for our wine category?
3.	How do we fit into that future for you?
4.	In what channel are you strongest? Can you really bring my wines to the attention of the on-premise trade? Chains?
5.	What wineries about my size and price range should I call to get a reference for your work on their behalf?
6.	Who will be my primary contact at the distributor?
7.	How much time should I spend in your market?
8.	What kinds of educational programs do you have for your sales people?
9.	How can I get involved in those?
10.	What kinds of sales can I expect in the next twelve months?
11.	What kinds of sales can I expect in the next three years?
12.	How badly do you want to represent my wines?

HOW TO WORK WITH A DISTRIBUTOR

As in any good relationship, the most important element is good communication. You have to make sure that you feel at ease discussing the key elements of your business, and you have to feel comfortable that you are getting honest and respectful answers in response to your questions. The more you can communicate that you understand the tough issues facing your distributor, and are willing to help him or her overcome these challenges, the more likely it is that they will give you the kind of enthusiasm and support you need to effectively sell your wines in the market.

Establishing Sales Goals

The place to start this kind of communication is right at the beginning when you work with your distributor to establish realistic goals for your brand in their market. Traditionally, wineries often set very high sales goals, because they know how much wine they have to sell, and they don't really have any other option. By the same token, distributors are likely to suggest more modest goals, because they will then have an easier time achieving them. So where should you begin?

Start by taking a look at your sales history in the market. A good distributor can provide you with a detailed analysis of where your wine is being sold, and in what kinds of volumes. Key factors that you should evaluate are listed in Table 10.2.

Table 10.2: Points to Evaluate in Setting Sales Goals with Distributors

✓ Number of on-premise accounts
✓ Number of off-premise accounts
✓ Key accounts in each segment that play a major role in your overall volume
✓ By-the-glass accounts
✓ Total sales volume for the whole market
✓ Sales trends in the market

This information is absolutely critical to a good meeting with your distributor. Ask for this information a month before your meeting, and make sure that you really understand it. In the same way that last year's budget is usually the foundation for this year's budget, last year's sales figures are the foundation for your conversations with your distributor. They are the starting point for any discussion about sales volume, channels, or product mix.

Be aware that it could be counterproductive to discuss generalized sales volumes with your distributor. While your winery may have the goal of increasing sales by twenty percent, this usually also implies a constant price point and distribution mix. If you tell your distributor that your goal for the next year is to increase sales by twenty percent, you may well achieve that goal. However the increase may also come via major price discounts at the chain level, lowering the overall image of your brand.

You are far better off working with the kind of detailed information you have requested from Table 10.2. If you are currently on the list in seventeen on-premise accounts, then a good goal may be to increase that by adding four new accounts. If you have two of your three varietals in the off-premise stores, then a goal might be to add the third varietal at half of the retail stores. If Pinot Noir in the overall market is growing, then you might suggest that you can provide thirty percent more Pinot Noir to take advantage of that trend.

By focusing on the very specific goals above, you will have achieved two very important things. The first is that you will have demonstrated to your distributor that you understand the market, and appreciate the challenges and opportunities they face. This is a basic element to good communication, and will pay dividends throughout the life of your relationship. The second thing is that you will have worked out a sales-goal plan with your distributor with very specific and attainable goals for the sales team.

Keep in mind that distributor salespeople are a critical and complex audience within the wine industry. Without them, sales of wine in America would plummet. Their time and attention are pulled in a hundred different directions every day, and you are only one of thousands of wineries that would like to direct their daily activities. It is unrealistic to expect that you will be able to maintain a strong hold on their attention for the course of a full year. Given the competition for their energy, you won't get their attention for more than a few days of each year. By giving them very specific goals they can achieve in a relatively short period of time, you make the most of these few days.

Establishing Long-Term Growth Plans
Once you have analyzed your sales in the market, set up a meeting with the distributorship management to discuss your plans for the

next year. Present the information they have given you, so that everyone is aware of the current status of your wines. Do not expect the distributor management team to be able to cite your sales statistics off the top of their heads. Give them the information in writing, and compare the current status with your records from previous years.

With that information as a background, you are now in a position to work with them to adopt your growth goals for the future. If you demand it, you will find the reception rather cool. In many cases, it is better to present the current sales figures and ask the distributor management where they see opportunities for growth. The goal of this meeting is simple. You want to get the distributor management to endorse your plans for brand promotion, and you want to achieve the long-term sales growth and positioning that your winery needs to be successful.

In markets that you feel are significantly underachieving, it is sometimes helpful to provide sales information from another market where your brand and distributor are being more successful. Look for ways to work with the distributor to get your sales figures up to the volume and positioning that has been achieved in your better markets.

A good solid discussion with distributor management should put you in a position to make a strong presentation to the sales force. This presentation will include not only your specific goals for the year, but can now also include an endorsement by their top management. Now you are ready to take your case to the sales team, and sell them on selling your wine.

THE DISTRIBUTOR SALES MEETING

Traditionally, every Friday morning from 9 a.m. to noon, distributor sales forces gather to listen to fifteen-minute presentations by wineries and producers. It is critically important to understand the dynamics of these presentations. For the presenting winery, this is the most important fifteen minutes of the year in this market. For the sales team, the winery presentation is one of twelve for the morning, and one of five hundred that they will sit through in the course of the year. The difference between the perspectives of the two groups can often lead to disappointment on the part of the winery.

Let's break this down to the lowest common denominator. Educators know that most students will remember only three major things from any educational lecture. While it may be flattering to think that the distributor sales force will remember three things from each of the twelve presentations made on any given Friday morning, it is far more likely that they will remember three important things from the entire morning of presentations. The question then becomes a simple one: How do you make sure that they remember what you tell them about your winery and wines?

For large companies with big budgets, these presentations can be quite spectacular, and often involve everything from very sophisticated multi-media effects to personal appearances by the Swedish National Bikini team. Your own talk about the unique character of the soils of your vineyard may not get the same kind of attention. In fact, unless you are a very effective public speaker, you may look out at an audience whose eyes have glazed over and whose attention may slowly be drifting back to some of the more attractive elements of previous presenters. This is not a good situation for the most important fifteen minutes that you will spend in that market this year.

The good news is that there are mitigating factors. Each of the salespeople in the room has his or her own special skills and interests. While it is unrealistic to expect them all to be riveted by your presentation, you don't have to rivet them all to achieve your goals. For most wineries, twenty percent of the distributor sales force will sell eighty percent of their wine. With this in mind, the goal of your presentation is simple. You cannot expect to thrill the entire sales force. What you absolutely must accomplish is to identify that twenty percent of the sales force that is selling your wine, and give them the information, incentives, and support they need to do a better job. And yes, that all has to happen in fifteen minutes.

The first step in solving any problem is to recognize it—and the problem here is that most of the people in the room are probably not going to get very excited about your presentation. Use the first few minutes of your time to pick out those in the room who are responsive to your message, and who may have the best contacts to sell your wine. This is pretty hard to do if you are the one doing all the talking. Therefore the first few minutes of your presentation should be inter- active with the audience, asking them questions, encouraging them to get involved, have fun, and start to build a relationship with you and your wines.

You can do this by asking the group questions about your winery, your wines, your category, and the market in which they compete. Those who know the answers are also those who are most likely to make an effort to use that knowledge to sell your wines. These are also the salespeople you want to connect with later in the day when they begin to make their sales calls. These salespeople are also the ones you want to cultivate over the long term. As they build their contacts and strengths in the market, you want them to use your wines to build their reputation and their sales volume.

Some of these salespeople can become more than just successful sellers of your products. In every market, you should have the goal of developing one salesperson as a kind of brand ambassador—the one person who is recognized as the leading expert and advocate for your wines. You can help this person succeed by giving them additional support and information, as well as the kind of encouragement and personal attention that make them feel special. In return, they see their expertise as a way of helping them achieve sales success for them- selves. As you help them build their reputation, they help you build your sales volume and position your wines appropriately.

The rest of your presentation should be concise, and focus on the key elements of your marketing and sales message. Make sure the sales force understands the positioning of your wines, and your unique selling proposition. Also, make very sure that they understand all of the various elements of marketing and sales support that you will provide to them. This is your one chance to really promote these campaigns and programs to the people who are most likely to take advantage of them. Don't waste it.

This is also the time for you to share sales successes from sales-people in the room, or from other markets. Tell them what works, why it works and how it was done. Give them everything from the strategic concept to the nuts and bolts of the actual sales conversation. Most of all, give them the proof that your wines do sell, and sell well with the right approach and effort. Make it simple and easy for them. That, in the end, is how they will be convinced.

The following week, as they make their sales calls, they will try out some of the tactics, strategies, and programs that you presented in the sales meeting. If they work easily and well, you are well on your way to achieving your goals. If they do not work as advertised, you can expect that your sales goals for the next year will suffer.

As an example, when Jean and Hubert Trimbach travel in the USA, they always make a point of telling a story about each wine, and relating it to their family that has run the winery for 13 generations and more than 350 years. It works. The wines have a great reputation for quality, and everyone in the business feels that they share a part of that success—primarily because they have come to know and love the Trimbach family. Wine is more than just a beverage, and a good producer will always give the sales network a good story to tell about each wine.

The Sales Call

Making a sales call, either on your own or with a distributor salesperson, is the real meat of any market visit. This is where you can do something more than just talk; it is where you can make a real difference in your business and the lives of the people in your sales and distribution network. Wineries who do this well succeed over time. Those who do this poorly not only struggle in the market, but the individuals involved often struggle in their careers.

Where should you call? Don't spend all of your time on your existing accounts, even though the distributor may like to do this. Look for challenges and new markets for your wine. Look for ways you can stand out, ways for you to use your direct connection to the winery to solve a problem, or deliver a benefit to the customer. Search for ways to demonstrate the sales strategies and tactics you presented at the sales meeting, so that the distributor salesperson can see those in action, and see that they work. In every case, pave the way for future sales calls by both the distributor sales person and you. The rules for a good sales call are simple.

Be Professional

Make your appointment in advance, and give yourself enough time to make it from one appointment to the next. This allows you to be on time, and mentally prepared for your sales presentation, rather than racing in late and making it up as you go along.

Dress appropriately for the market and your position. Winemakers can sometimes get away with wearing blue jeans and a nice shirt, but those in marketing and sales positions should dress in accordance with their counterparts in the market.

Make your presentation professional and concise. Introduce yourself, present your card, and explain your role in the winery or with the brand. The goal of being professional is more than just presenting a good image for your company. In a saturated market, everyone is looking for reasons to eliminate companies, brands, and salespeople from the seemingly endless list of suppliers. Don't give your customers a reason to eliminate you from consideration. Keep your manners polite, your conversation appropriate, and your doors open.

Respect Your Client

A good salesperson does more than just try to close a sale. If you really want to sell wine, you need to understand your customer's business. That means you have to listen as much as you talk. Paraphrase what they have to say to show that you have heard them. Respect their time by making each word count, and by adapting your presentation to their needs and interests. Know what kinds of wines sell in their shop, and what is selling in other shops like theirs. Become a source of industry information for them—and learn to cultivate their comments as well. The information they share with you not only helps you understand their business, but also the market as a whole. Listen to them.

Understand the Market

Don't make the mistake of selling wines that are destined primarily for supermarkets to restaurants or fine wine shops. While the supermarkets can get pricing discounts for their volume, the restaurants and retailers cannot. The result is that consumers come to the conclusion that the restaurants and retail shops are somehow not being fair in their pricing. Also, the restaurateurs and retailers don't like this feeling any more than the consumer does. Nor should you make the mistake of loading up a customer with a lot of wine that won't sell. You may find a client who is willing to help you out and buy a lot of something, but just remember that excess wine in the pipeline is everybody's problem.

Build Relationships, Not Account Lists

Your goal must be larger than just selling a certain number of cases of wine per day, week or month. In the end, you must become more than just a supplier. You must work to become a trusted ally, a reference for the customers on your list. You should always try to sell your wines, but sometimes the long term goal means that you may have to break the rules of brand loyalty to built trust and confidence. The concept of brand loyalty is sometimes taken to extremes in the beverage business, and salespeople will sometimes refuse to even speak about another brand. But if your goal is to become more than just a salesperson, then you need to think outside of this tiny box. If you want to build trust and credibility with your accounts, you need to show that you know the market, are aware of the strengths of the competition, and give them credit where credit is due. A salesperson who proposes a wine list exclusively of their own products will never have the same kind of credibility as one who carefully selects from various producers appropriate to the account, even going outside their own portfolio.

Service, Service, Service

Products come and go, but a good salesperson knows their customers and knows what they want. Just as a good server can save a meal in a restaurant, a good salesperson can go a long way towards helping a winery over a difficult stretch. Always keep your commitments and do what you say you are going to do. Always exceed your customers' expectations for service. Make yourself into someone they simply cannot live without.

SALES SUPPORT

What kinds of sales support programs do salespeople want? They want the kinds of programs that make selling your wine easy. They want the kinds of programs that encourage retailers or restaurateurs to request the wines, even when the salesperson doesn't have time to present them. Salespeople want the kinds of programs that get their accounts to pick up the phone and ask about the program, order the wines, and give the wines the perfect placement.

The biggest companies respond to this with big programs: huge in-store displays that feature moving parts, bright lights, and sound; incentives that include deep-sea fishing trips to Cabo San Lucas, and advertising campaigns that offer consumers the chance at free Super Bowl tickets. Those kinds of efforts always generate some positive results. The challenge for smaller wineries is figuring out how to compete with them. Since smaller wineries don't have the same budgets, they have to be more creative, more personal, and more cost effective than the big players.

Of course, the most cost-effective solution of all is to get very high ratings for your wines from the critics. A 98-point score from a leading publication will sell your wine far more effectively than anything else. However, you cannot count on those kinds of ratings. While a negative rating doesn't usually do as much damage as a great rating does good, there is still the danger that a low score will slow down sales, or may even keep some distributors or retailers from carrying the wine. The sword of wine critic ratings cuts both ways.

If you can't deliver the high rating points, and your budgets are limited, then the answer is simple, if not easy. You simply have to roll up your sleeves and get to work providing the sales network with the kind of support they need to sell your wines. This often means hitting the road, visiting personally with the distributor salespeople, and providing them with information about your wines and winery. You also need to be easily accessible via telephone or email to provide quick responses to questions or requests from the field. The list below is not comprehensive, but every small winery should at least have these elements in place.

1. **An internet website** that is more than just a feel-good brochure for the owners of the winery. This website should

capture the essence of your positioning, and should make it clear from the start. Your website should be the billboard that conveys your unique selling proposition. It should include basic wine fact sheets on every wine you produce, including vineyard sourcing, winemaking style and technique, production technical information, sensory tasting notes, and food and wine pairing advice. The website should also include up-to-date wine reviews for all of your wines—and these should get updated within twenty-four hours of when you get a positive review. Like the press kit, the website should have biographies of all of the key personnel, a history of the winery, and any unique elements that add impact or credibility to your unique selling proposition.

2. Creating the website is only the first step here. You also need to **promote that website** so that everyone in the distribution and sales pipeline knows about your website and how to use it. Put the URL of your website on every label, so that store clerks and restaurant sommeliers can consult it when they need information. Also include it on every advertisement and piece of collateral material that you produce. Mention it in your sales presentations, and include it as a link in every email you send. Your goal is to make this website a well-known resource for everyone interested in your company.

3. Part of the website should be an **emergency telephone number,** or emergency email address that goes directly to someone at your winery who can respond to requests from the field. Every request should get a response within twenty-four hours, and this should be promised and delivered as part of the sales support effort of your winery. Salespeople work on a very short timeline. If you do not understand this, and cannot provide them timely service, then your wine sales will suffer.

4. **Over-communicate with your distributor sales teams**. They will always appreciate any efforts you make on their behalf. This includes everything from advertising in the *Wine Spectator* to pitching stories to their local wine writer, or visiting the market. However, salespeople are very busy, and you can't expect them to follow every development in the marketplace, and notice every small thing you do. So tell them. Every time you begin a new program, or achieve visible success with a marketing campaign, tell them about it via email. Put it on your website. Make sure they know that you care about them, and are working on their behalf. When you host one of their customers at the winery, follow up with a report to them about what you tasted, what you talked about, and what next steps could lead to increased sales.

5. The same is true of every customer. **Therefore keep your customers updated.** If you can get an email address for a restaurateur or retailer, add that to your list, and send them news from your winery. The best news is in the form of those great wine ratings, but good reviews, success stories from the market, or successful strategic alliances that reinforce your positioning are all important. Always include your distributor sales team on these communications. It is important that they see you as an ally in their efforts, not as competition.

COLLATERAL/POS MATERIALS

If you really want to understand the role of sales collateral materials, take a tour through any wine distributor's warehouse. After you are impressed with the organization and storage of the massive wine inventory, ask to see the Point of Sales (POS) storage area. The POS is all of the materials that the winery sends the distributor to support the sales of its wine, including brochures, posters, shelf-talkers, server cards, and other collateral materials. What you will find will usually shock you.

First of all, you will find that it is not usually as well organized as the wine inventory. Notice the number of packages or shipments that have not been opened. Then make an effort to find the materials from a given winery. It will be hard. This is perfectly understandable. Distributors get paid for selling wine, and they will always try to sell as much wine as they can, with as little effort as they can. If they can sell the wine without using the POS, they will do so. If they occasionally need some POS to support a sale, they will do that. However, they are not paid to distribute your POS. They are paid to sell wine. Therefore the POS storage area is most often on the wrong side of the tracks in the warehouse.

To confirm this impression, ask to take a look in the trunk of any salesperson's car. What you will find is what is called "trunk mulch." A microcosm of the warehouse POS area fills the trunk of the car, and includes everything from wine fact sheets and small merchandising displays to sample bottles, corkscrews, and even a tuxedo for those special occasions. A salesperson lives in his or her car, and the trunk is the closet of that home.

Once you have seen these areas, you have a better perspective on POS materials. The first question you should always ask, before you decide to create any POS at all, is how that POS is going to be distributed from your winery, through the sales and distribution network, and out to the retailer or restaurateur. If you are not completely convinced that your materials are really going to get out into the retail environment, you should save the money and spend it on something that is more cost effective.

One small California winery paid thousands of dollars to create a new label and shelf-talker for a low-price wine that included an expensive yacht in the graphics. While the promotional materials performed satisfactorily on the West Coast, it bombed in East Coast markets because it was perceived as "too snooty," and customers chose not to buy it because of the type of boat it portrayed.

Insert Figure 10.1: Examples of Sales Support Materials

A branded cork puller

A Waitstaff toolkit

A Floorstack display rack   *A deli rack display*

When you decide that you need POS to support your wines, make sure that the materials accurately reflect your positioning and USP. To make sure that they really are going to help sell your wine, it is a good idea to consult with a few of your top contacts in the distribution network and get their input. Finally, when you have good news to share, remember that it is news. If you wait too long to produce the materials, you will have lost the news impact, and some of the effectiveness of the whole project. Following is a list of POS, or collateral materials, that can help support your wine sales, if implemented correctly.

- **Wine fact sheet:** These are the bare facts about the wine, organized in a way that lets everyone in the distribution network get a quick picture of what makes each wine unique. These should include everything from vineyard and winemaking information to positioning, appropriate food pairings, and a reproducible label.

- **Shelf talkers:** These are simply cards that appear on the shelves of retailers with more information about the wine. The information usually includes a top rating, but can also have tasting notes or wine and food suggestions. Some stores love these, while others aggressively prohibit them.

- **Table tents:** The on-premise version of the shelf talker is the table tent, a simple card that is placed on restaurant tables to encourage customers to order your wine. Most restaurants will expect some kind of special pricing allowance or volume discount in return for using your table tents.

- **Neckers:** If you can't get your sales team to put the shelf talkers up in retail stores, sometimes you can place the same information on a card that fits around the neck of the bottle. You can greatly increase the likelihood that these will make their way into the marketplace by putting them on the bottles at the winery, before the wine is shipped. However, that has increased labor costs, as well as logistical challenges.

- **Waiter cards:** A simplified version of the wine fact sheet, these are smaller, and fit into a shirt pocket, so that waiters can quickly and effectively represent the wines on the wine list.

- **Coupons:** Coupons are illegal for wine in many states, so be careful about how you use these. The classic theory behind coupons is simple: the coupons encourage consumer trial of the product. That trial then leads to brand loyalty. There is a major problem with this theory. That is that many people who use coupons only buy products offering coupons. You don't get brand loyalty; you simply attract coupon clippers. Since brand loyalty doesn't exist in the classic sense in the wine industry, coupons can't really deliver it. They are now usually used by wineries to offer a temporary price reduction to gain market share, with the hope that the price reduction doesn't imply a lower price point for the wine.

- **Case cards:** Formed to fit behind a case to draw attention to your wine, a case card can send a number of messages, from simple statements of quality or style to complicated promotions involving coupons, tear-off recipe pads, or sweepstakes programs. As with all POS, each store will have its own policy on these. Case cards are more complicated, expensive, and difficult to distribute than smaller elements of POS.

- **Floor stacks and end aisle displays:** These are the Holy Grail of merchandising programs, and reward retailers who buy in huge quantities. The displays themselves can range from complex installations with moving parts and life-sized figures of celebrities to a simple bold graphic on the shipping case that creates a large image when the cases are stacked. These displays are tremendously effective, as they carry the implied endorsement of the retailer, as well as some kind of price reduction on the product.

It is important to note that there are at least a hundred brands in the US market with wines that sell well enough to merit end aisle displays at major retailers. If the floor stacks are installed, the wine will sell. The real challenge for these wineries is to not convince consumers of the quality and value of their wines; it is to convince the retailer to install the floor stack in the beginning.

Dealer Loaders, Discounts, and Incentives

Wineries are often faced with the challenge of winning the attention and approval of large retail customers, and some offer a variety of gift merchandise, special displays, discounts, and incentives to win that battle. All of these are common, but bear in mind that many of them skirt the fringes of legality. In most states there are very specific limits to the kinds and value of gifts and incentives provided to retailers. Producers often avoid this concern by simply explaining that the gifts are not gifts, but display items that belong to the winery. When the winery fails to collect them at the end of the promotion, the retailer takes possession of the gift.

Coupons are illegal in some states, and national promotions often require that the promotions be available in a large number of states. Balancing these two issues can be a problem. Another area of confusion for some wineries is retailer advertising. Producers are not allowed to share funding for retail advertising. On the other hand, if a retailer agrees to purchase a large quantity of a producer's product, that volume purchase often qualifies the retailer to a significant price reduction. If that price reduction should be equal to one-half the amount of a major advertising buy on the part of the retailer, it would be dismissed as pure coincidence.

In every case, it is important for you to understand the exact legal issues involved in these marketing areas. Do not assume that what another producer or winery does is legal. It is far better to consult with your own legal team and make decisions based on clear thinking and long-term results. While the various departments that regulate these issues are usually overworked in the extreme, it is not safe to assume that your own program will not come under scrutiny.

In conclusion, you can be successful in sales and distribution management by following the tips and procedures outlined in this chapter. Make sure to do your homework, know your target audience, and then identify distributors who can help you reach that audience. Then you need to approach them with a win-win proposition that will help both parties meet their goals. From there on out, it is a daily relationship management process in which you both provide ongoing support and feedback to one another in an effort to jointly service your end consumers.

Direct shipping of wine to customers is one of the fastest growing sales avenues for wineries. The question is what components of direct wine sales are best for your winery? Chapter 11 examines four of the five major arenas of direct sales (the fifth, tasting rooms, is discussed in Chapter 12):

- Wine clubs/mailing lists

- E-commerce

- Telemarketing

- Special events

C H A P T E R 11

DIRECT WINE SALES: WINE CLUBS, E-COMMERCE AND OTHER VENUES

---

irect shipping of wine to customers is one of the fastest growing sales avenues for wineries. According to a recent report (MKF, 2004), consumer-direct wine sales is an increasingly critical source of profit, especially for smaller wineries producing less than 10,000 cases. Indeed, average revenue from direct sales rose 9%, contrasting with a 2% average growth in revenues through the three-tier system (MKF, 2004). Based on these numbers, it makes sense for every winery to launch a consumer-direct program as part of their overall marketing strategy.

The question is, what components of direct wine sales are best for your winery? Consumer-direct wine sales include five major areas: 1) wine clubs/mailing lists; 2) e-commerce; 3) telemarketing; 4) special events, and 5) tasting rooms. Some wineries only implement one or two of these components; others use all five and integrate them to enhance sales and brand awareness. (This chapter will explore the first four options, beginning with an overview of the pros/cons of direct wine sales. Tasting rooms are covered in a separate chapter.)

THE PROS AND CONS OF DIRECT WINE SALES

There are actually more good reasons to sell your wine directly to end-consumers, than there are reasons not to sell in this manner. However, there are several challenges to launching direct to consumer. Following is an explanation of the pros.

Why You Should Sell Your Wine Directly

The major reason to include consumer-direct as part of your marketing strategy has simply to do with margin. In bypassing the distributor and retailer channels and selling directly to end-consumers, you receive the extra 30–40% margins you would pay them. Of course, this has to be offset by the cost of your consumer-direct program, but in many cases, those costs are quite low—with the exception of a tasting room.

A second reason has to do with building brand awareness and loyalty with your customers. The more you can connect with them directly in a positive manner, the more they will remember your brand and perhaps become "brand ambassadors" for you—inviting other friends and colleagues to try your wine.

A third reason to sell direct is because many small wineries cannot get the interest of the big distributors in carrying their wine. With more than 5,300 wineries in the U.S. (Wine Business Monthly, 2006), and with many of them producing second and third labels, the competition is extreme, and will only get worse. Compound this with all of the international brands flooding the market—currently one in every four bottles of wine sold in the U.S. is from a foreign country (Wine Institute, 2004)—and it is no wonder that the distributors find their portfolios overflowing with too many wine brands. Even if you can secure a place in their portfolio, if you are a new or smaller winery without a track record of 90+ ratings from *Wine Spectator* or Robert Parker, the chances are that you will be lost in the shuffle. Therefore, a good consumer-direct program to help you supplement sales makes smart business sense. Just make sure not to undercut your distributors and retailers from a pricing perspective, but DO include some wines that are only sold through your consumer-direct program.

A fourth reason to establish a direct-to-consumer sales program is because the upfront costs are relatively low to establish a wine club, mailing list, e-commerce, or telemarketing program. Tasting rooms and special events can be more costly, but it also depends on the state in which you operate. In California, establishing a new tasting room can include many regulatory hurdles, not to mention the high cost of real estate. In other areas, however, where states are trying to encourage wine tourism, wineries can easily open a rustic tasting room in an old barn, or even in their kitchen with relatively little cost, and even receive potential tax relief from the state.

A final reason is because much positive progress has been made on the legal front for direct shipping legislation. In the last ten years, many states have opened up and allowed direct shipping, and currently twenty-six states have approved this (Wine Institute, 2003). With the Supreme Court examining this issue, it is possible that even more states will do so in the future. Plus there are consumer advocacy groups, such as Free the Grapes, that are bringing this to the attention of the public. With so many people making purchases over the internet—and the projected increase of this sales method in the future —the prognosis is good that consumers will begin demanding that borders open up to allow them to receive wine in their states as well. For updates on direct shipping legislation, see http://www.wine institute.org/shipwine/.

Cons of Direct Shipping

The major con at this point is the fact that small wineries cannot ship directly to all fifty states. This limits your markets, and often causes disappointment on the part of a new customer who is delighted with your wine and wants to join your Wine Club to receive monthly shipments. Instead they are told they cannot receive it, and their elation over your brand may dissipate. Encouraging them to ship to a relative or friend in an open state is an option, but it doesn't usually appease the disappointed customer.

A potential second con is if your direct shipping program is in conflict with your contracts with distributors and retailers. In most cases, a well-designed consumer-direct program should support the efforts of distributors and retailers. Indeed, you can include them in special events and wine club dinners you schedule in various cities to help boost their sales and outlets as well. However, if you undercut them in pricing, or establish programs that directly compete with theirs, this could be a problem which could potentially result in the termination of a previously positive relationship.

A final con is the cost of establishing and running a consumer-direct program. However, as mentioned earlier, this is usually not as costly as other forms of advertising—especially since the margins are so high. The only caveat is the establishment of a tasting room, which can be quite costly. Table 11. 1. lists all of the current pros/cons of direct shipping.

Table 11.1: Current Pros and Cons of Direct Shipping

Pros	Cons
• Higher Margins	• Currently cannot ship to all 50 states
• Build brand awareness and loyalty with customers—create "Brand Ambassadors"	• Potential conflict of interest with your distributors and retailers
• Relatively low entry costs to establish basic program	• Cost of implementing a state-of-the-art consumer-direct program
• Much positive progress on direct shipping legislation in the U.S.	

CREATING YOUR OWN WINE CLUB

If you are the owner of a small winery of less than 10,000 cases, and you have not yet established a wine club or mailing list, you are missing the boat! According to wine club expert Craig Root (2004), the profit margins from wine clubs are the highest of direct sales and can range up to 50%.

There are two types of wine clubs (Penn, 2003; Berglund, 2003). Ideally, wineries should implement both styles of wine club into their direct-to-consumer program. They are as follows:

1. **Automatic Wine Club**: Requires that a customer give the winery a credit card number and agree to periodic wine shipments. Generally, the customer gets a discount on the wine they receive. The relationship is maintained by the winery until the customer voluntarily terminates it by requesting to cancel their wine club membership.

2. **Offering Club**: Does not require that the customer provide the winery with a credit card or agree to a scheduled shipment. Instead the customer agrees to have their name on a mailing list that provides them with a chance to buy various products "a la carte."

The Offering Club is very similar to a mailing list, and in some wineries, they are the same thing. Also, in some situations, customers may also be offered a special discount on the wine—just as they are in an Automatic Wine Club. However, there are other wineries—usually high-end luxury wineries which sell all of their wine on allocation—which use mailing lists as a means to invite customers to purchase a limited number of highly sought-after bottles or cases. In some cases, customers have to wait several years to even be allowed on the mailing list and have an opportunity to purchase the wine. Cult brands from wineries such as Screaming Eagle, Viadar, and Chateau Montelena are fortunate enough to use this method.

Establishing a Continuity Wine Club

In creating or revamping your wine club, there are certain steps which are useful to follow. These are outlined below:

1. **Create your wine club strategy and allocation**: A wine club should be part of your overall marketing and sales strategy for your winery. Therefore, it should be described in this strategy, with specific information on the purpose of the wine club, the type of wine club, and the percentage of wine you intend to sell through this channel. For example, a small winery in Virginia sells 100% of their wine direct to consumers, with 40% sold through tasting rooms and special events, 10% through e-commerce, and the remaining 50% through wine clubs.

2. **Conduct a wine club competitive analysis**: This is simply obtaining information on your competitor's wine clubs. You can do this by examining their wine club on their website or by obtaining a copy of their wine club literature. At a minimum, you should review at least ten other wine clubs to see what types of discounts, the number of shipments, special benefits, and other components they are offering. In a recent wine club research study of 66 Napa and Sonoma wine clubs (Teaff, Thach & Olsen, 2004), it was discovered that 52% of the wineries did quarterly shipments, and 24% shipped every two months, reducing their shipping costs respectively. Furthermore, 67% charged $75 or less per shipment, with the average being $40. The most common number of bottles per shipment was two, at 62% of the sample. Conducting a similar analysis of your competitors will provide you with information that is specific to your niche, and allow you to establish a structure that is competitive and provides extra incentives to join.

3. **Consider hiring a wine club consultant:** It may be worth the time to hire an expert to assist you in designing your wine club. If you can't afford them full time, then perhaps just purchase a couple of hours of their time in the beginning to help you establish your strategy and discuss design options.

4. **Determine resource allocations (hire wine club manager or outsource):** It is important to recognize that running a wine club can be a lot of work. If possible, it is useful to involve your wine club manager in the design of the club. You may also elect to outsource the wine club to one of several companies that are now providing this type of service, including tracking customers, credit card transactions, warehousing, shipping, handling customer complaints, cancellations, and advertising special events to support the club.

   Though most wine club shipments occur at a specific time of the month, most wine club managers report that they spend much of their time on the phone with customers. Many phone calls involve customers calling about missing or late shipments, or calling to order additional wine. If you link special events to your wine club, they may call to register, or to schedule a special tour of your winery with friends they plan to bring. It is important to have someone identified who can handle all of these customer service issues as well as all of the logistics and tracking that go into wine club management. Finally, this person should be good at resolving complaints, and attempting to institute loyalty programs so that customers stay in your wine club.

5. **Use the wine club design checklist:** Figure 11.1 below illustrates the three major design components for wine clubs.

The first category is **Essentials,** and describes the structure of your club including the price, frequency of shipment, and number of bottles per shipment. You may also elect to include multiple club levels—such as a basic club for $39.99, where members receive two bottles every two months, as well as a luxury level for $75, where members receive two luxury wines every two months. Some wineries have as many as six levels! If you are just starting out, however, it is recommended that you start with no more than two levels, because the logistics of shipping and keeping track can be quite complicated.

A key aspect of the Essential category is brand promotion. Make sure you include your logo, photographs, stories, and other important aspects of your brand that set you apart from your competitors. Ideally your logo should be listed on every page of your wine club brochure and website.

Figure 11.1: The Wine Club Design Checklist

THE WINE CLUB DESIGN CHECKLIST

Reprinted with Permission: Teaff, B., Thach, L.& Olsen, J. (2004) Sonoma State University Wine Business Program

Essentials (6)	Member Benefits (17)	Terms & Condition (9)
Price	Discounts	Age requirement
Frequency	Products to included with the shipment	Adult signature
Number of Bottles per shipment	Access to wine	Commitment requirement
Club levels	Special Events	Cancellation policy
Membership AND what it means to be a member!	Winery correspondence	Modification policy
BRAND Promotion	Complimentary tasting and tours	Shipping address
	VIP status for members	Billing address
	Personal service	Pick-up options
	Winery affiliated services	Additional charges
	Gift memberships	
	Incentives	
	Members ability to customize the club	
	Optional shipments	
	Limited membership?	
	Purchase limitations?	
	Club membership without regular shipments	
	Other benefits?	

The **Member Benefits** portion of your wine club is what can set you apart from your competitors. It can make your wine club the one that people want to stay in and encourage their friends to join. The most common benefit is to provide a 20% discount on wine purchases; 10-20% discounts on wine merchandise, and up to 30% discount on reorders from the wine club shipment (Teaff, Thach & Olsen, 2004). Beyond the discounts, which are expected, are many special benefits such as invitations to events, parties, and celebrations; yearly anniversary gifts for staying in the club; VIP services and status when visiting the winery, and many other unique ideas. For example, one winery in Sonoma County has a wine club that sponsors a free party once a quarter for all of their wine club members. The party includes free wine, free appetizers, a band, and dancing. When interviewed, many of the wine club members stated that they stayed in the club because of the fun parties. The winery also allows them to pick up their quarterly shipment at the party, which saves them money if they are local members, and allows members to purchase additional wine and non-wine merchandise at a discount while at the party.

The third component, **Terms & Conditions**, is very important in designing a wine club, because it primarily deals with the legal contract and financial arrangements of the club. It is important to have your lawyer review this portion of your wine club to make sure you are in legal compliance. You must insure that wine is not sold or shipped to anyone under 21 years of age in the U.S. You also need to make certain that an adult signature is received before the wine can be left at a customer's home or business. In addition, you want to insure you have the legal right to charge their credit card on a monthly basis, and you should include information on how people can cancel. You may elect to charge a cancellation fee, and/or require that people stay in the club for a period of time, such as 6 months. However, most winery owners report that it is very difficult to enforce these types of rules, and often upsets the customer more than it is worth.

A very critical component of this section is notifying customers of the states to which you are legally allowed to ship. It is currently against the law to ship wine directly to customers in 24 states, though this may change in the near future. For customers who complain about this, encourage them to contact Free the Grapes and/or work with their local legislators.

6. **Print and start small:** In almost every case, you will need to pay for a printed brochure describing your wine club, but ideally you will also have a copy on your website. You can launch a wine club from an existing mailing list, add it to your website, or promote out of your tasting room or at special events. You may even be able to ask local business partners, such as hotels, restaurants, and tourism bureaus to stock your wine club brochures for customers. It is recommended to begin a slow and small launch so that you have time to get some of the kinks out of the system. Recognize that you will have some problems in the beginning, even if it is only with your shipping company, or credit card rejections. Be patient and give yourself time to improve; then expand the club.

7. **Treasure and protect your database:** As more customers join your wine club, your database will increase in size. It is important to treat your database with the respect it deserves, because it is a treasure source of potential increased revenue. Protect the privacy of your customers and insure the confidentiality of their credit cards. Do not sell or lend

the database to others without your customers' permission. If you find someone wants to cancel, telephone them personally and find out why. If there is anything you can do to keep them as a loyal and happy customer, do so. If not, wish them well, and let them know they are always welcome to visit your winery at any time in the future. Remember, providing long-term customer loyalty gifts or deeper discounts for longevity is a great way to keep customers.

Do not overwhelm your customers with email advertisements and announcements, but stay in touch with them online or in print at least once a month. You can send a short newsletter, recipes, special promotion information, or invitations to events. Allow them to purchase gift memberships for family and friends, and give them a discount or gift if they get someone else to join your club.

If you find someone's credit card has been rejected or has expired, instead of deleting them from your database, call them first and politely ask them for their new credit card. Tell them how much you enjoy having them as a customer, and invite them to visit again. Treasure your customer database, and if you use it effectively, it will only grow in size and bring rich rewards for years ahead.

Establishing a Mailing List or Offering Wine Club

In addition to a Continuity Wine Club, it is recommended that you also implement a mailing list or an Offering Wine Club. As mentioned previously, these do not require that customers give you their credit cards and agree to regular shipments. Instead, they sign up to be on your mailing list or Offering Wine Club. To do this, you can have them complete a card in your tasting room, online, or in a brochure. Once you receive their information, you then have permission to send them your quarterly or monthly newsletter with exciting information on your wine, new releases, special events, discounts, etc.

The reason you want to implement both types of wine clubs, is that not all customers are willing to give their credit card and sign up for the Continuity Club. Therefore, your back-up option is to ask the question, "Would you like to be on our mailing list?" One important caution, however, is that you do not give your mailing list customers equal or better deals than your Continuity Wine Club customers. You can offer specials and some discounts to the mailing list, but the Continuity Club discounts should be deeper, and also include additional benefits.

You may choose, however, to begin with just a mailing list. This is a good way to "get your feet wet," before launching a Continuity Wine Club. If this is the case, then you can offer more discounts, because you are not competing with your traditional wine club.

If your winery is highly allocated you may want to offer a mailing list only. In this case, your "mailing list" is really an "offering wine club," in which members must sign up and then are offered the opportunity to purchase wine several times during the year. Some of the high-end luxury wineries will actually kick customers off the list if they do not purchase wine each year. This is because they have one and two-year "wait lists" for other customers to get on the mailing list and be allowed to purchase wine. In most cases, consumers are also limited to purchases of two to six bottles. This is a highly sought-after type of business model, but one which is only available to a few select wineries that have been fortunate enough to receive high praise and scores from wine critics.

A final implementation concept on the Offering Wine Club is represented by the second level wine club of Chateau St. Jean. Their first level wine club, Club St. Jean, is a traditional Continuity Club, but they also offer a second level club called the Vineyard Room Society, which is limited to 300 members. Once it is full, it is closed to new members, and customers are added to a wait list. However, this highly sought-after second level is also a Continuity Wine Club, because customers are required to give their credit card and agree to quarterly shipments of wine as well as pay a $200 annual fee. This suggests that there are various models wineries can use in implementing wine clubs.

DIRECT SALES THROUGH E-COMMERCE

E-commerce is a growing area in direct wine sales. Since 2002, internet wine sales have increased by 64% (MKF, 2004), and wineries have reported that they expect to see increased revenues from this channel in the future (Thach & Eaton, 2001). With more than 75% of all Americans online (Nielsen NetRatings, 2004), and worldwide commercial transactions estimated to be at $6 trillion in 2004 (World Intellectual Property Organization, 2002), ignoring direct sales via the internet would be a mistake for the wine industry. However, as previously stated, the major challenge to wine e-commerce is the current regulations on interstate shipping. As these improve, it is expected that e-commerce will grow even further.

Wine E-Commerce Definition and Methods

Wine e-commerce is selling wine via the internet. This is done through a winery's own website, or the website of other online wine retailers, such as www.k&L.com or www.wine.com. This section focuses on wine sold through a winery's website; done in two major ways.

Invited customers: With this method, the winery sends out emails to customers—usually those on its wine club, mailing list, or purchased list—advising them of wine that is available to purchase on the internet. This may be a new release, or a special promotion. A link is provided, and customers can go directly to the website to purchase wine and have it shipped to their homes. The winery may also elect to outsource this function to a professional wine e-commerce group which will manage the email promotions and handle sales and shipping.

Customer initiated: Though less frequent, some customers will seek out the winery's website on their own to purchase wine. This is often spurred by a great review of the wine or some other publicity which drives customers to the website.

Setting Up Your Website—Three Levels

When setting up any website, it is important to keep several aspects in mind. The first is that your website should be professionally designed and reflect all of the care and time you have put into your winemaking and labels. Some wine critics actually go to a winery's website to gather information, before writing a critique; therefore, you want your website to reflect the quality of your wine. Just because your teenager daughter learned how to create a website in high school doesn't mean she should design your professional winery website. Another important aspect of a website is the domain name. Ideally the domain address will be the same name as your winery, but if this is not possible, attempt to keep it similar. Customers will use search engines, such as Google, to find your winery, and you will want them to be able to easily locate your website. Finally, once you have a website—even if it is a simple single-page one—it is critical that you check your email at least once a day, just in case customers want to contact you by this method.

If you are just starting out, it may not be financially feasible to establish a sophisticated website with shopping basket, credit card transaction, and other e-commerce functions. The good news is that you don't have to start at this high level. There are actually three levels of websites.

Level one—the information page: At a minimum, wineries should establish a simple one-page informational website providing information about the wine, winery, directions, contact information, and an email address. In this way, customers at least have contact information for the winery, and the winery has internet presence.

When one small winery owner in Napa set up a simple one-page website such as this, he found that customers rarely contacted him in this way. Most preferred to telephone. However, when he received a great review in a top wine magazine, he found he was deluged with email requests to purchase his wine. He then had to create an email order form, and asked buyers to fax it in with their credit card number and address.

Level two—the online brochure: Once your informational website is up and operating, you can consider upgrading to the next level, which is referred to as an online brochure website. This has multiple pages and much more information on your wines, viticulture practices, awards, press releases, etc., but does not include e-commerce options.

Level three—the e-commerce site: The third and most expensive level of website is a professionally designed e-commerce website. When establishing this type of website, make sure you hire a skilled web designer with wine industry web experience who knows how to set up shopping carts for wine sales. Due to regulatory issues and interstate shipping laws, wine e-commerce sites are not as easy to design as e-commerce sites for other products. Also, once you advance to this level of e-commerce, you will need to hire someone to manage this function, or outsource it.

Figure 11.2: Web Pages From L'Ecole No. 41 Winery in Walla Walla, Washington. Website Designed by ZangoCreative

In terms of how to design the e-commerce site, there are many experts you can consult who will advise on the latest advances in technology. Providing a comprehensive manual on e-commerce web design is beyond the scope of this book, but with wine e-commerce, there are a few basic guidelines:

- Place your "Purchase Wine" link prominently on the home page.
- Provide descriptions, prices, and, ideally, photos of your wine bottle and label.
- Provide a mechanism to insure the Buyer is 21 years of age or older.
- Provide a mechanism to verify you can ship to the state and address, and a reminder that an adult signature is required to receive the wine.
- Provide online credit card security protection.
- Invite the buyer to sign up for your newsletter and/or mailing list, using a check box.
- Provide an emailed receipt verifying you received their order, which gives estimated shipping time, and contact information should they need to email or call you. Include a nice thank you.
- Consider giving them an online coupon for a discount on their next e-commerce order, and/or a coupon for a free tasting the next time they visit your winery.

Tracking and Monitoring E-Commerce Sales

Anytime you establish a new sales channel, you will want to track and measure your results. Begin by setting some goals on the percentage of revenue you hope to achieve through e-commerce in comparison with your complete sales and marketing plan. Then set up a system whereby you can examine monthly sales data; analyze website hits after an online promotion email has been sent; review abandonment rate of online shopping carts (which is an indicator of the perceived risk of buying at your site); and gather customer demographics if possible. There may be other metrics you will want to track as well, but the main point is to analyze the data and make continuous improvements to increase the profitability of your e-commerce channel.

Related to this is database management and analysis. As with your wine club, you will want to analyze your database of online customers to understand their backgrounds and buying habits. You may find that most of your online customers are also your wine club members, or maybe not. You may find you have many online customers from certain states or regions, and that specific varietals or brands are selling better with different customer segments. Your online database is a rich source of sales data and consumer behavior regarding your wine. Make sure you utilize it to its fullest extent.

TELEMARKETING SALES OF WINE

Though used less frequently now in light of new laws against unsolicited telemarketing, some wineries still use telemarketing to reach their customers and inform them about special wine releases and promotions. Many of these wineries have highly sought-after wines that are allocated, so the calls are primarily made to qualified customers so that they can place orders when the wine becomes available. Haffner and Windsor wineries in Sonoma Country are two wineries that sell most of their wine through telephone marketing.

Wine club customers often appreciate phone calls from the winery to notify them of special events, promotions, or that their wine shipment is available to pick up at the winery (if they are local customers). Finally, if the credit card of a wine club member is expiring, a more personal method to reach the customer is by telephone. During the call, the winery staff person can not only thank the customer for being a member and encourage them to stay, but also inform them of new specials for sale.

SPECIAL EVENTS

Hosting special events for customers is the fifth major direct sales method used by wineries. It is a great way to build brand awareness and create lasting customer relationships by providing them with a special experience they will remember long after the event.

Special events most often take place at the winery. However many wineries also participate in trade fairs, festivals and other events located off premises as a way to promote their wines. The range of events that wineries stage is quite broad, as event planners are continually coming up with creative themes and ideas to bring in new customers. Mardi Gras parties, Italian festivals and cuisines of all types provide popular themes for special events. Examples include the Robert Mondavi Winery summer concert series; classic car event at Valley of the Moon Winery in Sonoma, and the annual crab and wine festival in Mendocino County.

Though special events can be a lot of fun for customers, they are work intensive and costly for the winery. Though professional events planners can organize and even advertise the whole affair, the costs can add up. It is prudent to develop a budget and estimate revenue from the special event. In some cases, just breaking even may be the goal, because the goodwill, brand awareness, and publicity received may be considered to be enough. However, charging a nominal fee for visitors to attend the special event is a good idea, and will help to insure you attract visitors who are more serious about your wine and want to be there.

During the special event, make sure you gather information about your visitors so you can follow up with them at a later date. Consider asking them to drop their business cards in a bowl for a raffle prize, or ask them to sign up in advance or at the door. Afterwards, follow up with a nice thank you card and a special discount on wine or merchandise because they attended the event.

Chapter References

"Active Internet users by country." *Nielsen Net Ratings (2004)*. Available at: http://www.nielsen-netratings.com/news.jsp.

Berglund, L. "Is your wine club healthy?" *Wine Business Monthly, 10*(6). 2003.

"Direct Sales Survey Report—2004." *MKF Research Monthly*. Oct. 2004.

"E-Commerce: The Case of Online Wine Sales and Direct Shipment." Wine Institute. 2003. Available at: www.wineinstitute.org.

"Intellectual property on the Internet: a survey of issues." World Intellectual Property Organization (WIPO). 2002.

Olsen, J., Eaton, C. & Getz, D. "Direct Wine Sales," in Thach, L. & Matz, T. (eds) *Wine: A Global Business*. NY: Miranda Press. 2004.

"Number of U.S. Wineries Tops 5,300." *Wine Business Monthly*, Volume XIII Number 2, Feb. 15, 2006. http://winebusiness.com/html/MonthlyArticle.cfm?dataid=36590.

Penn, C. "Tasting room sales 101." *Wine Business Monthly, 10*(4), 2003. Ppg.17-18.

Root, C. "Direct to Consumer Workshop." Presentation made at Wine Institute Workshop, Nov. 25, 2004. Santa Rosa, CA.

Teaff, B., Thach, L., & Olsen, J. "Designing Effective Wine Clubs." Presentation made at Wine Institute Workshop, Nov. 25, 2004. Santa Rosa, CA.

Thach, L. and Eaton. "C.E-commerce adoption in the wine industry." *Wine Business Monthly* 8 (5), 2004. Pp.1-4.

"U.S. wine exports up 17% in revenues in 2003, volume jumps 29%." Wine Institute. 2004. Available at: http://www.wineinstitute.org/communications/statistics/exports03.htm.

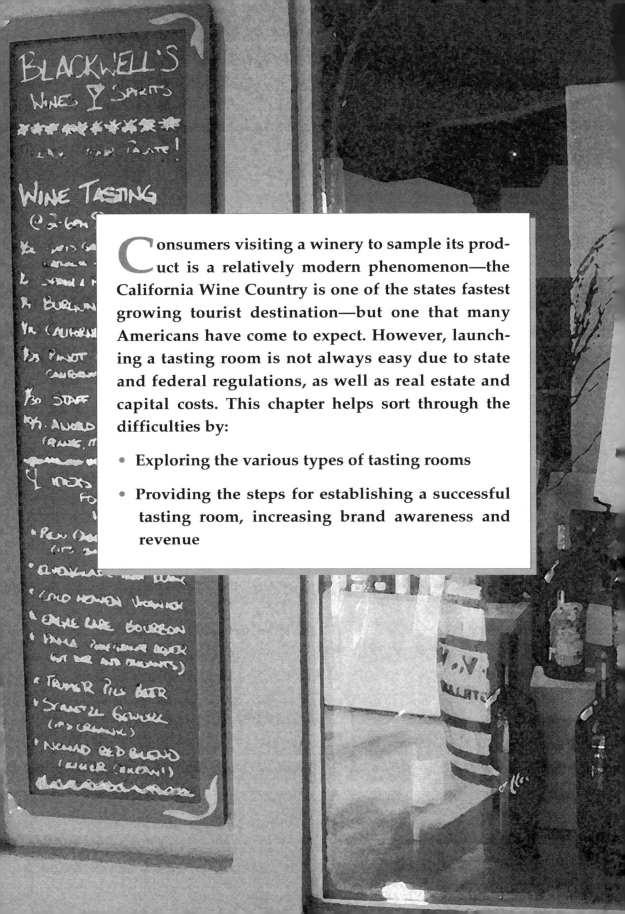

Consumers visiting a winery to sample its product is a relatively modern phenomenon—the California Wine Country is one of the states fastest growing tourist destination—but one that many Americans have come to expect. However, launching a tasting room is not always easy due to state and federal regulations, as well as real estate and capital costs. This chapter helps sort through the difficulties by:

- Exploring the various types of tasting rooms

- Providing the steps for establishing a successful tasting room, increasing brand awareness and revenue

CHAPTER 12

ESTABLISHING A TASTING ROOM

T he dream of many small winery owners is to have a tasting room where visitors from around the world can stop by to taste the wine and make purchases. Indeed, for many small wineries outside of California, New York, Washington, and Oregon, a tasting room is one of the major mechanisms for wine purchases. Some small wineries sell 80–100% of their wine from the tasting room (Teaff et. al., 2004).

However, launching a tasting room is not always easy, due to state and federal regulations, as well as real estate and capital costs. Then, once it is open, there is always the issue of driving customers to the tasting room, and working with regional tourism boards to help make this happen. Therefore, this chapter begins with an exploration of the various types of tasting rooms, and then provides steps you should consider if you want to establish a successful tasting room that not only increases your brand awareness, but brings in sales revenues.

VARIATIONS UPON A TASTING ROOM

If you are just starting out as a winery, and do not have the funds and/ or the regulatory clearance to build a tasting room, there are three options available to you for consideration. These can be part of your permanent marketing strategy, or a step on the path to opening your own tasting room.

The By-Appointment-Only Tasting Room

If you are not permitted to have a tasting room on your winery property, you can check with your local permit office to see if you can do tastings at your winery or other approved facility by appointment only. With this model, the customer must contact you in advance via email, telephone, or in writing, to schedule a time to visit and taste your wine. This is a useful model, because you have time to prepare for the customer, can learn about their needs through advance questioning, and can establish a positive personal relationship with them when they visit.

This model is also used by some of the higher-end wineries to segment their customers. For example, Caymus Winery in Napa Valley previously had an open tasting room, but switched to a by-appointment-only model and has been able to focus more on the serious types of customers who take the time to seek them out. The key to using this method is to insure that you have adequate advertising in local wine tourism papers, on your internet site, mailing list, wine club, with your distributor, and other methods to insure that customers are able to find the information that allows them to schedule appointments with you.

An added side benefit of this option is that the customers spend private time with you as the winery owner and, if impressed by your product, they are more apt to purchase. Generally this option does not include a tasting fee, but in some cases, customers are still asked to pay $5 to $10 to taste, which may include a private tour of the facilities.

The Co-op Tasting Room

This model is frequently used by small family wineries in wine tourism areas. It involves finding a group of fellow vintners who want to establish a cooperative winery tasting room. All members of the co-op agree to help pay the costs of running the tasting room, including permits, leases, insurance, taxes, staffing costs, and other financial considerations. Of course, it also requires that each winery provide enough wine to be tasted, as well as supporting literature, and potential wine related merchandise.

An excellent example of a co-op tasting room is the Family Wineries Tasting Room in Sonoma County on Highway 12 near Kenwood. A group of 5 to 7 wineries has established the tasting room, and share the staffing responsibilities. When it is one member's turn to run the tasting room, they make sure to learn about the other members' wines so they can describe them just as well as their own wines. In this tasting room, there is currently no tasting fee, and visitors can taste up to 30 wonderful wines at no charge. The small, intimate, and relaxed atmosphere, and the chance to talk with a small family winery member, encourages visitors to make purchases.

The downsides of a co-op tasting room are potential partner disputes, potential brand confusion to customers, and the time and cost responsibilities that come with running a tasting room. However, it is great experience before launching a new tasting room on your own.

The Virtual Winery Tasting Room

This concept is used by many start-up wineries, and is also used by some established wineries on a full-time basis, such as Patz & Hall, based in Napa, California. It includes making and branding a wine, but not having a tasting room facility of any type available to taste or sell the wine. The wine may be sold through multiple channels, such as the internet, mailing lists, the distributor/retailer channel, or special events. In order to taste the wine, customers are invited to visit the winery's booth at a special event. Examples may include events sponsored by a local winery association, tourism group, hotel, trade show, or other venue.

TEN STEPS TO CONSIDER
WHEN ESTABLISHING A TASTING ROOM

So you've decided to launch your own tasting room, or you currently have a tasting room, but want to increase sales. Table 12.1 illustrates a checklist of ten important steps to consider for both objectives. The following section provides more detail on how to implement each of the ten steps.

Table 12.1: Checklist for Ten Steps to Establish a Tasting Room

1. Identify Your Tasting Room Strategy
2. Research Regulatory Issues
3. Analyze the Competition and Differentiate Yourself
4. Design With Strategy in Mind ✔ Insure your signage and grounds are well-kept ✔ Design your tasting room to support your brand ✔ Determine your merchandising strategy ✔ Determine if a restaurant, weddings, picnic grounds are part of your design
5. Determine Your Tasting Pours and Pricing
6. Hire, Train, and Incentivize Your Staff
7. Establish a Professional Sales Environment ✔ Greet all customers within 30 seconds of entering the tasting room ✔ Engage in open-ended conversation with customers ✔ Welcome customers who do not drink ✔ Encourage visitors to linger with tours, picnic grounds, etc. ✔ Ask for the sale
8. Create Protocol for VIP Visitors
9. Invest in State-of-the-Art Sales and Inventory Control Systems
10. Get Involved in Your Local Community and Tourism Efforts

1. Identify Your Tasting Room Strategy

What is the purpose of your tasting room? Is it only to extend your brand and be a public relations vehicle, or do you want to sell wine in a serious manner from the tasting room? Though it may seem obvious that you want to do both, there are still many wineries—and some quite large—that only consider the tasting room as a brand awareness vehicle and do not expect much in sales. From a wine marketing perspective, however, this viewpoint is outdated. If you do not expect to generate decent sales from your tasting room, then perhaps it is not a good marketing channel for you, and you should consider investing money elsewhere—such as in enhancing distributor relationships or special events. The point is to become clear on the purpose of your tasting room, because it drives your tasting room strategy and impacts how you design, staff, train, and manage the tasting room. Remember the goal is to sell wine, and the best souvenir from a tasting room is a bottle of wine.

2. Research Regulatory Issues

Make an appointment with your local planning board, permit office, and other regulatory offices to make sure you understand all of the issues involved in establishing a tasting room. You may want to consider hiring a tasting room consultant to help you with this process, and/or consult your lawyer. Though permits and other regulatory issues differ by state, some you will have to consider are: permit to taste and sell wine from a tasting room; zoning issues, road access and parking spaces; noise issues with neighbors; disabled access and restrooms; types of merchandise allowed for sale; sanitary issues with any food you are offering; permits to hold special events, such as weddings; and waste disposal, utilities, taxes, etc.

In some areas of the country where there are already hundreds of tasting rooms, such as Napa and Sonoma, it is more difficult to obtain tasting room permits and licenses. In such cases, it may be easier to purchase an existing tasting room and re-brand it.

3. Analyze the Competition and Differentiate

As always, you want to know what your competitor wineries are doing. Visit the tasting rooms in your area and observe how they are designed and managed. Once you have this information, make sure you conceptualize a tasting room design and style that is different—something that sets you apart from the others in a positive way and highlights your brand. For example, if you are in an area where everyone has rustic tasting rooms in old barns, and you are selling Italian varietals, perhaps you design your tasting room to resemble an Italian villa. Or perhaps you are in a tourist destination that caters to golfers and you have created a wine brand and label featuring this sport; then you may want to design and style your tasting room with golf in mind. You could use architecture that resembles a golf club-house, include a small putting green, and insure you have plenty of golfing merchandise in your tasting room to complement your wine.

4. Design With Strategy in Mind

Once you are clear on strategy and regulations, and know how to differentiate yourself from the competition, you can begin designing your tasting room. There are a few simple elements that will assist with both brand awareness and sales.

Insure your signage and grounds are well-kept. Ideally customers should be able to see your tasting room sign ideally at least ten seconds before your entrance. If possible, consider using advance signage and advertising to let visitors know your tasting room is coming up. The grounds should be clean, with clear signs for parking, tasting rooms, and restrooms.

Design your tasting room to support your brand. Research has shown that for brand awareness, your tasting room does not have to be fancy, such as a French chateau design; it just needs to be clean, accessible, friendly, and support whatever brand image you are attempting to project (Olsen & Thach, 2005). Ideally the front door should be wide enough for two people to enter. If possible, eliminate stairs, or you will have to install a ramp. When customers enter the tasting room, they should see your brand-supporting merchandise first, with the tasting bar in the back. This way they have to pass through the merchandise before approaching the bar.

The tasting bar should be designed to be large enough to accommodate guests on crowded days. There should be enough room in front of the bar so that guests can linger, but if you find you have a very crowded day, there should be a second tasting area or room where visitors can go. This can be part of your winery, or an outdoor area where people can continue tasting.

Locate your cash registers near the door, so that visitors have to pass by the cash register when they leave. This not only cuts down on theft because you have a staff member near the door, but it is also a subtle reminder that visitors should purchase something. In addition, make sure you have enough cash registers to handle your visitor flow, so people don't have to wait in long lines. Don't forget to include small displays of enticing merchandise near the cash register, such as corkscrews, magnets, chocolates or other small brand-related items for people to pick up as a last minute temptation.

Determine your merchandising strategy. It is not necessary to sell other merchandise in your tasting room, except for your wine and potentially some wine serving implements, such as corkscrews, decanters, glasses, etc. However, if you discover or expect many visitors who do not want to taste wine, such as designated drivers, spouses, partners, children, etc., then you may want to have brand-supporting merchandise. These visitors are looking for something to occupy their time when they visit a tasting room, and merchandise can assist in this and also provide additional revenue to your tasting room. Some wineries achieve 10 to 30% of their tasting room revenues from merchandise alone.

If you do choose to sell other merchandise, make sure it is tastefully arranged and supports your brand image. For example, if you are focusing on French Bordeaux-style wines, you may want to have pottery from France, but not Italy. Be consistent in your imaging. Also, make sure merchandise is restocked as needed, dusted, and maintained. If you include food items such as chocolate, nuts, mustards, olive oils, etc., insure that they are fresh and up to date. You may want to consider hiring a professional buyer to purchase merchandise that is unique and supports your brand. Be careful about trying to sell the same type of merchandise that is sold at other wineries. Yours should be different. Some wineries, such as Sebastiani in Sonoma, have such extensive and well laid out merchandise in their tasting rooms, that they are considered to be a major shopping destination for the holidays.

Figure 12. 2: Sebastiani Tasting Room, Sonoma, California

A final caveat on tasting room merchandise is to be careful with pricing. Customers will often use the price of basic items such as t-shirts and cork-pullers to judge the winery as a whole. Since many tasting rooms have these basic items for sale, customers often benchmark tasting rooms by their pricing on these items. A winery that charges an extra $1 for the cork pullers may find that customers notice that....and not in a good way.

Determine if a restaurant, weddings, picnic grounds are part of your design. This issue is often determined by the zoning laws in your state and county. Depending on where your tasting room is located, you may be able to open a restaurant, host weddings, and include a picnic area for visitors—which might suggest that you have a deli to sell picnic food. The first step here is to check on your zoning and other regulations, and then decide if this should be part of your overall strategy. Keep in mind that each of these activities involves much more work and staff. You may decide to consider this at a later date, and in the beginning focus only on opening a tasting room. The advantage of including any of these extras as part of your overall winery tasting room is potential increased revenues, as well as other reasons for customers to seek you out. For example, the wedding business at a winery can be quite lucrative, but may require that you hire a wedding planner. Specific tactics on how to establish a restaurant, picnic grounds, wedding or other special venues are not in the scope of this book, but should be considered as options in your overall tasting room design strategy.

5. Determine Your Tasting Pours and Pricing

This decision is linked directly to your strategy and competitor analysis. Some wineries elect to allow visitors to taste all of their wines at no charge. Others choose to provide two to four complimentary tastes, and then charge for additional tastes—basing the price on the retail cost of the wine. For example, reserve wine might be $2 per taste, whereas a library or late harvest might be $5 per taste. You may also elect to organize your wine by flights, and let customers select a red reserve flight which includes four tastes for $10, or something similar. Some wineries charge a flat tasting fee and allow visitors to keep the glass and/or apply the fee to a purchase.

Whatever your decision in this area, it should be driven by your overall direct sales strategy as well as by what your competitors are doing. If everyone else is charging for tasting and you are not, you may well become the winery that is known for free wine and become a target for party drinkers with no intent to purchase. However, if you are the only winery in a wine-trail region to charge for tastings, you may receive fewer visitors. On the other hand, the visitors you receive may be more serious, with intentions to purchase. Also, if you are in the luxury price segment—with all of your wine priced at more than $25 per bottle, and with limited inventory—you may have no choice but to charge for your tastings.

One tactic that seems to work especially well is to charge a nominal fee for tastings, but to apply the tasting fee to the purchase of wine. This not only eliminates the non-serious taster, but encourages purchases of your wine, which can lead to increased brand awareness when the wine is taken home to be shared at a dinner with friends and family. The downside of charging for tasting fees is the administrative issues of collecting the tasting fee, and then having to reimburse at the time of purchase. An effective accounting system and supporting cash register models are required to insure this process works smoothly.

6. Hire, Train and Reward Your Staff

In the U.S., the majority of tasting room staff are part-time employees who are paid minimum wage or a little above (Thach & Olsen, 2003). This is unfortunate, because research has shown that their jobs are critical to tasting room sales, and there is a direct correlation between their friendliness and positive brand recognition (Olsen & Thach, 2005). Simply stated, customers who visit a tasting room and have a positive interaction with the tasting room staff are more apt to make positive comments about the winery and its brand after the visit, and are more apt to purchase the wine. Therefore, **hiring the best tasting room employees** is crucial to your success.

It turns out that **wine knowledge** alone is not enough to insure good customer service. Indeed, sometimes a long-winded lecture on the viticultural background of a specific wine can be a huge turn-off to customers. It is for this reason that wineries should first hire tasting room staff for their **friendly demeanor and positive attitude**. This is a similar strategy used by Southwest Airlines and Disney, because they realize that having enthusiastic employees who are "always on" is more important, in the long run, than having someone who knows everything about the product. Ideally, you want to hire employees who are both positive and have good wine knowledge, but keep in mind you can always train them on your viticulture and enology techniques. It is not always possible to train people to have a friendly, upbeat attitude.

If you are the winery owner, make sure you spend one day a month behind the tasting room bar waiting on customers. You can then see how exhausting it is to keep a smile on your face, pour wine for the 37th customer, and engage in the same conversation about the wine. Therefore, make sure you hire the right people the first time, and train them well. This includes the following two areas:

Insure responsible drinking: Make sure to train your staff on how to promote responsible drinking, as well as how to deal effectively with visitors who may have imbibed too much. Federal law dictates that it is a crime to serve someone who is intoxicated, so your tasting room staff must know how to politely cut someone off, without offending them or other customers. They should also learn how to effectively I.D. people, as well as how to deal with obnoxious visitors. Most local police offices or state liquor boards provide free training on these types of issues. Penalties for serving alcohol to under-age or intoxicated persons can range from a small or large fine, to prison terms, and/or loss of winery license, which could result in the winery and tasting room being shut down.

Incent and motivate your staff: If possible, attempt to pay your tasting room staff a decent wage so they can continue to live in a respectable way within the community. If they are part-time, make sure that they receive extra incentives such as wine and merchandise discounts. Many wine tourist areas develop a reciprocal tasting policy, so that all tasting room employees can taste for free at other local wineries. This can be a nice incentive. Also, many part-time tasting room employees want to work in tasting rooms because they love wine and want to learn more about it. Another positive benefit is continuing wine education, which can be a simple as in-depth discussions with your winemaker or a chance to spend some time in the vineyard.

Some wineries have established commission structures for tasting room employees, which provide for some type of bonus based on the amount of wine sold. This can be an individual commission, a team commission, or both. Sales goals for both wine and merchandise can be set for the day, week, and/or month. For example, a medium-sized winery in Washington State sets a daily revenue goal. If the employees achieve it, they each get to take a bottle of wine home for the day. They also set a monthly revenue goal, and if that is achieved, employees receive a bonus in their paychecks. Another tasting room in Sonoma County sets an annual revenue goal. If this is achieved, the company pays for the whole tasting room team to go on a group vacation and bring a significant other. Providing some type of commission structure is highly recommended in order to get your staff motivated about wine sales. It helps them feel a sense of ownership, encourages commitment, and can be highly motivational if the goal is achievable.

A few wineries have established skill-based pay systems, so that there is a career progression within the tasting room. This can be very motivational, and can also promote loyalty, which can improve your staff retention rate, and reduce hiring and training costs. For example, an entry-level, part-time employee may begin at $8 per hour, but after 6 months on the job, they may qualify to take a wine education test. If they pass, their wages may be increased to $9 per hour, etc. Likewise, full-time staff should have the opportunity to move forward in their careers, and perhaps move into sales, marketing, or other functions. It is especially critical to insure that you hire, train, and incent your tasting room manager so that he/she is a good role model and coach for other employees.

Finally, if you have a wine club, make sure to give employees a bonus for each new customer they sign up. This can range from $5 to $15 per sign-up. Go one step farther and consider giving them an additional bonus for each year their customers stay in the club. Consider giving them training to follow up with customers and make sure they are satisfied. This can help with your overall management of the wine club, improve customer satisfaction, and promote long-term sales and brand attachment.

Overall, keep in mind that your tasting room staff is your front-line face to your customers. Treat them well, so that they treat your customers well.

7. Establish a Professional Sales Environment

Even if you are only opening a tasting room for public relations reasons, you still want to insure that you develop a professional tasting and sales environment. This does not mean being pushy and encouraging customers to buy wine. Instead it means treating each customer with respect and insuring they have such a positive and memorable experience that they will tell their friends about it. They may not purchase wine or merchandise from you that day, but it is highly likely that they will when they return home via your wine club, e-commerce, or their retail establishment. Creating a professional sales environment includes some of the following activities:

Greet all customers within 30 seconds of entering the tasting room: Ideally, it should be sooner than 30 seconds, but sometimes the tasting room is crowded. In this case, the tasting room employee should say, "Welcome. I'll be right with you."

Engage in open-ended conversation with customers: This includes asking them if this is their first visit, where they are from, have they tried your wines before, etc. It also includes trying to understand the needs of the customer and their taste preferences. Questions such as, "Do you prefer sweet or drier wines, reds or whites.." can be helpful in determining customer preferences. Also, employees should be careful not to lecture customers and/or speak above or below them in terms of wine knowledge. A highly knowledgeable wine consumer does not want to be lectured to about what Brix means, but on the other hand, this could be very intimidating to a novice wine consumer.

Welcome customers who do not drink: Often tasting room visitors bring a non-drinking friend or spouse, designated driver, or children. These visitors should be treated with just as much courtesy as the customer who is tasting. Indeed they could be potential customers of your merchandise, as well as brand ambassadors in the future. Provide juices, waters, sodas, and perhaps crackers. Encourage them to wander through the merchandise, and/or provide a nice place for them to sit.

If you often have children in your tasting room, consider setting up a kids' corner with games, coloring books, and other toys. Some wineries such as Sterling Vineyards in Napa even provide small snacks for children. Because of their tram ride up to the winery, they are a favorite of families with children. Therefore, they provide a small welcome kit to kids which includes juice, pretzels, raisins, crayons, and a greeting card with their logo for kids to color, and then mail to friends and family. This is not only nice for the children, but allows the parents to spend some quality time tasting the wines.

Encourage visitors to linger with tours, picnic grounds, etc: If you can get visitors to stay at your winery for a longer time than they do at your competitors', and have a positive experience, you will have a greater chance of creating positive brand attachment. This is why some wineries require or suggest that visitors go on tours. This allows them to "tell their story," which is critical to brand awareness and differentiation. If the visitor can see the caves, the historic house, the ancient tree, or other items that make your winery different, they will remember this long after they have forgotten the taste of your wine. If you don't want to do tours, you can consider scheduling special tastings or events at your winery, or even encourage visitors to picnic on your lawn. Darioush, a beautiful winery in Napa Valley designed to look like a Persian palace, does a great job of encouraging visitors to linger and admire their lovely architecture, unique gardens and fountains, and picnic area.

Figure 12.3: Darioush Winery, Napa Valley, California

Ask for the sale: Research has shown that only approximately 30% of winery tasting room employees ask visitors if they want to purchase anything (Olsen & Thach, 2005). Most believe that their job is only to pour and talk about wine, and don't see sales as part of their duties. However, professional selling is not pushy, and if done correctly, is actually helpful to the customer. By asking at the end of the tasting, "Is there anything I can get for you to take home today?" or stating, "This wine is actually on sale today at a 20% discount," the tasting room employee creates an environment of positive support for the customer. Therefore, employees should receive some type of training and incentive on professional sales techniques in the tasting room.

8. Create Protocol for VIP Visitors

This includes distributors, retailers, wine critics, press, wine club customers, or anyone else who has shown a special interest in your winery. Ideally every customer who walks through the door will receive outstanding service, but your VIP customers should receive even more. They may require a private tasting and tour, additional information, or a meeting with the winemaker or owner. In most cases, they will call in advance. However, on some occasions, they will just drop by the tasting room and hand their business card to the first employee they meet. Your employees should be trained on how to handle VIP visitors. For example, in some wineries, special rooms have been set aside for wine club members. At Domaine Carneros in Napa, they greet returning wine club members with a "Welcome to Your Chateau" salutation and offer them a free glass of wine. These types of practices make the wine club member feel special.

Other wineries establish separate departments to manage VIP visitors, and will even provide accommodation and meals for their distributors. Whatever your protocol, it should be clear and well communicated to all of your staff, so that everyone knows what to do when one of these special guests arrives.

9. Invest in State-of-the-Art Sales and Inventory Control Systems

If you can afford it, it will be beneficial in the long run to purchase a first-class sales and inventory control system. This starts with the inventory in your cellar with a link to your tasting room registers. Ideally your tasting room register will be user-friendly with touch keypads so employees can quickly ring up a sale, including the ability to easily apply appropriate discounts, give tasting reimbursements, and recognize wine club members. It should also be designed so that employees can quickly be trained to use it, and you should have enough registers in your tasting room to accommodate traffic. You do not want customers to have to wait in long lines to purchase their items, or they may get fed up and leave. Don't forget to position tempting merchandise near the cash register so that customers may be enticed to make an additional purchase.

Figure 12.4: Winery Cash Register

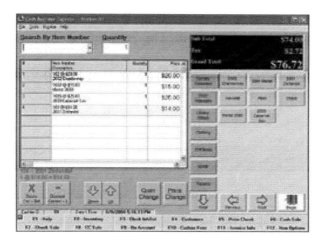

This system should be able to quickly show you the number of bottles/cases that have been sold at any time that day in the tasting room, and linked to your larger warehouse inventory. Ideally, employees can easily see when they need to stock more wine or merchandise on the floor. Likewise the system will communicate with your inventory control staff so they know the number of cases that have been depleted and need to be replaced for the next day.

Finally, the system should be able to give you and your employees a running total of the sales for the day at any given time. This will inform them as to whether they are meeting revenue goals or not. It will also tell you what types of wine and merchandise you have sold, and how well promotions and discounts are working. This type of state-of-the-art information management system will go a long way towards increasing your efficiency and quality of decision making around your tasting room profitability.

10. Get Involved in Your Local Community and Tourism Efforts

If you have a tasting room, you definitely need to be involved and support your local community and tourism efforts. Consider joining the Chamber of Commerce and any regional wine tourism groups that organize festivals and events for your wine-trail area. Even if you don't participate in all of the events, the goodwill you create by being a member will come back to you.

Remember that you are part of a greater community, and that by referring visitors to local restaurants, stores, hotels, B&B's—even other wineries—you are helping the whole area thrive. Once you have established positive relationships within the community, ask them to return the favor by recommending your winery tasting room for tours and other events. Provide these local partners with coupons for free tasting at your winery to distribute to their customers, and make sure you include the employees who work in those establishments. Consider advertising in local tourism magazines by providing a free tasting coupon or other ad to promote your winery.

Some wine regions, such as Alexander and Dry Creek appellations in Sonoma County, form networks of winery tasting rooms to help support one another and promote their region. Each winery emphasizes something different or special that is not competitive with the other wineries. For example, one winery has a restaurant, another has a special varietal such as a Tempranillo, and a third has a wonderful picnic area. They each promote one another, and even give free tasting coupons to visit other wineries. This unique system of "interwinery" referrals can be very lucrative, and helps to promote the whole wine region.

CHAPTER REFERENCES

Boone, V. "Virtual Vintner: Patz& Hall Has No Winery, Fancy Chateau, or Even Its Own Vineyards, Just Critically Acclaimed Wines." *Press Democrat*. August 31, 2005.

Olsen, J & Thach, L. "The Role of Service Quality in Creating Brand Attachments at Winery Visitor Centers." Paper Under Review for Publication. 2005.

Penn, C. "Tasting room sales 101." *Wine Business Monthly, 10*(4), 2003. Ppg.17–18.

Teaff, B., Thach, L., & Olsen, J. "Designing Effective Wine Clubs." Presentation made at Wine Institute Workshop, Nov. 25, 2004. Santa Rosa, CA.

Thach, L. & Olsen, J. "Customer Service Training in Winery Tasting Rooms: Perception of Effectiveness by Tasting Room Personnel." 2003. Accessed 9/24/2004: http://www.wine.unisa.edu.au/wmc/Colloquium%202003%20CD/File%20001.pdf

Thach, L. & Olsen, J. "Enhancing Tasting Room Service to Drive in Revenue." *Practical Winery & Vineyard*, March/April 2004. Pg.50.

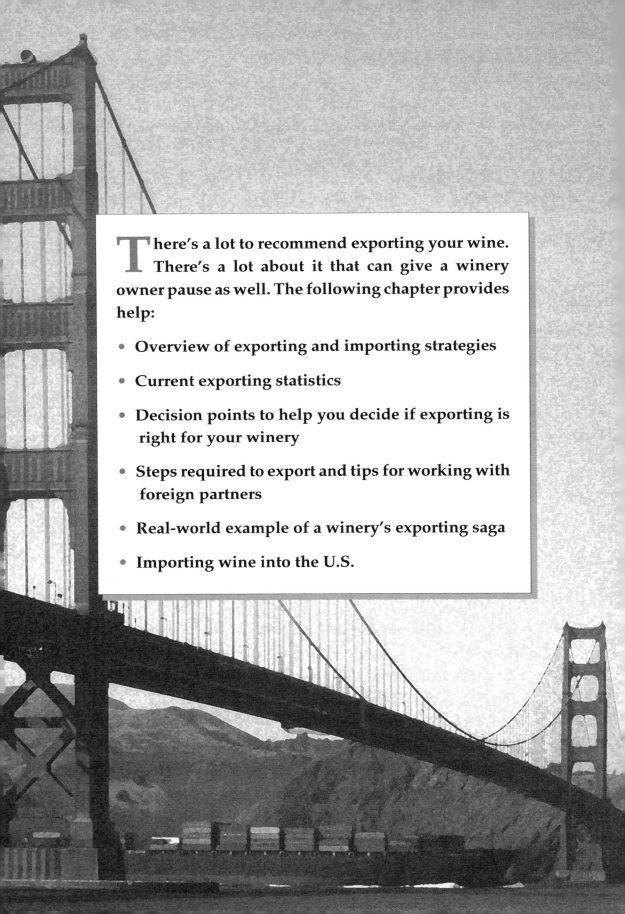

There's a lot to recommend exporting your wine. There's a lot about it that can give a winery owner pause as well. The following chapter provides help:

- Overview of exporting and importing strategies

- Current exporting statistics

- Decision points to help you decide if exporting is right for your winery

- Steps required to export and tips for working with foreign partners

- Real-world example of a winery's exporting saga

- Importing wine into the U.S.

CHAPTER 13

STRATEGIES FOR EXPORTING AND IMPORTING WINE

From the earliest times, wine has been exported from one country to another. Evidence has been found that the ancient Greeks transported their wine by ship in the 3rd century B.C. (Matheson & Koehler, 1989). Wine was one of the earlier products of commercial exchange. Today this tradition continues, as wine firms from many countries have come to rely on export sales as a profitable means to grow their businesses.

There are many reasons wineries elect to export their wine. Exporting provides wineries with an opportunity to diversify their markets. New consumers, previously unaccustomed to drinking wine, are emerging all over the globe. And consumers in Latin America and Asia are becoming more familiar with wine, and the easing of trade regulations has also made exporting more appealing to wine producers (Spawton and Lockshin, 2004). Despite these enticements, there has not been a huge increase in the number of US wineries exporting (Gallagher, 2004). Several wineries have indicated that they would like to begin exporting, but are still reluctant to move forward (Gallagher, 2004). Many do not know what is involved in exportation and are cautious of expanding into foreign markets.

Current Wine Exporting Statistics

The nations that export the most wine are Italy, France, Spain and Germany (Castaldi, Silverman, & Sengupta, 2002). However, other countries such as Australia, New Zealand, South Africa and Chile also have in the last decade rapidly increased the amount of wine they export. The degree to which wine-producing countries rely on export markets compared to sales within their domestic market varies greatly. For example, although France is the world's second largest exporter, only 21 percent of its wine is sold in other countries, while Chile, the seventh largest exporter, exports over 80 percent of its wine (Cellarnotes.net, 2005).

Figure 13.1: Chart of Global Wine Exports, Market Share, 2005

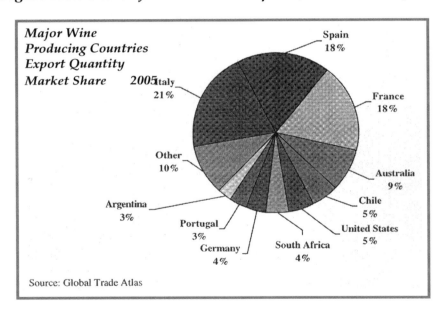

Major Wine Producing Countries Export Quantity Market Share 2005
Italy 21%
Spain 18%
France 18%
Australia 9%
Chile 5%
United States 5%
South Africa 4%
Germany 4%
Portugal 3%
Argentina 3%
Other 10%

Source: Global Trade Atlas

Exports of U.S. wines have grown dramatically in the past 10 years, increasing 300 percent in value since 1994. US wine exports were over 339.6-million liters with revenues exceeding $600 million in 2003 (Penn, 2004). However the export numbers for the US are improving. By 2004, total U.S. wine exports reached a record $736 million in revenues. Although the growth is impressive, US exports represent a mere 5 percent of the world's market share. Less than 15 percent of US wine is exported. In comparison, France, Italy and Spain each exports over 25 percent of their wine production (Castaldi, Silverman, & Sengupta, 2002). The United Kingdom is the top market for U.S. wine exports, followed by Canada, Japan the Netherlands, Germany, France, Ireland, Denmark, and Mexico. Sixty-six percent of US wine exports, over $487 million, were shipped to countries in the European Community (Wine Institute, 2005).

At the same time the US is increasing its wine exports, it also is importing more wine from other countries. Italy is the country that currently sends the most wine to the US, but Australia, in second place, is gaining steadily (Castaldi, Silverman, & Sengupta, 2002). Both Italy and Australia are far ahead of the third country on the list, France. The size and growth of the US market, however, insures that wineries from all parts of the world are working hard to capture market share. In the global marketplace, US companies must work hard to keep their market share at home while exploring foreign markets.

THE DECISION TO EXPORT

Should all wine firms export to other countries? Clearly the answer is no. Many small wineries do not have the resources and prefer to dedicate their scarce time and money to developing a stronger presence in their domestic market. Some wineries are in the envious position of having all their wines already allocated to domestic customers and do not have enough wine to sell to other countries. For other wineries, their strategic goals as outlined in their marketing plans do not include an export focus at the present time. Sooner or later, though, almost every winery will encounter an opportunity to export and must decide whether the time is right. So what factors should wine marketers and owners consider? Following are a few key points.

Top Management Support

Support from the owner and upper management is critical if the winery is going to succeed in exporting over the long term. The necessity for strong management support means that exporting wine, especially initially, is not an easy endeavor. There are many new aspects of the business that will need to be learned and skills that must be acquired. This learning process does not occur all at once, and exporting should be seen as a long-term commitment. Upper management must decide whether they are willing to devote time, either theirs or their employees', to learning the steps and procedures involved. If the current owners and managers don't have a strong desire to export, they probably will not be willing to take the time away from other tasks to see that exporting is accomplished.

Financial Commitment to Export

Not only the time commitment must be considered. Financial resources must also be available to establish an overseas presence. While these funds may be recouped in time, the initial outlay for market research, travel, and other marketing activities can be substantial. Here again, wineries that have relatively small marketing budgets may find themselves unable to commit the funds. This is especially true if the winery is trying to establish itself in other domestic markets at the same time. The resources would be spread too thinly to be effective in any of their markets.

Wine Allocations

The decision to export can also be influenced by the amount of wine the company has available to sell. Some wineries are in the envious position of having to allocate their wine among current customers, including their distributors and retailers. They just do not make enough wine to fill all of the demand in their domestic market.

In some situations it may be possible to increase production so that the winery can expand abroad, but if the wine is marketed as coming from a particular vineyard or appellation, it may be difficult to ramp up production to fill the unmet demand. In this situation, any wine that is directed to international markets must be taken away from a customer in the domestic market. As one might suspect, restricting or removing much sought-after products would not make for good relations with customers, especially those who have loyally supported the winery's brand over the years.

Even though exporting may not be an appropriate decision for every winery, a growing number of firms have made the commitment, and have the human and financial resources and the product available to make exporting a good option to explore. The following section provides a basic overview of the exporting process.

THE EXPORT PROCESS

Exporting requires managers to learn about a new, and often very different, market, as well as different procedures for selling wine. This is a process that never stops, but with experience, most winery managers find that exporting becomes easier over time. Table 13.1 illustrates the procedures. Once a winery has made the decision to export, including securing management support, financial commitment, and dedicated wine allocation, then it is useful for them to implement the following steps.

Table 13.1: The Steps to Wine Exporting

Step 1: Conduct Market Research on Target Countries
Step 2: Research Business Practices and Distribution Channels
Step 3: Learn Compliance Laws for Labels and Packaging
Step 4: Understand Pricing Structure
Step 5: Select an Exporting Partner

1. Conduct Market Research on Target Countries

When someone at a winery is first considering exporting, he or she will have a lot of questions. Learning where to find the answers and knowing where to go for help is probably the most important step in exporting. A prospective exporter will need information about wine consumers in other countries, and their wine culture. Marketers may wonder who currently drinks wine, and if the consumption rate is growing or declining, where wine is consumed and which types of wines are preferred. They also would like to know the image of US wines in general and if consumers view imported wines favorably. Marketers would like to know who is currently selling wine to the market and what their competitive strengths are. This type of marketing information helps marketers determine if there is sufficient demand in a market to make exporting worthwhile.

A good resource for market research and assistance is your local wineries association. Many such associations sponsor annual tours of wine shows in different countries. Going along with an expert the first time is a great way to get your feet wet and learn the ropes before investing a lot of time and money. You will also learn which countries are most open to U.S. wines, such as Canada, the UK, Germany, Japan, U.K, Switzerland, and the Netherlands (McCampbell, Mark, and Thach, 2005).

Other sources of country market research are Agriculture Trade Offices in U.S. Embassies and Consulates, as well as government trade offices, industry trade groups, and regional associations. For example, the Wine Institute and Wine Vision both provide a wealth of information on international markets. See Table 13.2 for Exporting Resources.

Table 13.2: Sources of Wine Export Assistence

Organization Name	Website	Assistance
Wine Vison	www.winevision.org	Advice on Global Exporting
U.S. Dept. of Agriculture	www.fas.usda.gov	Attaché reports and directory
Wine Institute	www.wineinstitute.org	Industry statistics Wine laws and regulations
California Wine Export Program	www.calwinexport.com	Market reports Importer lists

Once you've had a chance to do some market research, select only 1 to 3 countries for exporting. Experts advise using a targeted versus a scatter approach to successful wine exporting. Try to become successful in one or two countries first before expanding to others.

2. Research Business Practices & Distribution Channels

It is also helpful to know about business practices within the wine trade in other countries. This may include information about typical margins, commissions, terms of payment and delivery, and the marketing support expected from the winery. Wine marketers also need to know about the structure of the distribution channel in terms of availability of import agents, brokers, distributors, retailers, freight forwarders and other logistic facilitators. Marketers not only need to know if firms exist that serve the market, but how to best contact them to see if they have an interest in carrying a new imported brand of wine.

3. Learn Compliance Laws for Labels and Packaging

Another complicated issue for wine exporters is compliance with domestic and foreign laws. Marketers need to know what changes need to be made to the label and packaging materials, and what documents are required to ship wine into another country. For example, the term *reserve* has very specific meaning in Europe, and most wines with this term on the label would not be allowed. There may also be requirements on how the wine is made, and documents must be furnished to support the claims. Wine laws are often very complicated and vary from country to country, so making sure that all of the required information is provided and that it is in the proper form is a huge undertaking, at least the first few times that exports are attempted. With experience, however, wineries learn what the requirements are for each country, and the process goes more smoothly.

4. Understand Pricing Structure
First of all wineries need to make sure they understand all of the additional export costs they will incur so they can set their prices such that each export isn't a loss. In addition the price that must be charged to consumers in foreign markets is often a function of currency exchange rates. Thus it is not unusual to find that exported wines cost 2 to 4 times as much in export markets as they do in the domestic market. Needless to say, the high prices of US wine in many markets limit their market potential.

SELECTING AN EXPORTING PARTNER
When asked, most wine marketers will tell you that the most important decision they make with regards to exporting is to determine which importer they should use to represent them in the chosen foreign market. As we have seen, the import agent plays an important role in providing market information to the exporter. They are also responsible for carrying out the marketing plan according to the direction of the exporter.

Most importers provide assistance with label design and the development of marketing collateral. In fact, some wineries rely on their importers to handle all of these activities with very minimal input from the winery. It is very important that a winery select the agent that best fits with their overall objectives and has the resources to carry out the marketing activities that are needed to establish the brand. While a few large wineries are able to sell directly to retail accounts in foreign countries, most will find the services of an import agent necessary for them to succeed.

Methods to Identify Foreign Partners

There are several ways to find out the names of potential importers in a particular market. Some places a wine marketer may want to contact include the Wine Institute and the Agricultural Trade Office in the U.S. Embassy in the target country. They should also speak to other marketers at wineries that export to see if they can recommend an importer. Finally, attending trade shows is often a good way to meet and interview potential importers (www.winevision.org).

So what is the next step once an importer has been found? What should be included in a letter of introduction? First, a potential exporter should let them know how they found out about them and the reasons they are contacting them. Next, they should provide information about their wines and winery. They should let them know what makes the wines special and different from other brands that are available. They should inform them of the price range in which they are interested in selling the wines. It is also helpful to make any trade packets and marketing materials available to them, and most importantly, the exporter should let them know that they will follow up with a telephone call, and do so.

Screening Potential Partners

A potential exporter will probably want to interview several importers before selecting the one that is the best fit with their overall objectives in a particular country. Visiting potential importers and meeting with the managers and staff on site is very important. An exporter wants to make certain that the importer they choose has the staff and experience to sell the wine. They also want to see if the importer has too many other foreign brands, ensuring that their wine will get lost in the portfolio and languish in the warehouse. Only after a careful screening and selection process should an exporter be ready to commit to an arrangement and sign a contract.

Developing a Win-Win Relationship

Once the importer has been selected, it is very important that the exporter develop a close working relationship that is mutually beneficial to both parties. As with your domestic distributors communication is the key to making sure the relationship works. Even though there are many ways to keep in touch, such as telephone and email, many wine exporters feel it is necessary to travel to visit their overseas representatives and meet with them face-to-face on a regular basis. Just as with distributors in the US, wineries bring in foreign visitors to help foster excitement and interest in promoting the brand. It is also a good opportunity to make sure the importer understands the strategic goals of the winery and is involved in implementing the marketing plan correctly.

Insuring Timely Payment

One question that is at the top of every exporter's mind is whether they will get paid in a timely manner. The methods of payments that are used vary from company to company, but include cash in advance, 50 percent payment in advance, or terms of 30, 60 or 90 or 120 days. Letters of credit are also used. They are more expensive for the importer, but are a good form of payment if the exporter feels there is risk of non-payment. Most wineries find that their export sales are profitable, but there have been costly situations where payments were not received from buyers as expected.

Exporting is not easy, but most wineries that have persevered claim that exporting contributes greatly to the company, both in terms of profits and enhancing their image. More wineries are expected to expand into export markets in the future and take advantage of the opportunities in growing markets abroad.

OVERVIEW OF ONE WINERY'S EXPORTING SAGA

In the early 1990's a 30,000 case winery in Napa Valley made a management decision to begin exporting. This decision was a result of an annual strategy review meeting with the owner, board of directors and top management team. They decided that they were doing sufficiently well in U.S. markets and wanted to begin to become a global company. In the beginning the Director of Marketing was asked to assume the exporting responsibilities, but a year into the process, he was allowed to hire an assistant to help with compliance, shipping, communication, and payment issues. The management team made a decision to allocate 15% of their production to exports.

The winery began the exporting process by joining a regional winery group committed to exporting. The association organized trips abroad so that wineries could showcase their wines at foreign trade shows, such as Vinexpo, the London Wine Trade Fair and ProWine. As a result of these trips, they met importers in Canada, the UK, and Germany who expressed an interest in importing their wines. They met several times with the various importers, and ended up selecting three partners they felt would work best in representing their wines.

The next step was to negotiate agreements with the importers in the three different countries. The agreement was setup so that they sold their wine directly to the importers, who managed all of the paperwork and distribution issues within their home countries. In the first few years, the process moved slowly, but the Napa winery discovered that staying in close contact with the importers via email and telephone was very helpful. The winery CEO and Director of Marketing also visited the importers in their countries at least once a year, as well as inviting the importers to visit the winery in Napa. They found this was very helpful in promoting a positive work relationship and insuring their wines were sold overseas.

About two years into the process, they began to have difficulties with their importer in Germany, who didn't seem to be selling their wines. They investigated the situation, by flying to Europe to meet face-to-face with the German importer. In Germany, they found that there was an abundance of regional importers and that it was difficult to get their wine placed with the importer they were using. Therefore they ended up dissolving the relationship and selecting a new importer for their wines in Germany.

Regarding payment and margins, the winery found that, for the most part, payments arrived on time, although occasionally they were delayed. In the beginning the margins were not as large as in the U.S., but they have now caught up, and in some cases, have surpassed U.S. margins. The winery now has a positive brand following in the UK, Germany, and Canada, and is considering increasing the percentage of wine allocated for exports to 20%. They are also currently researching other countries' markets to penetrate.

In terms of lessons learned, the winery reported that a key issue is being able to communicate the quality of the wine, because U.S. wines are usually more expensive than the competition, but the quality is great. Working closely with the export partner is the major way to help make this happen, as well as visits to the country markets to meet with key customers. They also said it is important to follow the media and current events in the export markets to stay on top of changing conditions. They also caution that it is important to get your domestic business well in hand before beginning to export. Finally, they said that having an aspiration to be a world-class winery with a global presence and top commitment from management is critical to success.

IMPORTING WINE INTO THE U.S.

Imported wines make up a growing percentage of the US marketplace and come from many nations around the globe. Just as with domestic wines, the strategic challenge is to position the imported wine to appeal to a segment of the market better than competitive offerings. Fortunately, there are many consumers in the US market who enjoy exploring wine from producers around the globe and collectively create market segments that importers can reach. This is not true of all markets outside the US, where in many locations consumers tend to prefer locally produced wines, and imports receive almost no visibility.

Imported wines coming into the US face the same challenges in finding a spot in a crowded marketplace as domestically produced. Wine importers must follow the same steps outlined thus far in this book to create a unique positioning that will allow them to survive in their chosen categories. As with domestic marketers, if the category is crowded with many producers selling a similar product, they must either reposition themselves or find a niche segment of the market. Some importers have taken the approach of creating a new category which was unknown before, for example, selling Carmenere wines from Chile or Malbec wines from Argentina.

Once the marketing plan has been developed, the distribution strategy is essentially the same. Importers operate at the same level as producers in the three-tier system. Importers are not the same thing as distributors; however, they sell their wines through the same distribution network as domestic wineries do. Therefore, they must face the same challenges in finding and working with distributors. Anyone who has traveled outside the US and found a wine they are enraptured with naturally thinks that they should import the wine immediately to the US. Reality usually sets in when the person realizes they will be competing with thousands of wines competing for the same attention from distributors.

CHAPTER REFERENCES

Castaldi, M. R., Silverman, M., & Sengupta, S. "Export assistance needs of US wineries." *International Journal of Wine Marketing, 14*(1), 2002. Pp. 14–21.

"Exporting 101." *WineVision.* 2004. Available at: www.winevision,org.

Gallagher, N. "Weak dollar, strong export Sonoma County businesses beginning to reap rewards of going international." *The Press Democrat.* Feb. 15, 2004.

Matheson, P.M. W & Koehler, C.G. "Amphoras: a database on ancient wine jars. Paper presented at the conference of the Association for Literary and Linguistic Computing." Toronto, Canada, June 1989. Available at: http://www.chass.utoronto.ca/amphoras/allc89.htm.

McCampbell, C., Marke, M., & Thach, L. "California Wine Exporting: Successful Practices and Challenges." *Wine Business Monthly.* Oct. 2005.

Penn, C. "Insider Analysis—US Wine Exporters See Slight Value Uptick." *Wine Business Insider, 14*(1), 2004.

Spawton, T. & Lockshin, L. in Thach, L. & Matz, T. (eds). *Wine: A Global Business.* New York: Miranda Press. 2004.

"Wine Institute" 2005. Available at www.wineinstitute.org.

"World Comparison." 2005. Available at www.cellarnotes.net/world_comparison .htm.

"World Wine Situation and Outlook—2005."Special Report from the United States Department of Agriculture. 2005. http://www.fas.usda.gov/agx/Processed/Wine/. , Chart on p. 284 from *Global Trade Atlas.* P. 5 of report.

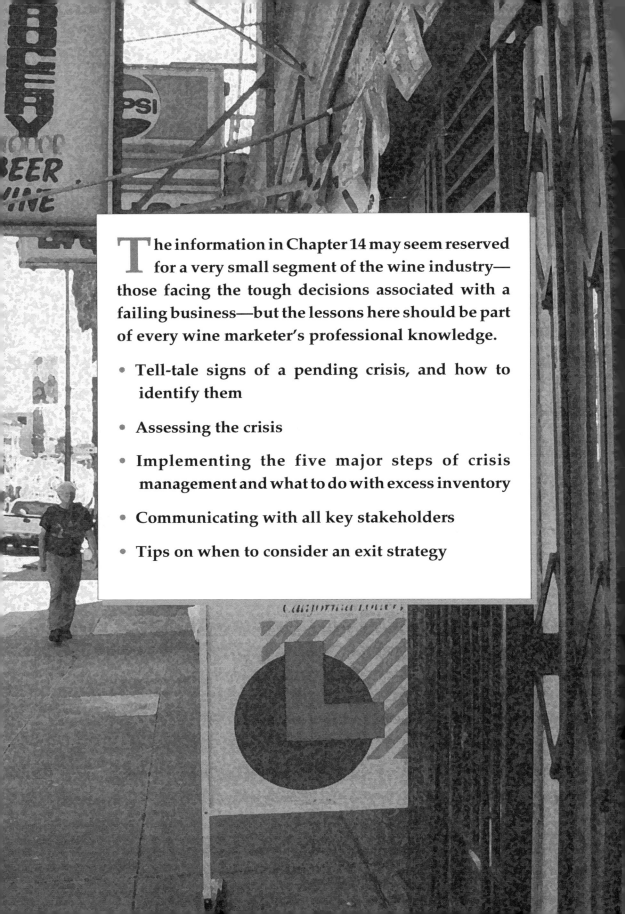

The information in Chapter 14 may seem reserved for a very small segment of the wine industry—those facing the tough decisions associated with a failing business—but the lessons here should be part of every wine marketer's professional knowledge.

- Tell-tale signs of a pending crisis, and how to identify them

- Assessing the crisis

- Implementing the five major steps of crisis management and what to do with excess inventory

- Communicating with all key stakeholders

- Tips on when to consider an exit strategy

REPOSITIONING AND TURNAROUNDS

It would be wonderful to think that your winery will always be successful or that you will only work for a winery that is achieving success. It would be wonderful, but unrealistic. Some of the biggest opportunities in marketing are those presented by a winery or brand that is struggling. Jumping in a Ferrari and driving fast is rewarding, but so is retooling a car with no engine, and turning it into a competitive vehicle. While many in the industry may respect those who work at successful wineries, their real adoration is reserved for those who have turned around a winery that looked as if it were on its last wheel.

That kind of result is particularly challenging in the wine industry. A poor track record in the marketplace is a big hurdle to overcome. All too often, distributors, retailers and consumers are looking for a reason to eliminate wineries or brands from their purchasing decisions, and your lousy image and slowing sales are a good reason for them to do that. Once the negative momentum takes hold, it takes even more effort to get the vehicle righted and turned in the proper direction. The good news? If you can do it, your resume will be the envy of just about everyone in the wine business.

The information in this chapter may seem as if it is valuable to only a small segment of the industry—those facing the very tough decisions of a failing business. However, this is not true, as there are lessons here that every wine marketer should learn by heart. These lessons will certainly help you turn a business around. Just as importantly, the issues and decisions covered here will indicate where a healthy business may be facing a real problem, with the potential of sinking slowly into a quagmire. In fact, taking action early, before the crisis becomes too serious, is a perfect way to avoid that fate. If you don't do this type of analysis on a periodic basis, then you can expect that sooner or later you will run into trouble, because every company faces a crisis eventually. Without adequate planning, the wheels may come off, and everyone will ask what to do about it.

This chapter provides some basic advice on a few things to keep in mind, so that you can be prepared to take a leadership role in helping to reposition and/or turn around your wine company when needed. It begins with how to identify a crisis, then explains how to assess your situation. Next, it describes how to implement the five major steps of crisis management, including tips on what to do with excess inventory. Finally it explains how to communicate with all key stakeholders, and provides tips on when you should consider an exit strategy.

IDENTIFYING A CRISIS

A crisis almost never becomes a crisis without some kind of prior warning. Slowing sales, declining quality of the wines, less effective marketing activities and lowered financial success are all indicators of a problem. When that problem hits the bottom line, it should get everyone's attention. The combination of declining revenues and low profits is a problem that's easy to read. When those factors become part of a larger and longer trend, it is an obvious crisis.

The first secret to a successful turnaround is to notice the problem before everyone else does. The key here is to measure your success against two very important yardsticks: your competition, and your long-term plan. If you are meeting your financial goals and are doing as well as or better than your competitors, your problems may be the result of larger industry trends. Those will be difficult for a small winery to escape. But if you are falling behind your competitors in the category, the time to act is now, and quickly.

By the same token, if you are achieving your long-term goals for sales volume, pricing, and profits, then you might well have reason to celebrate. However if your competitors are doing even better, then you are being left behind. When the market tightens up—as it always does—you will be among those slower zebras that get eaten by the lions. You want to be at the head of the herd, not one of the hapless stragglers.

ONGOING ASSESSMENT OF THE BIG PICTURE

Obviously, circumventing a crisis requires that you have effective and regular ways to measure your brand and winery against your competition. In this business, it is relatively easy to gain sales volume by reducing your price. Unfortunately, that has long-lasting repercussions with your image of quality. As you develop your parameters for measuring your business against the rest, make sure that you are addressing all of these issues: sales volume, price points, wine quality, and marketing efforts. It is recommended that you conduct this type of assessment at least once a quarter. If your sales are lagging, and your wine quality continues to be as good as or better than your competition, then you are simply being out-marketed. If that is the case, then it's time to get to work.

The first item on the agenda is to make an inventory of everything that you are doing. As you list each program and item, make sure you clearly understand the effect each one is having on your business. The goal here is to identify those activities and products that are working. If you have something that is working, your first decision should be to keep doing it well. Also, attempt to find ways to do more of it on a broader scope, but more cost-effectively.

In some situations, that will be the easy part of the job. Most wineries have a pretty good idea of what works for them. In a turnaround, those should become the power that drives you back into the race. Beware of those products and programs that are "what we have always done." Remember that what you have always done is why you are having problems. Instead, ruthlessly scrutinize each product and program to verify it is performing well.

A much more difficult analysis is that of deciding which of your products or marketing efforts are truly failing. A company in crisis has a tendency to hang on to every potential sale. It will try to maintain a vast product line only because a few customers in a few markets want to buy small amounts of one product or another. Why should you stop making those wines, lose that revenue, and further put your company in financial stress? Because every one of those products takes your time and energy away from the much bigger task of solving the crisis. Every minute you spend sourcing grapes, making wine, or marketing for some tiny segment of your portfolio is a minute that was not spent making your core wines better, your marketing more effective. Can you afford to do that? Not in a crisis.

There is a simple, two-part question that will help you decide the fate of every product in your portfolio and every marketing effort that you undertake. Does the product and program enhance the image of your winery and brand? Does it make a profit? If the answer to both of those questions is yes, then you should throw your heart and soul into it. If the answer to either one is no, then you really don't have time to spend on it. You would be better served focusing your energy in another direction.

Categorizing Your Products and Programs
Here is a quick menagerie of terms that can help you work your way through your portfolio of products in an effective manner:

Table 14.1: The Four Product Categories

Cash Cows	Products that perform well. Milk them for all they're worth.
Dogs	Products that do not perform well. Put them out of their misery.
Stars	Products that perform exceptionally well. Use them as a flagship to lead the brand forward.
Problem Children	Products that are not working well. Make them wok, or get them out of the house.

Cash Cows are those products that seem to sell all by themselves. They have a solid reputation in the marketplace, they make a nice contribution to the bottom line, and they don't require massive amounts of marketing support. Cash cows can and should be the source of funding for your turnaround budgets. Don't let them dry up.

Dogs are the opposite of cash cows. These are products that are hard to sell, and don't make much of a profit. They may well be the dream of the winery owner, but they are slated for the doghouse. Be merciless, and get rid of these as quickly as possible. They hurt your bottom line, and the problems they create in the marketplace reflect poorly on the rest of the brand. Every minute they are on the shelves is hurting the sales of your other wines.

Stars are wines that do more than just sell well; they add a halo of quality to every wine in the portfolio. The product quality is high, the reputation is excellent, and sales are brisk. Stars are a great place to assess your inventory during a crisis. What are your stars? Why are they successful? How quickly and effectively can you replicate that success with other products? While cash cows continue to provide funding, your stars will provide the strategic direction for the future. Understand them completely, and they will provide many of the answers that you need for a turnaround. If you don't have any stars, then your first real decision must be to create some. A winery without a star in the portfolio is doomed. Every winery should have at least one wine that is so popular that customers stand in line to get it.

Problem children are products with some very positive aspects, but which for some reason have not been successful. As the name suggests, these are more difficult to resolve. While cash cows and stars are a good bet, problem children are a long shot. It is important to ask yourself how long you can wait for them to achieve success, while continuing to invest in their uncertain future. These are decisions that should be made with great care.

It is ironic that successful wineries can always afford to wait longer and invest a little more in problem children—which means that those wineries will usually have more success. Success, in this case, does breed success. However, a winery in crisis is well advised to take a much more conservative approach to problem children.

MANAGING AN EFFECTIVE TURNAROUND FOR YOUR WINERY

If your assessment of the big picture of your winery and other external indicators show that you are truly in a crisis, then there are effective methods to instigate a turnaround. However, it is important to do this correctly, because the market generally only gives you one chance. If this doesn't work, you may have to consider alternative options, such as selling the winery. However, there have been many successful turnarounds, and by following the steps outlined below, you may find that you are in a much stronger position than you were before the crisis. In these types of cases, crisis can actually be positive, because it forces you to change and become more strategically focused and competitive.

Table 14.2: Steps to Implement a Crisis Management Process

1. Create a Crisis Team
2. Gather All the Information You Can
3. Develop a Turnaround Strategy
4. Communicate the Strategy
5. Implement the Strategy

Step 1: Form a Crisis Team

It is often difficult for a winery management team to make these decisions on its own. After all, these are the same people who made the decisions that created the crisis in the beginning. Each member of the team may have his or her own perception of which products and programs are most effective and which are least effective. To ask them to come to consensus on which products and programs to delete is likely to create as many problems as it solves.

It's time to form a crisis team to help make the hard decisions, without the baggage of past history. The team should include members of current winery management, but should also include outside experts who can give a more objective perspective on some of the harder questions. Key distributors, retailers and restaurateurs should certainly be consulted, because they can provide valuable input. However it would be a mistake to get them formally involved in the decision-making process. The crisis team may well have to decide to focus exclusively on one market segment or another, on one distribution channel or another. Partisans from those market segments or channels will make it even harder to make what is already a very difficult decision.

Step 2: Gather and Analyze Data

The next step is to gather and analyze data from all relevant sources. This includes distributors, retailers, customers, employees, community members, and other potential parties. The goal here is to get an absolutely honest appraisal of your current situation, how you got there, and the best direction to head in the future. It is always easy to include your strongest supporters in the distribution and sales network in this process. However, you should also include some individuals who are not strong supporters of your brand. They will give a different perspective, and in some ways, theirs is the perspective that must be changed. After all, your supporters should not need much in the way of incentive to continue to support you. It is those who are not big fans who will need the most convincing. If you do not include them in the process, you will find it much harder to achieve your goals.

As you collect input from various sources, identify a method to catalog it. Make note of what each contributor says. This will become tremendously valuable in the future. Once you have determined your new strategy, it will be very rewarding to tell some of these contributors that you remembered their advice, and can show how it has affected your policies for the future. This may also promote their ownership in the turnaround process, because they may feel an obligation to help implement your strategy effectively. If you have a distribution network that understands your solutions and feels a certain ownership towards making them successful, you are well on your way to turning the crisis around.

Step 3: Develop a Turnaround Strategy
Once the crisis team has gathered and analyzed the data, the next step is to develop a solid, serious, turnaround strategy. There is a tendency for wineries in crisis to begin to float trial balloons, as each member of the team shares what he or she hopes will happen. Avoid this at all costs, as it gives the impression that your team is disorganized and dysfunctional. Once you have admitted that your winery is in crisis, it is absolutely critical that every step you take is a step forward. You must control every statement that is made, and make sure that everyone is on exactly the same page.

The crisis team should meet for long hours as a group. It should consult with a wide range of resources, experts, and staff, but it should not make any promises or statements until everyone on the team has agreed upon the final turnaround strategy. The team should proceed as if one of the problems of the past was a lack of consensus in management, but act in such cohesive a fashion that this can never again be said of the winery. It means long hours of discussion, and intensive team building. The result, however, will be well worth the effort, as it will be a focused strategy to which everyone is committed.

Step 4: Communicate the New Strategy

After the long hours of deliberation, the resulting strategy should include the new direction and focus of the company. For example, this might be that the winery will elect to focus only on Cabernet Sauvignon and Merlot, and is dropping their low-performing Chardonnay, Chenin Blanc, and Syrah products. They may update labels, change distributors, and enhance direct-to-consumer programs. Whatever the new turnaround strategy, the results should be clear, focused, and highly supported by the crisis team.

Now the job of the crisis team is to communicate the new strategy to all key stakeholders, including the press. The team must be able to articulate a very clear and rational strategy for the future, and it must be able to list a number of the steps to be taken to achieve success. In many ways, this will become the new mission statement for the winery. Everyone must understand it, believe it, and endorse it. To assist in this endeavor, it is strongly recommended that a top public relations professional be part of the crisis team.

The winery staff is one of the first and most important stakeholder groups to be involved in the communication. They have been with you all along, and are usually aware of the crisis. They are hoping to hear some positive news from you regarding the new strategy and the future. Therefore, avoid talking too much about what happened in the past, and why it didn't work. Most people don't care what happened;

they want to know the future. They want to know exactly what you can promise them for the future, and they will expect you to deliver it.

Step 5: Implement the New Strategy

In order to implement the strategy, the crisis team should be given strong authority and a firm timeline with checkpoints. It is important to evaluate every marketing program as it evolves, but it is even more critical to do so in a time of crisis. By giving the team the power to make necessary decisions, you will avoid the "paralysis by analysis" that often plagues companies in crisis. By giving a firm timeline with checkpoints, you not only encourage the team to move forward, but you also give them confidence that you are not expecting instantaneous success. A series of intermediate checkpoints should give everyone the opportunity to determine which of the solutions are working, which need to be improved, and which should be jettisoned because they are simply not having the desired effect.

Almost certainly some of the strategies will fail. In times of crisis, these failures are often magnified, and their effects are amplified. However, it would be a mistake to approach the turnaround project as if any small mistake would spell immediate disaster. If you can't afford to take any chances at all, then it is really too late. Expect that there will be some setbacks as you move forward in implementing the new strategy, but with your crisis team, analyze each one and make a decision to move forward or not.

MANAGING AN EXCESS WINE INVENTORY

If you find yourself in an excess situation, however, the options are not as attractive. The comforting news is that most wineries have been in this position at least once, so you are not alone. Also, you can learn a lot from managing an excess inventory that will be helpful to you in the future as a marketing professional. Following are some decision points and options:

Wine format: Is the wine still in barrel or tank, or has it been bottled? If it has been bottled, has it been labeled? These are important questions because they determine the options available for you, and the costs associated with each.

Bulk wine sales: If the wine is still in tank or barrel, consider contacting a bulk wine sales house to see if they can assist you in selling it. Sometimes you can achieve a decent return via a bulk wine auction. You can also keep your name and brand anonymous, and only disclose the varietal, appellation, and winemaking techniques. This can help protect your brand image.

Private party label: Another option if you have bottled the wine, but not yet labeled it is to sell it to a third party, such as a large corporate client, airline, cruise ship, retailer, or other entity that is interested in this option. You can often still achieve a decent return, and if the wine is of good quality, the third party will appreciate your winemaking efforts and may continue to seek you out as a long-term supplier. Even if you only break even, this option may be better than dumping the wine elsewhere or writing it off. If you have already labeled the wine, you may consider taking off your labels and re-labeling; however, this is often more costly, and may not make financial sense.

Airlines and cruise lines: Even if you've already labeled the wine, airlines and cruise ships are a good target, because they are often looking for a great value and can move a lot of product. If you are confident of the quality of the wine, these venues can give you great visibility with a highly desirable demographic audience. They will be in the best possible mood to enjoy your wine, and if they have a positive experience with it, your sales should benefit in the long run. On the other hand, these markets are extremely price competitive, and you cannot expect to make a lot of money in this part of the business. And if your wine quality isn't what it should be, you will be in even worse shape. Consumers won't like it, and that will lead to problems with the account as well.

Discount houses: Another option, if the wine is already bottled and labeled is to sell it through a discount house, but be very careful with this option. If the discount is too deep and the retailer is not well-regarded, you will not only hurt your margins, but you will damage your brand image. Attempting to recover from a poor brand image is very difficult, and is almost more expensive than starting over developing a new brand. Therefore be very careful with this option. Be sure you know the retailer well, and have a good working relationship with them personally or through your distributor. The last thing you want is to walk into a store and find your wines sitting in a "last chance" wine bin, covered with dust, and marked down to $3 per bottle.

Direct to consumer: If you cannot find a reputable discount house to work with, consider selling directly to consumers. This can be done through any of the consumer-direct channels, such as your tasting room, e-commerce, wine club, etc. With this option, you can discount the wine and make the consumers feel like they are getting a good deal, but you will most likely still achieve a decent margin, because you are not sharing it with distributors and retailers. The caution here is to not dump "bad wine" on your good direct consumers. If wine club members begin to believe that you are selling them the "dregs" and saving the good wine for distribution, you will lose your loyal following. So be careful of the image you project, and if you sell excess wine in this manner, give your direct customers a good deal.

A related option of direct-to-consumer sales is to hold a special sale for friends and family of the winery. Since they will most likely know you and your brand, they will be less critical and may be excited about the chance of getting some of your good wine for a discount.

Donations: Another option for excess wine is to donate it to a charity or other cause. Though you won't make any money on this, you can write it off as a donation. The caution here is the same as above. Be careful not to dump "bad" wine on local charities, because it could come back to haunt you. Your brand is still being shown, and therefore you want to make sure you still have quality in the bottle.

Write off the wine: The final option, of course, is to write off the wine as a loss. Sometimes this is the best option, because it will protect your brand image. If none of the options above make sense, then this is always a fallback option. Remember your brand is your reputation. You have to decide what is most important during this time of excess —your long-term image or your current cash flow.

ONGOING COMMUNICATION WITH ALL KEY STAKEHOLDERS

Just communicating and launching the new turnaround strategy is not enough. A critical key to long-term success is ongoing communication. A winery in crisis needs to address the questions and requirements of every element of the sales and distribution network, as well as its own internal audiences. It won't be enough to simply announce that you have seen the problem and solved it with your new turnaround strategy. You will need to get very specific with each audience, and you will need to provide not only explanations, but tangible proof of change for all of them.

There is sometimes a tendency for individuals at a failing company to identify the problem as living in one department or another. This may be psychologically comforting, but it is certainly bad business practice. A successful company is a like a good sports team. When a team loses, it's easy to point the finger at one of the weaker players and complain. If only that player were better, then the whole team would improve. But what most people overlook in that situation is that the same could be said of every player on the team, even the very best ones. If they had played better, the team would have done better.

One of the key elements to any winning team is that all the players help each other out. If one is having a bad day, or even a bad year, the others step in to pick up the slack. They know that the team as a whole has to win. It's not enough for a good player to play well—he or she has to play well enough to help the team beat the competition. If your team is losing, don't just look at the weaker players and demand that they improve. Look to the good players, and ask them how they are going to make a difference. Ask them how they are going to help the weaker players be more effective. That's what winning teams do.

Table 14.3: Key Stakeholders to Communicate With During a Crisis

Winery Ownership
Winery Staff
The Distribution Network
Retailers and Restaurateurs
The Media
Wine Organizations: Professional, Educational, Appreciation
Consumers

When it comes to turning your company around, you will need to look at every part of your operation, and develop a plan for improving your performance. As you do this, look for ways that you are going be able to show this improvement to your key audiences. If you make a lot of changes that they can't see, then you will get far less benefit from them. If you focus ahead of time on how you are going to develop tangible evidence—a specific way to communicate and emphasize each change—you will find your turnaround will happen more quickly. In every case, that tangible evidence of change should be specifically designed for each audience, and should specifically address their concerns. In short, every single one of your plans should answer the question: Why should I care? — for one of your key audiences. Following are examples of key stakeholder audiences and some issues to consider:

Your Production Department

In the production department, a turnaround begins with making better wines, or making good wines more cost-effectively. That is a simple equation. For every suggested change, the criteria must be the same. Are these changes going to improve the quality of the wine, and make the wine more cost-effective? If so, then they are good changes. If not, then you will need to evaluate the risks of making changes that are not as effective as they could be.

Focusing on key elements of production to strengthen your marketing position is always a good idea. Limiting your production to estate-grown wines, or wines from a particular vineyard or region, will be easy to document and will provide a guarantee of quality. Better production practices, better equipment, or even better winemaking personnel are all changes that should be considered. As you consider these changes, always keep in mind that you will have to demonstrate the differences they have made. If you can't demonstrate them, then your audiences will certainly ask why you have bothered to make this change!

Your Distributors

For distributors, the question is always a very direct one. How are you going to make their lives easier? How are you going to make wines that are easier for their salespeople to sell? These people have seen wineries come and go over the years, and you can expect them to be pretty skeptical about anything you propose. That is why it is critical to give them something that gets their attention and captures their imagination. This is the time to boldly go where no winery has ever gone before. One example of a winery that has implemented a successful turnaround strategy with their distributors is Beringer-Blass Wine Estates. Acquired by Fosters' in 2000, Beringer-Blass worked closely with their distributors to develop a strategy to integrate all of its wine brands along with the Foster's portfolio to create a more streamlined and efficient system.

The solutions you propose should address everything from pricing and wine quality to outdated inventory and stale marketing plans. They should build a comprehensive foundation for the future, and remove some of the problems of the past. Your ability to deliver this presentation to the distribution network will play a critical role in the success of the winery, and it is a good idea to have top management take the responsibility of delivering the key messages. It is their plan, their winery, and it is their credibility that is being questioned.

To help support that credibility, give this audience some solid examples of what you are doing and the positive effects these changes have generated, making sure that some of these address the real concerns this audience has about your winery. Then promise that there are more positive changes to come as your turnaround strategy continues to be implemented. Then deliver on those promises. That's the only way this is going to work.

Another excellent way to gain credibility with this audience is to show them that you have really heard their concerns. If you admit that some of their concerns are valid, they will immediately give you the benefit of additional trust. By showing that you are not oblivious to their questions, you can also show them that you have some of the same concerns. You will build trust and credibility.

Your Retailers and Restaurateurs
The strategies for retailers and restaurateurs are similar, but it will be hard to get your top management to each and every account. Making the effort to reach out to a large group of these accounts during a

market visit will help, but some of the communication will have to be entrusted to your sales team and the distributor.

Because retailers and restaurateurs often have conflicting interests, it's not a good idea to make a standard presentation to both kinds of accounts. Restaurateurs want to make sure that major discount retailers aren't going to get the kinds of big discounts that make their own on-premise pricing seem out of line. Retailers often want to make sure that they have access to the same wines that the "A" list restaurants get. Be honest with both audiences, and work hard to develop a plan that gives each the opportunity to succeed with your wines. In the end, these two audiences are going to continue to be your primary interface with the general consumer, and they will have a huge amount of control over your image.

Because your winery is in trouble, they will question your credibility as well as your strategies and tactics. Welcome that discussion. Give your sales team the information and training they need to address the concern of these markets. In these markets, it is their credibility that is being questioned. Don't hang them out to dry.

Your End Consumers

Consumers, in some ways, are the least critical of all of the audiences in a turnaround. Wine consumers like to try wines from a wide range of producers, and if you can get the support of your distributors and retailers, the customers will buy the wines. But in a time of crisis, it is not enough to simply push the wines through the system and wait for consumers to buy them. This is exactly when you need to build a much stronger relationship-marketing team, and reach out to those consumers directly. Create some pull-through to complement the push from the sales side, and you will be well on your way to making some of those promises you made come true.

Now is the time to get out in the marketplace and let the wine-buying public put a face next to your name. Now is the time to develop a more effective email campaign to current and past customers. Every interaction with a customer, whether in person, on the phone, or via email, is an opportunity to build demand in the marketplace. Far too often, wineries decide that this kind of intense consumer interaction is too time-consuming and too costly. Yet this is exactly the kind of consumer interaction that builds brand loyalty—one of the hardest things to do in the wine industry. A time of crisis is not the time to cut back on your efforts with your consumers. It is the time to give them all you've got, because in many ways, they are all you've got.

As you are doing this, make sure that the people on your staff who are in direct contact with the customers really understand this, and give them the same kind of support and tangible evidence of change that you have provided to the other key audiences of your company.

Your Winery Employees

In the end, your staff is the most critical audience of all. If the management team develops a series of comprehensive changes that will turn the winery around, it is your staff that will have to believe in these, and make them happen. This is your first audience. If you can't convince them, then the rest of your plan will simply fail to get off the ground.

Tell them how you are changing. Give them examples of how the future will look, and explain why that will make you a better company. Show them how things will be done in the future, and clearly demonstrate how that will turn your company around. The goal here is to gain their trust and engender their enthusiasm. Without that, no turnaround will achieve its goals.

YOU ONLY GET ONE CHANCE: KEEP YOUR PROMISES

In the end, you really only get one chance to launch a turnaround. Companies in crisis are under a magnifying glass. Every statement they make is scrutinized more critically. Every promise they make is looked at with skepticism. Every action they take is viewed through particularly pessimistic lenses. If you make a series of promises that you cannot deliver, then your fate is sealed.

This means that you must be both very careful and very courageous. While successful companies are often given the benefit of the doubt, companies in trouble have no such luck. The wine business is not a an overly cutthroat one, and a company that is trying hard to turn itself around will usually be given a chance to explain itself. However, if any part of the explanation should prove to be misplaced, little mercy or patience will be shown. There are simply too many other wineries, too many other brands that can fill that slot in the shelf.

When you make a promise, you must follow through completely. Not only that, you must also tell your entire range of audiences what you promised, and how you followed through successfully. Nothing can be taken for granted. All of this is intended to restore one of the most valuable assets of any company—its credibility. When a company is successful, people often remark on the perception that "everything they touch is gold." When a company is in trouble, people may react in the opposite fashion. By proving to your audiences that you can make promises and then deliver against them, you can begin to establish your credibility again. Credibility, whether it be with distributors, retailers, or consumers, is money in the bank. Invest a great deal of the effort of your turnaround in building your credibility back up to the point where it can compete in the marketplace.

Making such promises requires courage. Living up to such promises requires superb execution. This can be intimidating. Of course, if you make no promises, then you will not have much to worry about in terms of execution. You will also not earn much in the way of credibility. If you think of your company's credibility as a kind of credit report, all of this will be quite easy to understand. The way you raise your credit rating is not by avoiding credit, because if you pay cash for everything you may be an excellent credit risk, but nobody will know about it. If you buy on credit, and then default on the payments, your credit ratings will plummet. Instead, you have to buy things on credit and then pay in a timely manner. Do the same with your credibility, and over time it, too, will gain a much higher rating from your audiences.

WHEN TO PULL THE PLUG: THE EXIT STRATEGY

This may seem like a pretty brutal question to ask in the middle of a crisis. Often you will find that those in a crisis don't want to consider this option, for fear that they will be perceived as having a negative attitude. That's short-sighted. This is not only a question that should be considered in times of crisis, but is one of the strategic questions you should ask at least once a quarter as you analyze your statement. "Is this business still worth running, or should we look for an exit strategy?" If you don't ask yourself that question every once in a while, you are not doing a good job of managing your business.

Of course, asking the question is the easy part. Answering it is always a bit harder. You will really need to add up the plusses and minuses on each side of the equation, and somehow reach a total you can use to make a decision. That is easier said than done, because many of the pluses and minuses are in the realm of the unknown.

How much is your business really worth? There is only one answer: What you can get someone else to pay for it. However, what every good wine business consultant will tell you is that you can always get more for your business when it is healthy than when it is in a crisis. That's why it is so important to ask the question on a regular basis, not just when you are in deep trouble.

Accountants can often give you some good estimates of industry benchmarks for the value of some of your assets, and others will obviously be based on the book value alone. Each of these is a building block, but each is somewhat less than concrete. As you stack them one on top of the other, bear in mind that the variations in these estimates can easily create a situation where the estimated value of your business is quite a wide range of figures.

Do not become so jaded in the process that you forget to consider your options. As your company struggles, it may be well worth your time to consider an offer that is somewhere in the middle of the range of estimates for its value. When compared to the kinds of investment that are frequently needed to achieve a full-scale turnaround, in some cases the exit strategy is the wisest choice.

CONCLUSION

Though nobody welcomes a crisis, keep in mind the dual meaning of "crisis" in the Chinese language: it signifies both "danger, and "opportunity." A business crisis forces change, and sometimes change is the healthiest option for a stale business strategy.

Therefore, understanding the steps for managing an effective turnaround can be a good set of career skills and competencies to possess. In the long run, they are the same as implementing a new strategy—you are just forced to do so. With this in mind, the best prescription to maintain a healthy wine business is to conduct a strategy reassessment every couple of years, to make sure you are on track. The steps are the same as a turnaround: 1) gather and analyze data; 2) develop several viable strategy options, including an assessment of an exit strategy; 3) select and implement the best choice; and 4) communicate and follow up. In the best-case scenario, you will validate your current strategy. If not, you now have the information you need to reposition your strategy and avert a crisis.

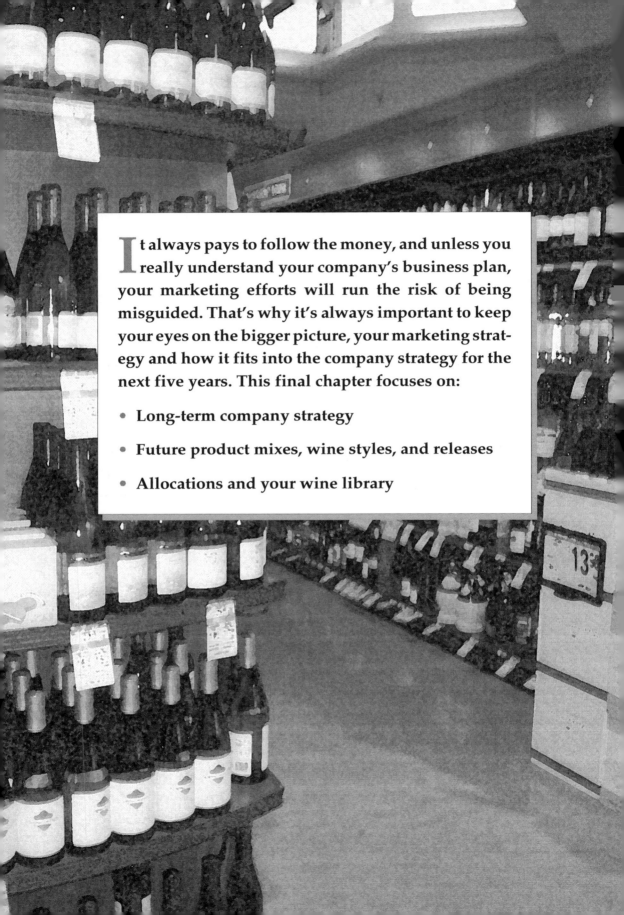

It always pays to follow the money, and unless you really understand your company's business plan, your marketing efforts will run the risk of being misguided. That's why it's always important to keep your eyes on the bigger picture, your marketing strategy and how it fits into the company strategy for the next five years. This final chapter focuses on:

- Long-term company strategy

- Future product mixes, wine styles, and releases

- Allocations and your wine library

THE BIG PICTURE AND EVOLVING TOPICS

LINKING WINE MARKETING STRATEGY TO BUSINESS STRATEGY

R oughly defined, strategy is *how* you will implement your company mission, values, and long-term goals. Ideally, then, your marketing strategy should be linked into this overall company plan, so that marketing and sales receive the appropriate resources and focus. Figure 15.1 illustrates the big picture of the strategic planning process and linkages.

Figure 15. 1: Strategy Linkage Diagram

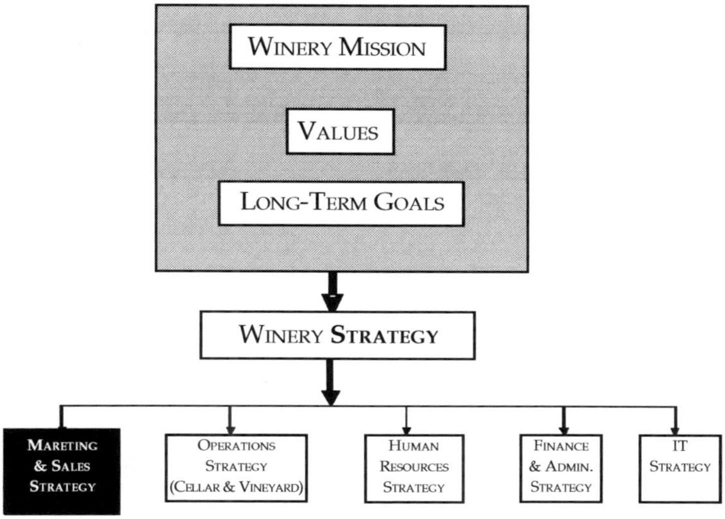

Based on the diagram above, everything begins with the mission of the company. In the wine industry, however, this is not always clear. A mission statement "to produce the highest quality wine in a small family winery environment" may sound impressive, but is actually not precise enough and sounds like the mission of 1,000 other small family wineries.

A mission should be specific and describe what makes you unique. In the wine industry, trying to produce a multitude of varietals to please all palates is not very realistic, unless you are one of the few multi-million-case wineries. Instead, you should focus on producing a varietal and style for which you have passion, and one which is also suited to your appellation. For example, a mission to "produce hand-crafted single-vineyard Petite Syrah and Zinfandel from the Amador region" is much more focused, and not only drives corporate strategy, but provides a clear and compelling direction for your marketing strategy.

After getting clear on company mission, the next step is to link this to company values. These can range from a focus on traditional winemaking methods to processes which utilize the newest technology. Other values can include family-run, team-oriented, environmental sustainability, a focus on specific charities, and other ideals that the winery owner and employees take pride in espousing. These should also be linked into company and marketing strategy through policies, practices, and allocated resources. For example, a value of green farming could be demonstrated by a policy of purchasing only certain types of organic pesticides, using recyclable containers, and communicating these efforts on all point-of-sale materials.

The next step is to identify long-term goals. These generally include revenue growth, profitability, return on investment, contribution to shareholders, and other goals for the overall business. Ideally these goals are quantitative and established for a three to five year period. They are established by the winery board of directors, executive team and other relevant parties. An example of a long-term goal may be to achieve revenue growth of 15% per year for the next five years.

Then based on the winery mission, values, and long-term goals, the comprehensive strategy for the company can be created. Again, this should be at least three to five years in length, but may be tweaked each year based on competitive and market conditions. Ideally the executive team will conduct a strategy review meeting at least once a year to make sure they are on track.

The overall strategy should describe what the winery will do to achieve their mission, values, and long-term goals. This could include product focus, sales channel methods, operational emphasis, research and development philosophy, and methods to deal with customers, suppliers and employees, etc. The strategy may also reflect the launch of new product lines, such as a second or third label, new varietal or blend, or a related product, such as a late harvest wine, olive oil, or wine jelly. In addition, the strategy may address such long-term issues as acquisitions or divestitures, as well as expansion into foreign markets. Finally, the strategy should include sources of competitive advantage and synergy, such as a distinctive distribution channel, higher-quality human resource practices, a shared IT infrastructure, or other competencies that help the winery compete.

From this high-level corporate strategy, the marketing strategy is born. Ideally, the winery owner and the rest of the executive team should assist in the formation of the marketing strategy, so it is something that is not done in a dark corner by a solo wine marketing professional. If you are the only wine marketer in your company, you may be asked to create a first draft of the marketing strategy, but it is highly recommended that you seek involvement and buy-in from the rest of the executive team. If you work in a larger winery with several people in the marketing and sales department, it is best if they can all be involved in the development of the marketing strategy. If you wear both hats, and are both the winery owner and the marketing guru, then you will obviously want to work with your other winery partners to develop both your long-term business strategy and marketing strategy.

Process to Create Your Marketing Strategy

The marketing strategy is composed of most of the elements that have been discussed in this book, but are linked specifically to corporate strategy and therefore should also be in a document that covers three to five years. This can then be used to create your annual marketing and sales plans, which include specific tactics, budgets, timelines, etc.

The marketing strategy document begins with a direct linkage to the corporate strategy document. In fact, both can be formatted using two columns on one page to illustrate this linkage. Beginning with mission and values, the marketing strategy document can describe how all marketing and sales efforts will reflect both of these. Using the examples from above, the marketing strategy would be to target all high-income Petite Syrah and Zinfandel drinkers in a certain geographic territory, e.g., California; the five major top wine-consuming cities in the U.S., and/or the U.K., France, Germany, and Japan. Target market definition is a key piece of the marketing strategy document, as well as a description of the long-term market development plan. Regarding the values, continuing with the example from above, implementation of the value of green farming could include a communication strategy to describe all green farming specifics, such as use of solar energy in the winery, etc., on all marketing and sales materials.

Other marketing strategy items that are linked to corporate mission and values are a description of branding policies, product line depth and breadth, and any potential product line extensions or eliminations. For example, if the Petite Syrah and Zinfandel winery in the Amador region has just secured a long-term grape purchasing contract from a new vineyard that has 150-year-old vines, then the company will most likely be planning a new launch of that vineyard designate with acclaim for the vineyard's age. Likewise, if the winery forecasts that they will run out of the 2003 vintage by 2006, with the exception of reserve or library wines, then this needs to be noted in the long-term marketing strategy.

Next the marketing strategy document should describe specifically what it will do to help accomplish the long-term corporate goals for the next three to five years. This is where marketing metrics are matched to corporate metrics, and includes forecasts for sales, market share, margin, and customer satisfaction metrics. Again, these are high-level forecasts, and will later be fleshed out into an annual marketing plan with more specific numbers for each marketing program (see Budget chapter).

The marketing strategy may also provide a high level allocation of how resources will be spread across the marketing mix elements: This includes most of the items covered in the previous chapters, but specifically deals with product, price, place, and promotion, and is tailored to the needs and wants of potential customers in the various target markets. Finally, the marketing strategy should also describe the special competitive advantage and synergies that your marketing efforts bring to the company. This could range from effective product positioning to superior promotion capabilities compared to your competitive set—the other wineries with which you compete for market share. For a large winery with multiple brands, synergies could include sharing of resources across multiple marketing departments to achieve economies of scale. A small winery might achieve synergies through a unique partnership with a distributor or retailer, or even a regional winery association.

Figure 15. 1 illustrates an abbreviated example of the fictional Petite Syrah and Zinfandel winery described above. Though the detailed marketing strategy is not represented here, most of the major components are listed. The next step is to break these down into an annual plan and budget, focusing on target audiences, product mix, and corresponding marketing programs as described in the budgeting chapter.

Figure 15.2: Example of Abbreviated Strategy Linkage Chart for XYZ Winery

COMPANY MISSION	Produce hand-crafted, single-vineyard Petite Syrah and Zinfandel from the Amador region.
VALUES	Traditional winemaking methods; family-run, team-oriented, green farming; fun place to work; give back to charity.
LONG-TERM GOALS (3–5 years)	1) Increase operating profit margins from 11%–16% within 5 years 2) Streamline our supply chain 3) Maintain current low production costs and high quality 4) Increase direct sales by 15% 5) Continue to donate 1% of revenues to local charities 6) Launch successful advertising campaign for 2 new wines 7) Achieve 15% return on investment over next 5 years 8) Achieve recognition as 1 of the top 5 Petite Syrah producers in the U.S.

WINERY STRATEGY *(To Achieve Mission, Values & Goals)*	**MARKETING & SALES LINKING STRATEGY**
• Continue to focus on Petite Syrah and Zinfandel from Amador County. • Launch 2 new wines: Petite Syrah, Dry Rosé and Zinfandel Port within the next three years. • Use traditional winemaking methods with natural yeasts and hand-harvesting. Only use American Oak. • Long-term contracts with sustainable grape growers, plus 100 acres of our own 100-year old grapes using green farming techniques (key competency)	TARGET AUDIENCE: High-income Petite Syrah and Zinfandel drinkers in the 5 major top wine-consuming cities in the U.S., Canada, Japan, and Germany. BRANDING (Competitve Advantage): Promote green farming, ccharitable contributions, wine awards, and traditional family-run winery with 100+ year-old vines. NEW PRODUCT LAUNCH: Create campaign to launch new Rosé and Port.
• 50% of sales via distributors. • 50% of sales direct to consumers through tasting rooms; Internet sales and wine club. • Increase international sales from 5–10% of production focusing on Japan, Canada, and Germany. • Maintain cost-effective and safe operations. • Invest in employee training and our local community.	• Enhance distributor relationship program. • Develop program to increase direct sales by 15%. • Target international trade shows and partners to increase foreign sales by 5%. • Achieve 15% return on investment for marketing programs. • Achieve average of 4 on a 5-point scale for customer satisfaction on tasting room survey. • Develop effective PR program with wine critics and competitions.

NEXT STEP: DEVELOP ANNUAL MARKETING /SALES PLAN AND BUDGET TO IMPLEMENT MARKETING STRATEGY

DETERMINING PRODUCT MIX, WINE STYLES, AND FUTURE RELEASES

It is difficult to forecast what consumer wine tastes will be in the future, especially since something simpl as a movie release (remember *Sideways*) can cause the public to seek out certain varietals and ignore others. Therefore, how do you determine your product mix, wine style, and future releases? The answer lies in a solid business strategy, as well as ongoing market research.

Each year when the executive team and board of directors come together for their annual strategy meeting—if this isn't currently happening, push for it to occur!—this strategic issue should be addressed. The session should begin with a review of current and forecasted customer needs, and then an analysis of how or if this impacts your current strategy. However, if the mission and values of the winery are clear, there shouldn't be too much jumping around and changing of focus. Once the winery decides what business they should be in regarding a specific focus on certain varietals, regions, etc., then they should "stick to the knitting." This doesn't mean, however, that there cannot be offshoots of current product lines to meet new consumer demands. For example, if rosé is suddenly becoming popular, and you currently only produce big Petite Syrahs and Zinfandels, it may be prudent for you to consider developing a unique rosé out of your Petite Syrah. The key is to link the new product to your existing brand image and varietal/appellation focus.

Likewise, if you have a tasting room, and are selling much of your wine direct, you may find that many of your customers are requesting a sweet wine. You may elect to stand fast to your original market mix of big Petite Syrahs and Zinfandels, or you may decide to honor customer requests and develop a late harvest Zinfandel or something else to meet their needs. You could even expand to include Zinfandel truffles or syrups—just as long as you continue to honor your original mission. The danger is trying to become everything to everyone, because this only breeds mediocrity. It is important to stay true to what you do well and are passionate about. This will support your strategy and help you build a strong and consistent brand in the eyes of your customers.

The issue of future release dates should also be discussed during this annual meeting, with, ideally, a consensus decision being reached. This is especially important for the winemaking, marketing, and finance teams. Often there is disagreement between departments, because the winemaker wants to hold the wine until it reaches its peak, whereas the marketing team wants to release it so added publicity can be obtained and sales can increase for the short period after the release. The finance group is usually concerned about release dates as well, because the longer the wine is aged and held in inventory, the more costs climb. Another variable that often throws a wrench in the works is wine critic opinion regarding the overall vintage. If they predict that 2006 will be a poor year, it makes it that much more difficult to sell your 2006 releases, regardless of how good they may be.

Therefore, the best advice regarding releases is to listen carefully to your winemaker—they know when the wine will taste the best— and to keep an eye on what your competitors are doing. As the marketing and sales guru, you can invite distributors, retailers, and press to an advance tasting in the winery, and let the winemaker explain how the wine will only get better by the time it is released. However, if everyone else is releasing at a certain date, then you may want to follow suit. A caveat to this is if you are a high-end luxury brand. Then it may be expected that you hold your wine an additional year before release. Likewise, you may even decide not to release a vintage wine for one year if the wine is not up to your usual quality. This not only demonstrates your commitment to quality, but can add some nice public relations if you communicate the news well. A final thought is to consider selling futures on your wine, if your brand is well established and you have the accounting system to do so.

ALLOCATIONS AND YOUR WINE LIBRARY

What do you do when you are running out of wine, and how much wine should you keep in your wine library? Obviously having so many customers request your wine that you find you are running short is more desirable than having too much wine (see Chapter 14 on how to deal with excess wine issues). However, running short of wine can also present problems with customers. Chateau St. Jean, for example, tells the story of when their now famous Cinq Cepages was identified as the number one wine in the world by *Wine Spectator*. The next day, their phones were ringing off the hooks with over-anxious customers trying to buy the wine, and they ran out almost immediately. This caused a negative customer backlash, with some customers actually threatening not to buy wine from them in the future, because they couldn't get the bottle they coveted. Chateau St. Jean now says that they make sure to hold back some of their high-end wines and do a second release later in the year to preserve customer satisfaction.

Guidelines for Managing Allocated Wine

On the flipside, many customers are intrigued with a bottle that is in tight demand. The very fact that it is hard to get, and they have to wait for it, makes it that much more valuable in their eyes. Wine marketers usually refer to this customer segment as Prestige Seeking or Connoisseurs. If you find you have to allocate your wines, then you will most likely be working with this customer segment. Here the guidelines of allocation are simple. Determine the amount of wine you have to sell, then calculate a forecast of how many customers will want the wine. Divide the number of cases (or bottles) by the forecast, and develop your allocation plan.

Next create a communication plan for customers, letting them know in advance when the wine will be available and how much it will cost. Inform them of the case/bottle limit and the timeframe for purchase. Generally these types of communications go to all members on your mailing or wine club list, as well as key distributors and retailers. You may want to make a limited quantity available for sale through your tasting room, but ensure that customers are aware of how rare it is, and how fortunate they are to be able to purchase it. Finally, if you are highly allocated and have been selling wine this way for a while, you may want to consider holding back a certain amount of wine for a second release, or maintain a larger library collection than normal. In this way, you have some "insurance" against potential customer complaints.

Setting Up Your Wine Library

A wine library, or a collection of your wine from all of your previous vintages, has always been a good idea—if only to demonstrate the age-ability of your wine. There are no set guidelines on the amount of wine to hold back, but general it is a good idea to keep from a few bottles to 10% of the cases for future library wine sales and marketing/public relations events. Therefore, if your winery produces 10,000 cases, you'd want to hold back something between ten and a thousand cases for future sales. The obvious caveat is that you only want to hold back wine that can be aged. Of course, if your winery is focusing on making fruit-forward wines that show best when they are young, then this is neither practical nor advisable. But if you are making wines that should improve with age, you must assume part of the responsibility of demonstrating this to consumers, media and the trade. To do so, you will need an inventory of these older wines. The best way to determine the size of this inventory is to create the sales and marketing plan for these wines, and hold back inventory as appropriate.

THE FUTURE OF WINE MARKETING

The future of wine marketing is bright, because the marketing function will only become more critical for wineries in the future. It is predicted that the number of small wineries will only continue to grow in the U.S., whereas the larger ones will continue to consolidate in order to gain market share and economies of scale. Every once in a while, they will gobble up some of the smaller wineries that have managed to create a solid brand—if they are for sale, that is.

On the international front, more wineries will also come online in countries around the world, especially in Asia and Eastern Europe. This means the global wine market will only become more competitive, making effective marketing that much more crucial.

So what does that mean for you as a winery owner and/or a wine marketing professional? It means your role is changing and growing. Following are some of the areas you may want to consider to help you be successful in this exciting future.

Professional marketing expertise: It is no longer enough to sell wine through the traditional methods of "relationship marketing," in which you built a relationship with a distributor who then sells your wine. Now you also need to have professional marketing expertise within your winery. This means either hiring a professional with a degree and experience in marketing—ideally wine marketing—or becoming one yourself. You need to become actively involved in marketing, and help your distributors and retailers market your product. You need to be on the road, visiting restaurants and stores, meeting face-to-face with consumers, and continually staying in touch with your markets and developing markets. You need to understand and know how to use the latest wine marketing techniques, which have been described in this book.

Technology savvy: In addition to marketing expertise, you need to understand and know how to use all of the new technologies that are coming on the market for wine sales. This includes barcodes, inventory control systems, online depletion reports, customer database management, electronic data interchange (EDI) with distributors and retailers, and other up-and-coming technologies to enhance wine sales and marketing. Currently some of the largest wine retailers in the U.S. and elsewhere will not even consider working with you, unless you have the capability of using some of these systems. This will only expand in the future.

Niche marketing: As the division between the global mogul wineries and the small family wineries under 10,000 cases continues to grow, niche marketing will become even more critical. You need to understand the intricacies of doing this well, and build solid relationships within your niche market. This may mean becoming an expert in a specific varietal, region, or other specialty area. It may call for a tight regional sales strategy, in which you only sell your wine locally, or a sophisticated international niche strategy where your unique product is sold on a global basis, but in limited quantities.

Global mindset: Even though you may be a small winery focusing on a specific niche, you still need to develop a global mindset, because whether you like it or not, you are operating in a global marketplace. Just think of the source of your supplies—barrels from France, corks from Portugal, potential software developed in India, and perhaps bottles made in Canada. Therefore, it behooves you to pay attention to global fluctuations in the wine industry. Keep track of what is happening in key wine regions such as Europe, Australia, South America, and China. Is there a surplus of grapes or a shortage? What types of varietals are gaining in popularity? What are the taste profiles of customers in emerging wine markets? All of this has an impact on your future wine sales and marketing.

Sustainable winemaking and ISO classification: Sustainable viticulture and enology practices are erupting around the world, with some wineries pursuing ISO (International Standards Organization) classification for one or both of these areas. Though still in its infancy, this aspect of winemaking is expected to continue to grow in importance as more and more consumers seek companies which embrace environmentally-friendly practices. If you are not already doing this, it is something to look into for the future. Not doing, it could potentially become a barrier to selling your wine globally—if wine ISO classification follows the same path as computers and other commodities.

Innovative packaging: Though already widely available to consumers in other nations such as Australia, New Zealand, Chile, Argentina, and many part of Europe, non-traditional wine packaging is predicted to grow in the U.S. as well. This includes selling wine in boxes, plastic, pouches, and in different sizes. Some consumers want wine that is easily portable and has one or two servings, versus six or eight. Novel closures, ranging from screw caps to synthetic corks are also expected to increase in the U.S., as are colorful, fun and minimalist labels. This is not to say that traditional wine packaging will go away—there will still be consumers who want an elegant wine in a glass bottle with a real cork. However, there are times when a wine consumer wants to take a simple portable box of wine to the beach, without the stigma of drinking cheap wine. Other times, the same consumer will want an expensive bottle of Cabernet Sauvignon with a cork to be decanted at a meal in a fancy restaurant. This means that wine marketers need to be open to new consumer needs and packaging innovations.

Third-party labeling: A related sideline to innovative packaging is the growth of third-party labeling. This is expanding rapidly in Europe, as large grocery chains, such as Tesco, continue to request private labeling of their brands. In the U.S., Target, Walmart, the Oscars, and many restaurants have also pursued private labels for wines they carry. This whole area of the market is expected to continue to grow, and is something to consider as part of your strategy as you strive for innovation and revenue growth.

Changing regulations and social/economic issues: In the U.S., especially, it is important to keep track of changing laws in direct shipping and other wine regulations. In addition, changing social and economic issues impact the sales of wine. As the large and powerful millennial generation comes of age, they will most likely have a positive impact on wine sales—if they like your marketing. In addition, the increasing emphasis on food and wine as part of a healthy lifestyle, as well as changes in economic conditions, may cause fluctuations in your sales. Keeping abreast of these issues and making the necessary adjustments to your wine marketing strategy and tactics are crucial.

The issues listed above are the current hot issues that will impact the future of wine, but it is important to note that this list is not exhaustive. There are others as well, that may now be minor, but could erupt into major forces. Therefore, a good wine marketer is always scanning the environment in order to be proactive and not reactive when it comes to effective wine marketing and sales.

CONCLUSION

In conclusion, the future is bright for wine marketing. Wine quality has increased on a global basis, and the consumption rate in the U.S. is climbing. Innovation is welcome, and therefore, wine marketers have a green light to use some of the most creative strategies of any industry. By adopting some of the techniques described in this book, you should be well on your way to becoming a wine marketing expert, and helping to propel your winery into the spotlight in a positive way.

CHAPTER REFERENCES

Walker, O., Boyd, H., Mullins, J. & Larreche, J. *Marketing Strategy: A Decision-Focused Approach, 4th Edition*. Boston: McGraw-Hill Irwin. 2003.

INDEX

allocations/wine library, 329–30
excess inventory, 308–11
tasting room inventory control, 279–80
involvement levels/market segments, 36–37
ISO classification, 332–33

J
Jake's Fault, 35

K
key message
graphic design projects, 104–6
wine organization outreach, 165
key product attributes, identifying, 50, 51–52

L
labels, 22, 123–24, 126, 142–43
back labels, 130
contact information on, 160
design issues, 130, 131, 134–37
examples, 112, 135, 136
exporting compliance issues, 289–90
federal regulations, 131–33
micro labels, 130
neck labels, 130
See also graphic design; packaging
legal/regulatory issues
direct shipping legislation, 3, 59–60, 243, 250, 253
e-commerce, 255, 257
exporting, 289–90
retailer incentives, 238–39
in situation analysis, 59–60
tasting rooms, 267, 271, 273–74
tracking changes, 334
TTB label requirements, 131–33
U.S. distribution system regulation, 3, 17–18, 200, 201
wine clubs, 249–50
leverage, 22
Leverhulme, Lord, 69
licenses, tasting rooms, 267
Lodi-Woodbridge Winegrape Commission, 114

long-term goals, 321, 322–23, 325
low-cost positioning, 62
See also inexpensive wines; price categories

M
mailing lists, 250–51
advertising event participation, 161–62
offering wine clubs, 245, 251–53
management. *See* winery owners/management
marginal wine drinkers, 30
market, defined, 22
market categories, 11–13, 21
See also market segments
market changes, 40, 334
marketing basics, 4–23, 331–34
assessing success, 21
basic marketing goals, 9–10, 12, 20
challenges, 2–3, 5–6, 17–20
defining market category, 11–13, 21
five P's, 6–8
future of marketing, 330–34
key marketing audiences, 174, 190–91
key terms, 6–8, 21–23
sales vs. marketing, 15–17
strategic approach, 13–15, 19–20
wine vs. other goods, 2, 17
marketing budgets, 172–80, 188–97
advertising budgets, 77
challenges, 173–75
determining budget size, 175–79
donation budgets, 85, 194
examples, 196–97
export capability and, 286
frequently overlooked items, 194–95
image enhancement in, 174–75, 177, 188–89
important questions, 188–93
maximizing your investment, 193–94
presenting to management, 195–96
target audiences, 174, 190–91
winery size and, 2, 19, 177, 178–79
marketing companies, 201–2
marketing goals, 9–10, 12, 20, 174–75, 191

WINE BOOK PUBLISHER OF THE YEAR
Gourmand World Book Awards, 2004

The Wine Appreciation Guild has been an educational pioneer in our fascinating community.

—Robert Mondavi

Your opinion matters to us...

You may not think it, but customer input is important to the ultimate quality of any revised work or second edition. We invite and appreciate any comments you may have. And by registering your WAG book you are enrolled to receive prepublication discounts, special offers, or alerts to various wine events, only available to registered members.

As your first bonus for registering you will receive, free of charge, our bestselling, interactive GLOBAL ENCYCLOPEDIA OF WINE, on CD-ROM (a $29.95 value). This CD is compatible with PCs and Macs running Mac Classic. It has:

- Wine regions
- The process: from grapes to glass
- Enjoying wine: rituals and tasting
- Wine Guide, a fascinating database for choosing different wines
- Cellar Log Book, that will allow you to document your own wine collection.

You can register your book by phone: (800) 231-9463; Fax: (650) 866-3513; E-Mail: Info@WineAppreciation.com; or snail mail the form on the following page.

REGISTRATION CARD

for WINE MARKETING & SALES

Name_____Date_____

Professional Affiliation_____

Address_____

_____

City_____State_____Zip_____

E-Mail_____

How did you discover this book?_____

Was this book required class reading? Y N

School/Organization_____

Where did you acquire this book?_____

Was it a good read? (circle)   Poor   1   2   3   Excellent
Was it useful to your work? (circle)   Poor   1   2   3   Excellent

Suggestions_____

_____

Comments_____

_____

_____

You can register your book by phone: (800) 231-9463; Fax: (650) 866-3513; Email: Info@WineAppreciation.com; or snail mail.

THE WINE APPRECIATION GUILD
360 Swift Avenue
South San Francisco, CA 94080

www.wineappreciation.com

Fold Here ▲

Tape Closed Here ▼

4513468

Made in the USA
Lexington, KY
03 February 2010